Cultural Competence
in the Caring Professions

of related interest

Learning to Practise Social Work
International Approaches
Edited by Steven M. Shardlow and Mark Doel
ISBN 1 85302 763 4

Integrating Theory and Practice in Social Work Education
Florence Watson, Helen Burrows and Chris Player
With contributions from Lorraine Agu, Simon Shreeve and Lee Durrant
ISBN 1 85302 981 5

The Child's World
Assessing Children in Need
Edited by Jan Horwath
ISBN 1 85302 957 2

Meeting the Needs of Ethnic Minority Children - Including Refugee,
Black and Mixed Parentage Children
A Handbook for Professionals
Second Edition
Edited by Kedar Nath Dwivedi
ISBN 1 85302 959 9

User Involvement and Participation in Social Care
Research Informing Practice
Edited by Hazel Kemshall and Rosemary Littlechild
ISBN 1 85302 777 4

Permanent Family Placement for Children of Minority Ethnic Origin
June Thoburn, Liz Norford and Stephen Parvez Rashid
ISBN 1 85302 875 4

Innovative Education and Training for Care Professionals
A Providers' Guide
Edited by Rachel Pierce and Jenny Weinstein
ISBN 1 85302 613 1

Research in Social Care and Social Welfare
Issues and Debates for Practice
Edited by Beth Humphries
ISBN 1 85302 900 9

Cultural Competence in the Caring Professions

Kieran O'Hagan

Jessica Kingsley Publishers
London and Philadelphia

First published in the United Kingdom in 2001
by Jessica Kingsley Publishers
116 Pentonville Road
London N1 9JB, UK
and
400 Market Street, Suite 400
Philadelphia, PA 19106, USA

www.jkp.com

Copyright © Kieran O'Hagan 2001
Printed digitally since 2006

Library of Congress Cataloging in Publication Data
A CIP catalog record for this book is available from the Library of Congress

British Library Cataloguing in Publication Data
A CIP catalogue record for this book is available from the British Library

ISBN-13: 978 1 85302 759 8
ISBN-10: 1 85302 759 6

Contents

Figures and tables

Figures

Tables

*This book is dedicated to health and social care
professionals striving for a more culturally sensitive world,
pursuing the goal of culturally competent practice.*

Acknowledgements

The experiences which contributed to this publication have occurred over a long period of time, in different locations, and have involved many different people. A Bengali family with whom I lived over twenty years ago, in Calcutta, provided experiences of incomparable insights into culture, and of my own limitations in adjusting to cultures vastly different from my own. Mother Teresa's missionary Brothers in Los Angeles brought me into sustained contact with the cultures of Hispanic immigrants, for whom they provided shelter and care. Bangladeshi and Pakistani communities in Leeds and Bradford awakened me to the reality of child protection work still in the infancy of providing culturally competent services. A friend, Gordon Dawber, now retired in New Zealand, arranged a six-week Australian lecture tour for me; I met very few of the indigenous population during the tour, but the experience nonetheless gave me a powerful sense of the near total destruction of Aboriginal culture. Ironically, it was, however, on returning to N. Ireland, and working with an Irish speaking community, that the notion of writing the book took hold. This small community taught me most about culture; not just about their culture, but more significantly, why culturally diverse peoples throughout the world – and in Ireland itself – regard their cultures as so crucial. I am therefore most grateful to the Organising Committee of the ISPCAN conference held in Dublin, 1996, for granting me the funding to carry out research within the community.

My wife Maura once again selflessly ensured that I could maintain sufficient focus on the task, and this despite her own responsibilities of nursing and caring for others. Maurice Reid, a lifelong friend, provided interest, humour and encouragement in his weekly visits. His impatience with my cooking was strategically important, as it ensured ample time for him to investigate and solve the latest problems in my computer! Our nephew Michael Carr converted numerous thoughts on the meaning of culture into the diagrammatic presentation in Chapter 14. Maura Dunn and Margaret Mullany provided much needed secretarial and IT backup. Margaret Fawcett offered valued feedback on the chapter, *Culture and Religion,* and counselled me wisely on distractions and obstacles which continually appeared while the book was being written. One daily distraction, however, was welcome. It occurred around eight o'clock each morning, at the end of my first two-hour daily writing shift. My grand-daughter Niamh, all eighteen months of her, religiously knocked my study door. She then magisterially entered, demanded my full attention, and proceeded to explore anything and everything in her sight. I wonder if she will ever know how therapeutic and revitalising her daily visits proved to be.

PART I

Rediscovering Culture

CHAPTER I

A Tale of Two Cultures

Islamic culture

In a bleak and desolate landscape near the centre of a northern city, four sisters made their way across waste ground. The desolation made the sisters and their movement conspicuous, like newcomers arriving on a previously uninhabited land. But they lacked the curiosity of the newcomer: they had been here before and there was nothing to see. The four sisters were led by the eldest one, Ameera, 18 years old. Muhja, aged 16, followed closely behind. Then Haleema, 12, and Yasirah, 7. Only the eyes of the sisters were visible, and occasionally their fingers. They each wore the traditional Muslim yashmak. There was a strong wind daily whipped up on the wide open space, and the sisters hurried onward, looking neither to the left nor the right, preoccupied with the objective of getting to the end of the waste ground, and home. This was a short way home for them, from their Friday worship in the mosque. But it was not without its risk. Ameera was now burdened with the memory of her elders in the mosque advising her not to come home this way. Occasionally her anxious eyes scoured the land, then she would look straight ahead and quicken her pace. Her sisters just about managed to keep up with her.

The sisters were three-quarters of the way through the waste land. They heard a sound familiar to them, but in a tone distinctly unfamiliar. They reached the slight brow of a hill and looked in the direction the sound appeared to be coming from. Ameera was stricken with terror at the sight which greeted them. A large crowd of youths, only about 50 yards away, were on their knees, their hands raised above them, mockingly calling out 'Allah! Allah!' Ameera trembled. She realised this must have been planned. They had obviously watched her and her sisters enter the waste ground. They had obviously rushed along the left side of the ground, low enough to keep out of their sight, to re-emerge cutting them off. Ameera's sisters looked at her large beautiful eyes and, despite her attempt to appear calm and controlled, they sensed her terror. Ameera said: 'Don't look ... Walk on.' She slowed the hurried pace ever so slightly, and her sisters moved closer to her. But the mocking chant continued, almost as if it were physically accompanying them. Ameera saw the youths moving quickly forward and turning towards them. They divided into two groups, like a pack of animals in the closing stages of the kill. Again they went on their knees and chanted 'Allah!' Ameera trembled again; there was an unmistakable hostility and evil intent in their blasphemous mocking chants. And the space they had created for the sisters to pass them was nothing more than a den.

Yasirah began crying. Haleema put her hands around her and comforted her. Muhja, the most spirited of the sisters, stared defiantly at their would-be tormentors. She scoured the ground looking for bricks or stones. She saw some, near her. Ameera knew what she was thinking. She grabbed her arm tightly, and warned her. Then she turned to face the youths.

The apparent leader, a blond-haired tall youth, aged about 17, with tattooed arms, rings in his ears and a scar beneath his right eye, got off his knees and moved towards Ameera. The remainder continued chanting, more loudly. He stared at Ameera, gratified in sensing her terror. Her yashmak both attracted and repelled him. Her eyes were as fearful as they were beautiful. She was immensely mysterious to him, but he was acutely aware of her vulnerability and of his momentary power. Ameera stopped. He moved closer to her. He raised one hand towards her eyes, and she panicked. She ran past him. Her sisters tried to follow. The youths moved in on them. The sisters could move no further. The youths shoved them and spat on them. Then they tugged lightly on the yashmaks. Muhja flailed helplessly at them. Haleema and Yasirah began screaming. Ameera tried desperately to reach them, to protect them. But it was futile and their increasing helplessness and panic only fuelled the youths more. They tugged harder on the sisters' yashmaks and laughed more loudly. Then they threw the sisters from one side of the den to the other, whipping themselves into a frenzy with their continuing mocking chants of 'Allah! Allah!'

Some hours afterwards, the four sisters were being comforted in their homes by their parents and extended family members. They wore new yashmaks. The defiled ones were dumped, which was a cause of much consternation to the police who needed them for forensic analysis. But the crisis of the occasion was of such magnitude for the parents that the police sensitively did not pursue their need; they merely hoped that the yashmaks could be retrieved at a later time. Social services were there, as were significant representatives of the community. A GP had called and left, giving prescriptions for tranquillizers and advising that the sisters were in no fit state yet to be questioned by the police. The police and social services respected this, but nevertheless sought to remain in the home and establish some kind of useful contact with the family. The police asked the parents and other family members whether any of them had experienced racist attacks before, or any kind of racial harassment, from anyone. Numerous family members had and proceeded to describe their experiences in detail. As the discussions and questioning continued, more police officers arrived. They had been at the scene of the incident, seeking witnesses and material evidence. It was not the first time such an attack had taken place on the waste ground.

Ameera eventually felt able to talk. The police inspector thanked her. He was particularly keen to hear her version of events first, before speaking to her younger sisters. Together with a female detective constable, he proceeded to talk to her with great tact and sensitivity. Ameera's parents remained at either side of her, determined not to leave her, yet dreading once again having to hear the details of what their daughters had endured. The inspector encouraged Ameera to tell her own story in her terms, beginning from the moment the four sisters left the mosque. He listened carefully and his colleague took some notes. Ameera recalled the events in great detail. There were some outstanding memories for her: there was the relative ease with which they entered the waste ground and the increasing unease the further they went; there was the ghastly chant of 'Allah!' which she instantly recognised as mockery; there was the sight of the youths on their knees, blaspheming what was holy and sacred to her. The inspector and his colleague listened carefully, concealing well a genuine revulsion that they both felt towards the attackers. The inspector then sought Ameera's permission to ask her some questions. Ameera consented.

The inspector asked whether she or her sisters had been in contact with anyone since leaving the mosque. Was she aware of being watched or followed at any time? Had anything like this ever happened before? Was there anyone they could think of, at school or play or wherever, who she thought might have harboured racist views or feelings against her or her sisters? Ameera looked at the inspector, somewhat puzzled. There was no one, she stressed. Then the inspector asked her to describe the attackers. Ameera vividly recalled the many features of the apparent leader, his long blond hair.

'Not a skinhead?' the inspector checked.

'No, long and blond,' Ameera said, 'unclean.'

The inspector was convinced he would have been a skinhead. Ameera then mentioned the multiple tattoos on his arms.

'Oh yes,' the inspector said, 'What can you remember about those?'

'They were obscene,' Ameera replied.

'Obscene?'

Ameera nodded. The inspector, acutely conscious of and sensitive to her parents' presence on either side of her, dared to ask her what she meant.

'Naked bodies,' Ameera replied, and 'words ... '

The words could come later, the inspector thought. 'Did you see anything racist on his arms, National Front, Union Jack ... you know?'

'Nothing,' Ameera said.

'Any racist tattoos on his face?'

She shook her head.

'What was he wearing?'

'Jeans ... black, and Reebok trainers. He had a white T-shirt; I don't remember the design on his T-shirt; it was circular, orange and black.'

'Might it have been a racist design?'

Ameera looked at the inspector, slightly exasperated. 'I don't know.'

'And what about his face, what can you remember about his face?'

A face that she would never forget, Ameera thought; a voice that would never stop ringing in her ears. The inspector was well pleased with the description she gave and knew that with the help of a police artist a near perfect photofit portrait would emerge. He paused for a moment, leaned back on his chair and said, 'Now you've told us about this chanting, Ameera, what else can you remember hearing them say ... to you or your sisters, or amongst themselves?'

'Nothing. They didn't say anything else.'

The inspector looked at her, for the first time revealing the slightest incredulity. 'They said nothing at all. Nothing except "Allah"?'

The word seared through Ameera. Her parents stiffened. 'Nothing,' she said.

'You're absolutely certain about that?'

'Yes.'

'Did they say anything to your sisters?'

'No.'

He couldn't believe this. 'When they were hitting you ... throwing you around ... they said nothing more than "Allah"?'

She knew he did not realise what he was doing in uttering this word. She thought for a moment. How could she tell him? The exasperation in her voice was obvious when she said, 'They didn't just say it. They chanted it, together. They knew what they were doing. They didn't have to say anything else. There was nothing else they could do or say that would have injured us more.'

The inspector looked at her gravely: 'Ameera … I know how painful this must have been for you and your sisters … '

Ameera knew he did *not* know.

'Maybe your sisters can recall … You were trying to protect them after all. Maybe other things were said … and you didn't hear. These kinds of youth have their own trademark you know: the things they do, the clothes they wear, the tattoos they want, the racist insults they shout. It all helps with our inquiries.'

Ameera breathed deeply, and bit her lip. The inspector appeared not to notice.

'What about the rest of them, what can you remember about any of the others?'

'Three of them were black,' Ameera said.

The inspector stared at her. The grip on his pen loosened. 'Black?' he asked.

'Yes,' she replied. Then she spoke pointedly, but quietly: 'It wasn't a racist attack, inspector. It was an attack on our religion.'

Gaelic culture

In Belfast one Saturday evening, a mother and her two children, a girl and a boy, made their way towards the accident and emergency department of one of the city's main teaching hospitals, situated not far from where they lived. The girl was aged about ten and the boy about six. The boy held his mother's hand securely, and seemed driven by a necessity to keep up with her frantic pace. He had a pained and dazed expression. The girl trailed behind them, seemingly reluctantly and stubbornly, murmuring and sulking to herself, catching up only when her mother turned to utter an empty threat. Their mother was aged about 30. She was extremely worried-looking.

Saturday night was not a good night to visit accident and emergency. There were all classes of people there, all ages, all types of injuries. There were road accident victims, victims of domestic violence and destitutes. There was someone hobbling on one leg and another peering from beneath a makeshift bandage covering an eye. There were some who were sobbing and others who had previously wept. There were those who regarded accident and emergency as a great social occasion, and there were others inconvenienced and injured enough to respond as though it were a bad dream – cocooning themselves through silence and isolation from all the activity and people around them.

The mother and her two children joined the reception queue. There were two receptionists seated behind thick scarred glass screens. One was female, the other a young man with thick horn-rimmed glasses, entirely compatible with his serious, eyes-riveted-to-the-computer-screen countenance. He never once looked up.

'Yes?' (He asked this question while setting up a new questionnaire on his screen.)

'My son here… He fell off a wall.'

'His name?'

'Seosamh MacLiam.'

The receptionist *did* look up. He said quite emphatically: 'What?'

'Seosamh MacLiam.'

His colleague, the young woman, seemingly immersed in her own screen, glanced over. The young man looked at the mother and asked, 'Can you spell that?'

'S – E – 0 – S – A – M – H'

This had sounded like *Shosoff.* He typed it in and stared at the screen for a few seconds, focusing on the red underlining that told him this was a wrong spelling, or that it was a very strange name indeed.

'Date of birth?'

'Seventh of the third, 1993.'

'School?'

'Shaw's Road Bunscoil.'

He hesitated. 'Bunscoil?'

'Yes.'

'Can you spell it?'

She did. But she sensed that what he really wanted to know was the type of school it was. 'It's a primary school', she told him.

'Can I have *your* name, please?'

'Áine MhicLiam.'

She could read his thoughts again: MhicLiam was not the same as MacLiam. She anticipated the question he was reluctant to ask, though he did take the trouble to lift his head in asking it. 'Are you the child's mother?'

'Yes.'

'Could I have the father's name?'

'Proinsias MacLiam.' This sounded like something you eat, he thought. The sounds were getting to him and he relieved his tension a little by glancing over to his colleague. She was now straining herself to appear engrossed in her own inquiry, but the mother could clearly see a smirk on her lips.

'Can you spell that?'

'P – R – O – I – N – S – I – A – S.'

He had never seen nor heard anything like it before. It was a crazy language, he thought, pronouncing a spelling like that.

'Do you have other children?'

'One other, my daughter here.'

'And her name?'

'Caoimhe NíLiam.'

He looked at her and stared. 'What?'

'Caoimhe NíLiam.' It sounded like Keeva NeeLiam. He asked he to spell it and she did. He asked her what a fada (above the i) was. 'Like in French,' she told him. She sensed that he and his colleague were now finding it exceedingly difficult to control themselves.

He hurried through the remaining questions. He printed a handout with the details and gave it to her, along with a little booklet on patients' rights. As the mother walked from the reception, he deliberately dropped a piece of paper near where his colleague sat. He bent low to retrieve it, but more to conceal his head entirely from the view of those waiting. He whispered to his colleague, 'Keeva Proinsias Shosoff Bunscoil MacLiam, VicLiam NeeLiam, NoLiam … No no no no no Liam!' He raised himself and turned to face the computer screen again. His colleague bit her lips, trying to keep her laughter contained.

Áine looked around the waiting area. There were few seats available. They would have to separate. The children found two vacant places and their mother sat in another row. On one side of the children sat a rather heavy man, with arms folded. On the other side sat a teenage girl, her head heavily bandaged. Neither of them looked at or spoke to the children.

Caoimhe then spoke to her brother. 'Cad é mar a bhraitheann tú anois?' Her expression and the tone of her voice suggested she was asking how he was feeling then. He didn't respond, just shook his head glumly.

The heavy man and the teenage girl instantly came to life. Many others within earshot of Caoimhe and Seosamh also looked interested. Some in front looked behind. Meanwhile Áine sat reading the booklet on patients' rights. It was dominated by the hospital's mission statement, a great gushy outpouring of principle and good intent. She read about how much importance the authorities placed on 'respecting clients'; how determined they were to administer their services in a non-discriminatory manner; how sensitive they were to all peoples and cultures. She read that patients whose religion was other than the mainstream Catholic and Protestant could be put in touch with the city's multiracial centre, and that those who may not be able to communicate in English could have access to someone conversant in their own language.

A staff nurse appeared from behind an extended curtain leading to the treatment cubicles. She was struggling to read a form she had picked up from reception.

'Is that ... *Mac* ... Liam?' she asked loudly, her brow wrinkled and her eyes wide open to denote her perplexity. '*See oh Sam* ... Mac Liam!'

The whole congregation of patients looked up, some smiling, a few laughing. She smiled at them in return.

'Yes,' Áine said, instantly recognising the chemistry of mockery so familiar to her. The children sensed it too and hurried towards their mother.

'This way,' said the staff nurse. She explained, 'I'm staff nurse Reynolds, Mrs ... Mac Liam ... '

'Mhic Liam,' said Áine.

The staff nurse looked at the form again. She was more confident and forthright than the receptionist. 'How come your surname is different from that of your son, Mrs ... Hick Liam?'

'It's not,' said Áine, 'it's only the prefix that's different. *Liam* is the surname; *Mac* is there because he is a boy; it means *son*. *Ní* is used if it's a girl, and *Mhic* is used before a married woman's name.'

'This is Irish,' said the staff nurse, 'isn't it?'

Áine nodded.

'But isn't Liam a Christian name?'

'It's an Irish name.'

'Meaning what?'

'Williams.'

'Williams? These forms are in English, Mrs ... Williams? Why can't we write *Williams*?'

'My first language is Irish.'

'But if you can speak English and these forms are in English we need to have your names in English.'

'Why?'

'Because they're typed in English.'

'I have a right to be called the name I want.'

'Of course you have, we all have that right, but we are obliged to fill in this form in the language in which it's typed, English that is; the language that's on your birth certificate and your medical certificate.'

'Those are the names I've given you.'

'What?'

Áine opened her handbag and rummaged through it. She produced birth certificates and medical cards and handed them to her. The staff nurse looked at them. Her countenance betrayed a sense of defeat. She had argued this particular stance many times before. She had always convinced herself she was fair minded and logical, non-discriminatory, and sensitive too. Why, she had often demonstrated that sensitivity in dealing with non-English-speaking patients, contacting Belfast's multiracial centre, getting translators, ringing foreign consulates, etc. But someone who could speak English perfectly well, who knew the English equivalents of the Irish names they wanted to be called and who, she was convinced, used Irish and spoke Irish merely to assert if not antagonise – this she found difficult to take.

She handed them back to Áine. She lifted other forms from a pile on her desk and said, 'I need to ask you some more questions before the doctor sees your son.' Her tone and her manner were distinctly cool.

CHAPTER 2

Culture
A Global Concept

Ameera and Áine: Fact or fiction

Despite the title given to the first chapter, the two stories it contains are more factual than fictional. The first story is based upon a television news feature in 1998 which explored the increasing cultural awareness of minority communities in Britain. The main thrust of the argument was that culture (embracing, in particular, religion) was much more significant in the perceptions and feelings of members of these communities than their racial origins. So much so that their leaders had initiated campaigns to have the Race Relations Act 1976 amended on the grounds that its focus is far too narrow. They argued that discrimination, prejudice and attack upon minority communities and individuals are increasingly motivated by aspects of culture other than race. A young Moroccan Muslim woman, Arooj Khan, illustrated the point: she described how she and her sisters were attacked by a group of youths. At the time of the attack, which was sudden and totally unprovoked, the sisters were all wearing the traditional Muslim yashmak. This meant that only their eyes were visible. Arooj was convinced that she and her sisters were attacked because of the clothes they wore, and the Muslim religion they signified. She said, 'It was nothing to do with my race'; given the yashmak, they could not in any case have known. She also said that her sense of identity stemmed far more from her culture and her religion than it did from her race.

The second story is based upon the experiences of a family in a small community of Irish-speaking people which has established itself in West Belfast. The origins and development of that community will be described in a later chapter, but the point of the story was merely to illustrate how another family, in another location, regarded *language* as central to their culture and identity. The police inspector and the staff nurse missed the point in their respective stories, but given the neglect of religion and language in welfare and police training generally that is hardly surprising.

Motivating factors

A paradox to be resolved

The motivation for writing this book stems from numerous sources. First, substantial literature and research have revealed a high degree of cultural incompetence within health and social care work, and I want to explore the question 'Why?' There is a paradox here which urgently needs addressing: governments, agencies and individual professionals have all striven to ensure equality of opportunity and services within our increasingly multicultural society, yet the literature indicates an undiminished potential for culturally incompetent practice. One explanation might be that the focus of all these efforts has been on anti-racist and anti-discriminatory practice (ARADP). We can be certain that the police inspector and staff nurse (and many other professionals in their respective bodies) have recently digested lots of ARADP literature. The police officer was obviously alert to racist issues, but he could not see beyond race. He was unaware – as well might many of us be – of a component of culture more crucial in the victim's formulation of her own identity, namely religion. The staff nurse was incapable of believing that another component of culture, namely language, held an equally central position in the self-perception of her patient. Worse still, she could see no reason why the sound of a name in one language had a very different meaning for the patient than the sound of her name in another (other than that the patient must be a bloody-minded anti-British Irish Republican!). I want to explore further the paradox of massive training in anti-discriminatory and anti-oppressive practice and an undiminished potential for cultural incompetence.

Seeking definitions

The second motivating factor for me is the attempt to define *culture* and related terms within the context of health and social care practice. Cultural competence necessitates an understanding of the concepts of culture and *cultural identity*. These are fundamentally dynamic, global concepts, subject to powerful influences and pressures in an increasingly technological and rapidly changing world. The lack of adequate definition of culture and cultural identity is apparent in health and social care legislation, policy documents, and in professional codes of conduct. Take the Children Act

1989, for example, reputedly the most important piece of childcare legislation this century. Many have actually commented favourably on its clarity and detail, and on its obliging professionals to *give due consideration to a child's 'religious persuasion, racial origin and cultural and linguistic background'* s.22(5)(c) (Corby 1993; Dalrymple and Burke 1995; Seden 1995; White, Carr and Lowe 1991). But culture is not defined. This is a glaring omission in an Act that has been commended for the definitions it provides for so many other terms. If something is assumed to be important, but is not defined, then many will attempt to define it for themselves. This has the potential for developing a limited, unbalanced, even negative perception of culture, particularly the culture of others. There are literally hundreds of differing definitions of culture and cultural identity in literature other than that of health and social care. If cultural competence is the goal of health and social care agencies, then it seems a worthwhile exercise to seek useful definitions of culture and cultural identity for health and social care professionals. Such definitions should be based upon health and social care practice and research.

The use and abuse of 'culture' and 'identity'

The third motivating factor is a wish to counter the limitless confusion which results from the multiple uses and abuses of the terms culture and cultural identity. This is not a recent development, though there can be no doubt that the term culture has now become something of a cliché, with no corresponding enlightenment about its use. Probably no country in the world uses and abuses the terms culture and cultural identity like Northern Ireland. I returned there after a working lifetime elsewhere and heard and read these terms countless times each day. Even used intelligently, such frequency would irritate; but invariably used as a weapon, it is depressing. I recall, shortly after extremists in the Orange Order once again created mayhem during their annual July celebrations that dissident Republicans perpetrated the worst single atrocity in the Northen Ireland conflict, at Omagh. Such events generate even more abuses of the concepts of culture and cultural identity. The perpetrators of the former would contend that their actions were in defence of a Protestant and Orange culture and identity; while the perpetrators of the outrage in Omagh were mad enough to believe they could impose a Catholic and Green (i.e. Republican) culture and identity upon the Irish nation as a whole, whatever amount of bombs and bullets are required. These perversions of crucially important concepts like culture and cultural identity have to be challenged.

The abuses elsewhere are not so perverse, but r
Culture and cultural are attractive words. They have a s
which writers obviously find appealing. They are go
chosen more for their aesthetic worth and impact tha
adjective cultural can now seemingly be placed befor
unrelated nouns (e.g. cultural apartheid, cultural un
cultural landscape, cultural environment, cultural
racism, cultural oppression, cultural superiority, cultural blindness, cultural
violence, etc.), while the noun *culture* can seemingly follow a thousand or more
unrelated adjectives (e.g. partisan culture, political culture, popular culture,
dependency culture, modern culture, material culture, folk culture). All these
terms are used with such monotonous regularity as to give the impression that
they have been part of everyday speech over many generations. Few other
words have been subjected to such an etymological assault, and it will be
noticed in the examples given that so many negative appendages have been
attached to both the adjective and the noun (cultural apartheid, partisan
culture, cultural racism, etc.) that we could be excused for believing that
culture itself is a negative concept. Many health and social care writers
actually do believe that culture is a negative concept. Adequate definition may
help counter these trends.

Aim and objectives

The principal aim of this book is to promote cultural competence within
health and social care professions. Within that broad aim there are specific
objectives:

1. to share with readers the findings of a research project carried out
   within a culturally distinct minority. These findings will contribute
   towards enhancing cultural sensitivity and limiting cultural
   insensitivity

2. to provide comprehensive definitions of *culture, cultural identity* and
   related terms; which will reflect the multicultural world in which the
   caring professions now operate

3. to broaden the existing anti-racist and anti-discriminatory basis of
   training within health and social care professions

4. to focus on neglected aspects of culture such as language and religion:
   core components of identity for many minority clients

help practitioners understand and fulfil their statutory obligations relating to culture

6. to provide frameworks which facilitate self-exploration for the purpose of identifying potential sources of cultural incompetence.

Achieving these objectives will largely depend upon an international perspective and multidisciplinary approach. Culture is a truly global concept which all health and social care professions and their academic disciplines must consider. Other disciplines not traditionally aligned with health and social care have contributed significantly to the understanding of culture, and their contribution will be explored and acknowledged.

The book is divided into three parts. Part I (Chapters 1 to 6) uses a number of differing methods and perspectives to illustrate the rediscovery of culture. A beginning is made on the task of defining culture and three chapters describe the re-emergence of specific cultures in different parts of the world. Part II (Chapters 7 to 10) concentrates on the challenge of cultural competence. A pervading theme in this section is that achievement of the goal of cultural competence is hampered by a traditional negativity and hostility to culture evident in the early history of health and social care professions, and in current literature and research. Part II also focuses on two neglected components of culture: religion and language. Part III (Chapters 11 to 15) points the way forward, through recent research findings, definitions and training.

Chapter 3 begins by exploring the origins and evolving meanings of culture and identity. Some of the more prominent meanings attributed to culture and its derivatives will be considered, but there are aspects of the original meaning important enough to be incorporated into a modern definition. The contribution of anthropology to the understanding of culture will be acknowledged. This chapter should advance the aim of providing a modern, comprehensive definition and explanation of culture.

Chapters 4, 5 and 6 focus on three cultures which are re-emerging and reasserting themselves: Islam, American Indian culture and Australian Aboriginal culture. Common features and trends in these developments will be identified. The chapters explore the nature of the challenge this re-emergence has posed for public bodies, and how some are responding to that challenge. Chapter 7 explores the traditional lack of cultural awareness in the literature of the health and social care professions. It highlights the fact that many of these professions in the early years of their development contributed significantly to the destruction of indigenous cultures. This makes for uncomfortable reading, but the evidence is inescapable, not the least of which is that the relevant professional bodies have openly acknowledged the same and made formal apology. No effective foundation for culturally competent practice can be laid without exploring and understanding this regrettable past. Chapter 8 explores the perception of culture within anti-racist and anti-discriminatory practice. A good deal of the negativity and hostility to culture originates in anti-racist writings. Why this is so warrants analysis and comment. Macey and Moxon's (1996) challenge that anti-racist literature is 'theoretically inadequate, being informed by neither sociological, political nor economic theory or research' is examined. The chapter also differentiates between *culture* and *ethnicity*, terms which are often used synonymously.

Chapter 9 highlights the irony of the demise of religion and religious influence in the health and social care professions and the general population, at the same time as religion is reasserting itself as the core component of culture and identity within some minority populations. Some impressive attempts to ensure cultural sensitivity to religious minorities in different parts of the world are described. Chapter 10 explores another neglected and crucially important component of culture: language. Health and social care literature demonstrate that language differences generate much discrimination in practice.

Chapter 11 concentrates upon research carried out within an Irish-speaking community in Northern Ireland. This is probably the first piece of research that asks people to define their culture in their own terms, to identify the most important components within that culture, and to provide examples of professionals being culturally both sensitive and insensitive in the delivery of services to their community. Chapter 12 suggests numerous ways in which the findings of the research contribute to the literature and training on cultural competence. Chapter 13 provides an agency perspective on the delivery of services to minority cultures generally, and to the Irish-speaking community in particular. Managers, front-line practitioners and government officials all contribute.

Chapter 14 completes the task of definition of culture begun in Chapter 3, using much of the learning of previous chapters, in particular how research respondents defined culture in their own terms. Chapter 15 concentrates on training. It includes a review of the knowledge base underpinning cultural competence and stresses the importance of health and social care staff rigorously examining their attitude and approach to culture and to culturally distinct groups. It also provides challenging self-exploration frameworks, enabling students and practitioners to identify potential sources of negativity and hostility to culture.

A final word on Arooj and her sisters: victims of a sectarian attack

An author setting out on this particular journey can be under no illusions about the nature of the task. The dimensions of the challenge of cultural competence in our multicultural societies have magnified considerably. Yet in our technologically shrinking world, it is much easier today to learn about culture. At the touch of a keyboard, not only can we learn of diverse peoples, their cultures and ways of defining their cultures, but we can also communicate with them. There is some irony in the fact that many of the communities (including the Irish-speaking community of Northern Ireland) which are striving to re-establish their ancient cultures and identities have acknowledged their potential ally in the internet and in a global communications system which is commonly believed to be the mortal enemy of culture and cultural diversity. Thus they enthusiastically exploit the internet to the full (the various American Indian tribes boasting over 10,000 sites), loading their websites with a purity of culture that Matthew Arnold would be proud of! Such a rich source of material is certainly a new experience for this author who, throughout 20 years of writing for publication, has been entirely dependent upon traditional sources of learning. How refreshing then to be able instantly to reach out to the farthest corners of the earth, to share and probe diverse thoughts and feelings on culture.

All these sources therefore (namely, traditional methods of learning, recent research and modern technology) have made a valuable contribution to this text. They have, for a start, convinced me that Arooj Khan and her sisters, the Moroccan victims of a sectarian attack, are not alone. There are millions like them for whom race and racial origins, important though they are, are neither an abiding preoccupation nor a central pillar in their own definitions of their culture and identity. Arooj would probably protest against writers who think otherwise; who have conceived of race and racism as the supremely important factor in the lives of those served by health and social care professionals – a factor to which all other aspects of culture and identity must be subordinated. We can only guess how Arooj would react if she also discovered that many of those writers believed they were serving her interests and speaking on her behalf. On second thoughts, maybe this should not be the final word on Arooj's much more intelligent understanding of what she and her sisters endured.

CHAPTER 3

Towards a Definition of Culture and Cultural Identity

Introduction

Culture and cultural identity are crucially important concepts in health and social care work. Much has been written about these two concepts, but not in health and social care literature. Some health and social care publications do provide definitions, but they are invariably borrowed from other disciplines. Nothing wrong with that – this chapter too will spend some time looking at various perspectives on culture, particularly that of anthropology. But a start must be made on defining culture and related terms specifically for health and social care practitioners, based upon the experiences of those working with culturally diverse groups, and with reference to the 'culture-sensitive' legislation now governing their work. This chapter begins by looking at the origins and developments of the concepts identity and culture. It will draw heavily on sociological literature for the former and anthropological literature for the latter. It will then consider perspectives on culture from sociology, cultural studies, cultural geography, psychology, cross-cultural psychology and medical anthropology. It will reinforce the point that culture and cultural identity are complex concepts, with virtually limitless parameters, which cannot be defined or explained in the two or three sentences usually allocated to them in much health and social care literature. The contents of this chapter will be frequently referred to throughout the book and will provide a foundation for much of the content of subsequent chapters.

Origins, meanings and use

Identity

The term *cultural identity* is a relatively recent construction, but the words *culture* and *identity* have a heritage older than the English language itself. Both words have French and Latin origins. *Identity* stems from the Latin *idem* (meaning 'the same') and *identidem* (meaning 'repeatedly'). The *Oxford English Dictionary* defines *identity* as 'absolute or essential sameness'. This may surprise some who instinctively associate identity with individuality and difference rather than sameness. Psychology is probably responsible for that association, defining identity as 'a person's essential, continuous self, the internal subjective concept of oneself as an individual' (Reber 1985, p.341). If we ask the question 'Identity with what?', we immediately realise that the core of the original dictionary meaning remains intact: our identity is first constructed upon identification with, and a sense of belonging to, something or somebody, or (more accurately) some things or some people.

Identity crisis is a modern commonly understood term which facilitates our understanding of the original meaning of *identity*. We are likely to experience an identity crisis when our identification with 'something assumed to be fixed, coherent and stable is displaced by the experience of doubt and uncertainty' (Mercer 1990, p.43) The identity crisis will endure until it is replaced with an alternative identification. A number of writers (e.g. Horowitz 1975; Weeks 1990) define identity in terms of both these opposing attributes – sameness (or belonging) and difference – but we surely cannot experience a consciousness of difference until a sense of sameness and belonging is well established. The 'something' or the 'people' to which we feel we truly belong is the reference point that enables us to discern difference. It may be a community or a group, or a nation state. It may be a particular race, with specific physical features; it could be a geographical location, a system of values, a religion, or a language. More likely, however, the 'sameness' will embrace many of these. 'Identity ... is constituted out of different elements of experience and subjective position' (Rutherford 1990, p.9).

Aspects of identity

There are numerous aspects of identity which make it a more problematic and less transparent concept than common usage would suggest. The first and most obvious is that each individual may have numerous identities, each of which stems from that sense of belonging to, and sameness with, some thing or some group. 'Multiple ascriptive identities are the rule,' says Horowitz (1975, p.118). The individual could have a religious identity, a racial and linguistic identity, a national or geographical identity, an ideological or political identity. They could also have a sexual identity, an occupational and professional identity, or a developmental identity (i.e. for some, their age and stage of development may be the most potent source of identity). All of these may fuse to form an overall identity but by no means the complete inventory. A useful task for any group of trainees in the caring professions is to invite them to consider the 'some things' and the 'peoples' to which they belong (which have inevitably therefore contributed to their identity formation). The task (i.e. completing the inventory) often proves to be as difficult as it is illuminating.

The second aspect of identity worth considering is that (like culture) it is a dynamic concept undergoing constant change. Horowitz (1975) speaks of 'these processes of expanding or contracting identity' (p.118). Hall (1990) writes: 'Instead of thinking of identity as an already accomplished fact, which the new cultural practices then represent, we should think, instead, of identity as a 'production', which is never complete, always in process' (p.222). In a later work, Hall (1996) goes further, undermining identity's 'settled semantic career' and questioning its 'stable core of the self' (p.3). This applies to identity in total, and to the various strands of what Gramsci (1988) refers to as the inventory of identity. The sense of belonging to, and sameness with, any of the strands will be subject to differing pressures and challenges and will often strengthen or weaken. New allegiances will be made, the sense of sameness and belonging will gradually be transferred, and identity may be totally transformed. Professionals in health and social care, particularly in mental health, know only too well that the process of change in identity can constitute a major crisis for their clients. That process is often risk-laden, heightening alienation and vulnerability, and necessitates much understanding and empathy.

The third aspect of identity leads naturally from the second and is probably the most crucial one. Identity is normally perceived as both a necessity and an asset. It is often a source of confidence and assertiveness. But the core sense of *sameness* and *belonging* in the meaning of identity may not tolerate a perceived lack of sameness and belonging in others. A sense of identity constituted primarily through sameness and belonging may be threatened by difference. Identity may be maintained by separation from, suspicion of, or hostility towards difference. The origins of identity are often division and inequality. Rutherford (1990) exaggerates, but his point is worth making anyway: 'It is

within their polarities of white/black, masculine/feminine, hetero/homo-
sexual, where one term is always dominant and the other subordinate, that our
identities are formed' (p.10).

The fourth aspect of identity is its recent increasing prominence in the literature of disciplines related and unrelated to the caring professions. Nau (as
cited in Tickner 1997) argues that identity is a more powerful variable than
anarchy or power in understanding international relations. Tickner (1997)
believes that most current insecurities in the world are not about disputed
boundaries or power rivalries; rather, 'issues of identity are driving underlying
perceptions of threats and vulnerabilities' (p.147). Haynes (1993) writes
about religion in third world politics, but makes it clear that both religion and
ethnicity are important components of national and cultural identity. Fitzgerald (1993) regards identity as the 'action unit of culture'. It has an
executive role and is fundamentally the 'problem solving tool for coping in
particular environments'. Historically, social and international relations
theorists have convinced us that our sense of identity primarily stems from
loyalty and obligation to a nation, a state, or citizenship within that state.
Authorities have often exploited this linkage. Tickner's (1997) critique (compatible with much feminist social work writing) exposes the limitations in this
interpretation, including its hierarchical and exclusionary nature, its social
and gender inequality, constructed out of experiences more typical of men
(dominating the public sphere) than women (traditionally confined to the
private sphere of home, children and domestic responsibility). Feminist
writers in social theory and international relations advocate an alternative
concept of identity (Tickner 1997; Tronto 1993). They believe it must be
based on the assumption that human beings are interdependent rather than
autonomous, 'sometimes giving care and sometimes receiving it'. A person's
sense of identity is based more upon their caring, sharing and receiving in
whatever societal context they live than on an assumed prevailing consciousness of the state, and their loyalty and autonomy within that state. A vocabulary of care is 'the mechanism that offers the greatest possibility for trans-
forming social and political thinking' on identity. (Tronto 1993, quoted in
Tickner 1997, p.161).

Culture

The word culture and related terms such as cultured, cultivate, and cultivation
derive from the same French word *culture* and the Latin word *cultura*. All these

words referred to the tilling of the land, the improvement of crops and crop production. The words have undergone significant change in definition, but that original meaning, centring on a symbolically powerful earth and its soil, remains a core component in the subjective meaning many of us are likely to provide for the word today. The association with the land may be latent or even unconscious in our everyday use of the word culture, but if we are asked to define or explain the word, the land of our birth and upbringing is likely to influence, directly or indirectly, our responses.

In the thirteenth and fourteenth centuries, the meaning of culture was expanded to include *improvement* or *refinement* of human beings, primarily through education and training. Hobbes later wrote: 'The education of children is called a cultivation of their minds.' Milton wrote of 'cultivating friendship'; and the OED records the meaning given at the beginning of the nineteenth century: 'the training and refinement of mind, taste, and manners'. Matthew Arnold extended this notion with his famous *Culture and Anarchy: An Essay in Political and Social Criticism* (1869). He regarded culture as 'a perfection in which the character of beauty and intelligence are both present, which unites the two noblest of things'. Arnold contrasts this ideal with the political and religious indoctrination of the masses:

> The ordinary popular literature is an example of this way of working on the masses ... Culture works differently. It does not try to teach down to the level of inferior classes; it does not try to win them for this or that sect of its own with ready-made judgements and watchwords. It seeks to do away with classes; to make the best that has been thought and known in the world current everywhere; to make all men live in an atmosphere of sweetness and light, where they may use ideas, as it uses them itself, freely – nourished and not bound by them ... This is the *social* idea; and the men of culture are the true apostles of equality. The great men of culture are those who have had a passion for diffusing, for making prevail, for carrying from one end of society to the other, the best knowledge, the best ideas of their time; who have laboured to divest knowledge of all that was harsh, uncouth, difficult, abstract, professional, exclusive; to humanise it; to make it efficient outside the clique of the cultivated and learned, yet still remaining the best knowledge and thought of the time, and a true source therefore of sweetness and light. (Cited in Bryson 1967, p.493)

Raymond Williams (1963) thought this was a little over the top. He blames Arnold for the 'common English hostility to the word' manifest thereafter: 'There is surely a danger of allowing culture to become a fetish.' He concludes,

'The idea of culture is too important to be surrendered to this kind of failing' (pp.134–5).

An understanding and meaningful definition of culture should draw upon the knowledge and experience of disciplines and professions for whom exploration and meaning of the concept have been an enduring preoccupation. No subject area has contributed as much to our understanding of culture as anthropology. But we shall also consider contributions from cultural studies, cultural geography, sociology, psychology and medical anthropology.

Culture in anthropology

Anthropology has been more preoccupied with culture than any other discipline, and provides by far the most illuminating theory and comment on the subject. 'It is the most liberating of all the sciences,' stated Grace de Laguna, President of the Eastern Division of the American Philosophical Society, as far back as 1941; and has 'exposed the fallacies of racial and cultural superiority' (Haviland 1999). Anthropology is defined as 'the holistic study of humankind – its origins, development, social and political organisations, religions, languages, art and artefacts' (Helman 1994, p.3). A brief look at the theories and research of some of the most prominent pioneers is warranted.

Edward Tylor

In 1871, Edward Tylor formulated the most enduring definition of culture, equating it, as did Arnold, with civilisation: 'Culture or civilisation is that complex whole which includes knowledge, beliefs, art, morals, law, custom and any other capabilities and habits acquired by man as a member of society' (cited in Helman 1994, p.9). The all-embracing nature of this definition is explicit in the term 'and any other capabilities and habits acquired'; these include language. Tylor's study of ancient texts and ethnological reports, and of the recordings of explorers and missionaries, revealed that similar cultures had evolved among different races in different locations. He later formulated an evolutionary theory to explain cultural development. All cultures evolved along 'nearly uniform channels', because all human minds are similar and are governed by the same laws of cognition. The processes of cultural development are similar for all societies, irrespective of location and time. Culture itself is a 'cognitive construction created by similar human minds solving the problems of existence' (Moore 1997, p.22).

Franz Boas

In the USA, Franz Boas was to acquire a similar status to Tylor in England. He greatly undermined Tylor's theory on cultural evolution, by simply asking for evidence. Boas believed that cultures were integrated wholes, but concluded that Tylor's assumption of unilineal evolution was untested and untestable: 'As soon as we admit that the hypothesis of a uniform evolution has to be proved before it can be accepted the whole structure loses its foundation' (Boas 1920, quoted in Moore 1997, p.49). Boas did not dispute Tylor's assumption of the existence of general laws of human behaviour (upon which all cultures are based), but he (justifiably) refuted any claim that Tylor or his contemporaries knew precisely what those laws were. Boas attempted to discover them, but more importantly: 'The object of our investigation is to find the processes by which certain stages of culture have developed. The customs and beliefs themselves are not the ultimate objects of research. We desire to learn the reasons why such customs and beliefs exist – in other words, we wish to discover the history of their development' (Boas 1896, quoted in Moore 1994, p.49).

Alfred Kroeber

Alfred Kroeber's earlier career was concentrated on salvaging the remnants of the fast-disappearing cultures of the native peoples of California. His 1000-page *Handbook of California Indians* (Kroeber 1925) remains one of the great classic anthropological texts of this century, revealing, for example, that native Californians had the highest linguistic diversity of any region in North America ('the Babel of ancient America'). Kroeber designed the 'culture element distribution list', a tool that was to enable such cultural diversity to be measured and explained. He divided his observations of cultural features into units, which, he believed, could be understood qualitatively and quantitatively, and dispatched his army of student researchers among some 250 tribes and tribal subdivisions west of the Rocky Mountains. The technique was a major advance in anthropological research, but was later judged to be seriously flawed. Culture was being atomised into bits and pieces, each considered to be of equal significance; and when a cultural element already identified in one culture was discovered in another, Kroeber interpreted their meaning identically.

Ruth Benedict

Ruth Benedict, a former social worker and pupil of Boas, was, like Kroeber, preoccupied with the patterning of culture. She was specifically interested in the underlying values and ideas within cultures, and in the relationship between them. Benedict was the first major anthropological figure to concentrate on values underpinning cultural practices. Peoples' responses to situations are more likely to be determined by these underlying values and associated ideas than by any particular stimulus the situation presents. In her *Patterns of Culture* (1959) she sought to demonstrate the causal primacy of culture over biology in the lives of the tribes she was studying, and applied her reasoning to understanding the differences amongst modern societies. (Towards the end of her life, she wrote a powerful propaganda pamphlet in the service of the American war effort against Nazism, arguing that cultural differences were far more important than racial differences.) She believed that cultural differences among individuals and their societies emerged from differences in the societies' most basic core values. Benedict's concentration on values and her consciousness of the emergence of deviance in the relationship between the individual and society make her work relevant to current attempts within health and social care professions to understand culture.

Margaret Mead

Margaret Mead explored the cultural bases of personality. Like Benedict, she believed that culture was much more significant than either race or biology in personality development and human responses to life's transitions, particularly adolescence. Her main focus of study and research was on child rearing. Mead wrote about the 'cultureless' child at birth and how the child-rearing aspects of the culture of the tribe into which the child was born are instrumental in shaping the personality of the child. These cultural manifestations are transmitted from the moment of birth:

> When the Balinese baby is born, the midwife, even at the moment of lifting him in her arms, will put words into his mouth, commenting, 'I am just a poor little new-born baby, and I don't know how to talk properly, but I am very grateful to you, honourable people, who have entered this pigsty of a house to see me born.' And from that moment, all through babyhood, the child is fitted into a frame of behaviour, of imputed speech and imputed thought and complex gestures, far beyond his skill and maturity. (Bateson and Mead 1942, quoted in Moore 1997, p.109)

It is in such intensely cultural interactions that personality is formed. Mead was less concerned with the origin and development of culture than were some of her contemporaries. She was more interested in the dynamic, complex, culturally specific hour-by-hour processes she encountered.

These are only brief extracts from some well-known anthropological texts on culture. There are countless more (e.g. Geertz 1973; Haviland 1999; Leach 1982; White 1949, 1959) demonstrating that anthropology and its various branches have for centuries been preoccupied with core concepts of human existence highly relevant to health and social care.

Culture in cultural studies

Bennett (1997) remarks on the burgeoning industry of textbooks and primers on cultural studies. This relatively new subject is essentially interdisciplinary, embracing, if not relying upon, many other disciplines, notably sociology, anthropology and history. It seeks to influence all disciplines in respect of culture. Bennett believes cultural studies supply 'an intellectual field in which perspectives from different disciplines might be selectively drawn on in examining particular relations of culture and power' (p.51). There is a noticeable tension between two strands of thought about the definition of culture in cultural studies. One strand seeks to define it within narrower parameters of politics and power; the other, within virtually limitless boundaries of wholeness and total way of life. The latter is in the ascendancy, represented by Hall and Jefferson's (1996) definition:

> The culture of a group or class is the peculiar and distinctive 'way of life' of the group or class, the meanings, values and ideas embodied in institutions, in social relations, in systems of belief, in mores and customs, in the uses of objects and material life. Culture is the distinctive shape in which this material and social organisation of life expresses itself. A culture includes the 'maps of meanings' which make things intelligible to its members ... Culture is the way the social relations of a group are structured and shaped: but it also the way those shapes are experienced, understood and interpreted. (Hall and Jefferson 1996, pp.10–11)

This is a useful definition, easily transferable (with a few minor adjustments) to work within the caring professions. 'Systems of belief' needs some elaboration, to include (or to spell out) 'religion and faith', as religion and faith are often the origin and defender of 'meanings, values and ideas'. Another small addition could include 'language' in the 'maps of meaning', as language will surely be the potent means by which the culture and its 'material and social organisation' expresses itself.

Cultural geography

Cultural geography is an increasingly prominent offshoot of cultural studies. It is being treated here as a separate entity because it provides a unique perspective on culture which has not yet been acknowledged in cultural competence training. Cultural geography asserts that culture (and, consequentially, cultural identity) evolves from the interrelationship between human beings and their land, space and physical environment (i.e. mountains, valley, rivers, seas, sky, road, house, hearth, farmyard, field). Shurmer-Smith and Hannam (1994) write: 'If mountains, rivers and weather are not approached culturally, there is a terrible lie uttered every time the word "environment" is used' (p.216). This is a logical argument if one considers the original definition of culture, centring as it does on the earth, on the cultivation and products of the earth. What is also happening to the cultivator in this intimate relationship is one of the questions which cultural geography explores. The cultural geographer looks at 'landscapes and artefacts to try to discover the thought patterns of the individuals who constructed them' (Crossman and McLoughlin 1994, p.90). All the features of landscape, and of the relationship, impact not only on the individual, but on his or her family, community and society. More importantly, they not only mould and shape individual identities, but also the evolving pillars of culture (i.e. customs, institutions, beliefs, dress, diet, etc.). Lee (1997) explains: 'Space, when taken culturally, represents a relatively coherent and autonomous social domain which exercises a certain determinacy upon both the population and the social processes located upon its terrain' (p.127). Such a view may appear rather abstract, but there are occasions when it is expressed in a powerful simplicity.

This land is me

Nick, a farmer's son, born and reared in the Yorkshire Dales, was one of the participants chosen by the producers of a long-running television documentary series begun in 1964, when he and the other participants were seven years of age. The producer and his team returned to the participants every seven years, to see how they were getting on. By the age of 42, Nick was a successful nuclear physicist in a US university. The programme interviewed him and his wife in the university and in his former Yorkshire Dales home. He was asked about the significance of these roots and the surrounding Yorkshire countryside. He glanced around and said: 'Of course it's significant; just look at it; it's not beautiful by any means; but it's still spectacular. The hills are dour, but they are awesome too. They are part of me. They are what made me what I am; you can't escape the influence these surroundings have on people.'

Nick's comments encapsulate one of the central tenets in cultural geography: that it is the physical environment, and the ensuing relationship which develops between it and those whose lives depend upon it, which give rise to cultural processes. The relationship between the individual and the land is the most continuous and enduring aspect of culture, countering the claim that culture is always socially transmitted. Patterns of thoughts, feelings, spirituality and values evolve from this relationship (nowhere better described and explained than in many of the poems by Wordsworth). Over time, attributes like confidence, realism, practicality, patience, scepticism, conviction, predictive tendencies, resignation, etc., will be forged from this relationship and become features of personality. Differing physical environments will produce differing relationships and, therefore, differing attributes; and they will, most definitely, produce different dress codes and diet choice. Within the community as a whole, such attributes, shared by so many who have similar relationships with the land, will give rise to and continue to influence numerous aspects of culture such as rituals, habits and customs.

Contrasting lessons from cultural geography

There are two contrasting lessons to be drawn here, bearing in mind the ultimate goal of cultural competence in health and social care practice. First, there is the realisation that health and social care training have never considered the likelihood that a client's culture and identity owed anything to the features of the land of their birth and upbringing; or that their emotional life, thought sequences, conceptualisations, habits and rituals could in some way have been shaped and influenced by the space, landscape and climate of that land. Yet this is a universally applicable fact. It can apply to ex-crofters from the Scottish Isles, and African Caribbean people from the beaches and shanty towns of Trinidad; or ex-farmers from the West of Ireland, and homeless families from the streets of Calcutta. The challenge faced by any of these groups in the vastly different physical environments and in the demands of modern cities may be formidable. Combined with racism, it may be overwhelming.

The second (cautionary) lesson is that cultural geography's apparent 'deterministic' aspects (note the use of the word 'determinacy' in Lee's explanation above) may contain a potential for prejudice. Some may interpret Lee's explanation to mean that the culture of the individual and of the community is predetermined by the physical environment alone, and that neither individual nor community can significantly influence it. The potential for prejudice in this perspective is evidenced in some of the writings of E. Estyn Evans (1984). Evans moved from his native Wales to Northern Ireland in 1923. He wrote extensively on the cultural geography of Northern Ireland. He noticed that rural Protestant families lived in an entirely different physical environment from that of many Catholic families. He believed the rich and fertile lowlands of the former, systematically and monotonously tilled, hidden to the outside world and closed in on all sides by natural and artificial boundaries, provided the restricted horizons that limited vision and imagination. As for Catholics, occupying the wilder and economically poorer landscapes, he wrote about 'the open and naked bogs and hills which are naturally areas of vision and imagination, which are poetic and visionary and which represent the other tradition in Ulster' (p.7 quoted in Crossman and McLoughlin (1994) p.91). There is no evidence or research validating Evan's 'observation' ('academic licence' may be a more appropriate term); but potentially it could be culturally insensitive baggage indeed for any health and social care worker to carry.

Culture in sociology

Sociologists have borrowed from anthropology in attempting to articulate a sociological perception of culture. Giddens (1993) says culture

> refers to the ways of life of the members of a society, or of groups, or within a society. It includes how they dress, their marriage customs and family life, their patterns of work, religious ceremonies and leisure pursuits. It also covers the goods they create and which become meaningful to them. (p.31)

Sociologists are primarily responsible for popularising the concepts of 'mass culture', 'popular culture', and the theory of the 'culture industries'. These terms are seldom clearly defined, but the sociological interpretation is clear. Giddens (1993) believes that the chief focus of sociology is the study of industrialised societies (and, by implication, the study of cultures and cultural diversity within those societies). Probably the most significant start to that study was made by the Frankfurt school of sociologists (Kellner 1997). They lived through the European fascist era and witnessed how the modern industrial state could use instruments of mass culture to produce a subservient society, enslaved to the ideology pursued by that state. Later, in exile in the USA, they made similar observations about American popular culture:

> The culture industries were organised according to the strictures of mass production, churning out mass-produced products that generated a highly commercial system of culture which in turn sold the values, life-styles and institutions of American capitalism. (Kellner 1997, p.14)

Hence the coining of the phrase 'Fordism' to symbolise mass production and a 'homogenising regime of capital' producing mass desires, tastes and behaviours. It was, according to the Frankfurt school, 'the end of the individual' (p.14).

Here is a new meaning of culture. If culture is primarily the 'way of life' of a society, then sociologists are correct in identifying the 'cultural' consequences of industrialisation and more latterly of information technology. But this may not make sense to the millions of people who are striving to reassert a *traditional* cultural identity. Many of these people will say that 'mass culture' or 'popular culture' or the 'culture industries' have nothing to do with culture; and that these twentieth-century developments represent destructive, dehumanising forces which pose the greatest threat to culture (as the term has been previously understood).

Sociologists' perception of culture generally, however, acknowledges its importance. Giddens (1993), for example, devotes a whole chapter to the topic in his classic sociology text. Like the anthropologist Boas, he too believes a culture should be studied in terms of its own meanings and values, and he concludes:

> No societies could exist without culture. Without culture, we would not be human at all, in the sense in which we usually understand that term. We would have no language in which to express ourselves, no sense of self-consciousness, and our ability to think or reason would be severely limited. (Giddens 1993, p.32)

There are numerous sociology texts written specifically for the caring professions (e.g. Day 1987; Heraud 1970; Kelleher and Hillier 1996). Day writes about the need to familiarise oneself with the patterns of obligations and responsibilities in families, with the roles, networks and hierarchies operating in communities and families, with their child-rearing practices and their culturally influenced perceptions of their own problems. He speaks of the all-pervasive nature of the cultural dimension, whether one is attempting to arrange day care, improve housing conditions, or place children for fostering.

He cautions against interpreting real problems as nothing more than cultural differences, against the tendency to tolerate out of a misguided cultural sensitivity, and against evading responsibility for action through stereotyping particular cultures as perpetually self-sufficient.

Culture in psychology

The *Penguin Dictionary of Psychology* provides many derivative terms from culture, and is very precise in the meanings attributed to them. Here are some of the terms: cultural absolute, cultural conserve, cultural items, cultural relativism, cultural monism, cultural transmission, culture conflict and culture traits. The definition of culture itself is:

> The system of information that codes the manner in which the people in an organised group, society or nation, interact with their social and physical environment. A key connotation is that culture pertains only to non-genetically given transmission; each member must *learn* the systems and the structures (*operating within the culture*). (Reber 1985, p.175)

It is a neat definition and its emphasis on learning echoes a behaviourist interpretation. But 'interaction with the environment' need not always be a 'learning' process in the behaviourist sense of the word. It can equally be an aesthetic, an emotional or even a spiritual experience. Psychology has made a significant contribution to the understanding of culture in its research and exposure of such negative concepts as 'cultural blindness' and the related 'ethnocentric fallacy' (Atkinson, Atkinson, Smith and Hilgard 1987). These refer to a disposition to view the world wholly through the values and norms of one's own culture, entirely unaware of differing values and cultural norms which may be underpinning the thoughts and actions of another. Psychology has also been instrumental in exposing the cultural bias of psychological tests, to which virtually every individual has been subject, either in his or her educational or employment career (Atkinson *et al.* 1987). Many of these tests were designed on the biased perceptions and assumptions of a dominant prevailing culture. Consequently, those sharing in a minority or peripheral culture often failed to pass such tests, and were erroneously judged to be unable to fulfil the responsibilities designated. Psychology has taken the lead in attempting to produce culture-free tests, designed to eliminate, insofar as is practically possible, any advantage pertaining to cultural factors which one individual may have over another.

Cross-cultural psychology

Cross-cultural psychology is less concerned about defining culture than with exploring and comparing the influences of different cultures on human development (Keats 1996; Segall *et al.* 1990). Keats (1997) emphasises the centrality of values in culture, and that the individual's knowing, accepting, and internalising those values is a gradual developmental process. Useful research has been carried out in cross-cultural psychology. For example, Thomas's (1986) study in New Zealand concentrated upon the relationship between the degree of 'cultural knowledge' of four groups of children and their achievement in mathematics and language tests. The children culturally identified themselves as: (a) Pakeha (i.e. European); (b) mostly Pakeha; (c) mostly Maori; or (d) Maori. The Maori children who scored highest in cultural knowledge also scored higher on the achievement tests, leading Thomas to refute the idea that children steeped in Maori culture were educationally disadvantaged. Cross-cultural psychology contributes significantly towards countering prejudicial perceptions of cultures.

Culture in medical anthropology

Culture is now recognised as an important issue in the perception, diagnosis and treatment of illness. Ongoing research in many branches of medicine and health care has revealed persistent, and as yet inexplicable, occurrence of illnesses and vulnerability in respect of culturally distinct groups of peoples, and a corresponding ineffectiveness in treatment. This has dictated calls for a new agenda in training, literature and research, giving impetus to a comparatively new offshoot of anthropology, namely, medical anthropology. Medicine and anthropology have been closely related, and the former has adopted the definition and understanding of culture provided by the latter (i.e. Edward Tylor in 1871; see p.32).

Helman's (1997) authoritative work *Culture, Health and Illness* demonstrates the clinical significance of cultural and social factors in illness and in health, and in preventive medicine and health education. It draws new boundaries in which medical personnel must strive to understand, before treating: Helman says that health care programmes

> need to take account of the specific needs and circumstances of different communities, their social, cultural and economic backgrounds, and what the people living in them actually believe about their own ill-health, and how it should be treated. (p.11)

The forcefulness of this statement may be a response to the diversity of approach to culture in the various branches of medicine, ranging from acute sensitivity and impressive research (e.g. Currer 1991) to a conspicuous lack of awareness of the concept in medical publications. Recent exposures of medical negligence and incompetence have a cultural aspect which will be discussed in Chapter 7.

Definition: an ongoing task

All these contributions from differing disciplines should influence any attempt to find suitable definitions of 'culture' and 'identity' specifically for health and social care workers. They vary substantially, each perspective revealing the dominant theme or preoccupation within the discipline, and some perspectives with content which we may disregard or contest. The convention in textbook writing is to provide a definition in the early chapters and to impose that definition on the content of subsequent chapters. Here we may depart from convention. A significant start has been made towards definition, but it is too early to attempt to complete the task. All the above perspectives teach us that 'culture' and 'cultural identity' are complex, all-embracing and elusive concepts, and that there is much more ground to cover which includes:

- examining the challenge which culture has posed for health and social care professionals in the past

- critically reviewing how health and social care literature perceives 'culture' in the present

- listening to health and social care clients within a distinct cultural minority group defining their own culture in their own terms.

The definitions which eventually emerge should enhance workers' understanding of the concepts and, more importantly, should function as useful reference points in fulfilling the statutory obligations relating to culture.

Summary and conclusions

This chapter has laid the foundations for the promotion of cultural competence and for pursuing the objectives of subsequent chapters. It began by considering the origins and developments of the terms *identity* and *culture*. Some key sociological writing on identity was critically examined, with agreement on the pervading belief that it denotes 'absolute or essential sameness' with something, and that that something could be one or more of several things.

Our sense of identity could stem largely from our sameness with, and our sense of belonging to, a community or a group or a nation state; or a particular race of people with specific physical features; or a geographical location, or a system of values, a religion, or a language or a sexual orientation. More likely however, the sameness will embrace many of these, and each of them is subject to change (i.e. consolidation or dissipation).

Anthropology's contribution to understanding culture predominated in this chapter, with extracts from five of the pioneers of that discipline. They convey the complexity and the richness of the concept, and its crucial role in the development of all civilisations. Health and social care workers may note that two of the most famous names in anthropology, Ruth Benedict and Margaret Mead, concentrated their research on two areas of particular importance within the caring professions, values and child rearing. Additional contributions from sociology, cultural studies, cultural geography, medical anthropology and psychology were also considered. The contribution from cultural geography merits further attention, as it teaches us how our physical environments can be construed as culture. It asserts that for many people both culture and cultural identity evolves from the interrelationship between human beings and their land, space and physical environment. The cultural geographer, just as poets, novelists and dramatists have done for centuries, tries to discover how landscapes impact upon the thought patterns and emotions of the individuals who constructed them, lived on them and worked them. This is a subject area which has been neglected in health and social care literature and yet, for many minority cultural groups, the relationship with and the perceptions and memories of the physical environment in which they were brought up may have a fundamental influence on their responses to professionals and the services they provide.

CHAPTER 4

The Re-emergence of Culture
1 Islam

Introduction

Culture is re-emerging and reasserting itself. Chapters 4, 5 and 6 will concentrate on three well-known examples of the re-emergence of culture: that of Islam, the American Indian and the Australian Aborigine. Many western attitudes to culture today are rooted in the confrontation with and attempted annihilation of cultures in the past. Indigenous peoples never seriously threatened their colonial oppressors militarily, but their cultures posed major obstacles, for which the most convenient solution was to deny them this means of expression. This was particularly the case with American Indians and Australian Aborigines. Similarly, today, there are many aspects of the re-emergence of Islamic culture which pose difficulties for non-Muslim majority populations (including, of course, health and social care workers).

This chapter will begin by clarifying the meaning of Islamic culture. Islam is both a religion and an all-embracing culture. The chapter will briefly touch upon significant milestones in the origins and development of Islam and concentrate upon current anti-Islamic feeling. This has been reactivated by terrible events on the world stage which need revisiting, acknowledging and reassessing in a wider, more objective context. Islam is reasserting itself in numerous ways, each of which will be explored. Health and social care provision to Muslims in Britain and Europe will be reviewed in the light of four separate, differently located research projects. The consensus within the findings is that health and social care professionals remain largely ignorant of and disrespectful towards Islamic culture and way of life.

The all-embracing nature of Islam

Islam is the religion of Muslims. The word Islam derives from the Arabic *aslama*, which means resigning oneself (in peace) with God. All Muslims are obliged to fulfil five principal duties: faith, prayer, giving alms to the poor, fasting and pilgrimage to Mecca. Islam is also, inevitably, a culture. Vatin (1982) actually refers to the resurgence of Islam as 'an evident regeneration of *culture*'. Islam so comprehensively influences the everyday life of Muslims that one can confidently say it is a way of life. (Readers will recall that this phrase 'way of life' is commonly used in differing definitions of culture.) The resurgence of Islam has had a seismic impact on international relationships and politics, on governments and societies, on the global economy and on the numerous other cultures upon which it comes into contact. The origins of this resurgence have many interconnected strands: historical, political, religious, colonial and cultural. The roots of some of these strands reach back to Muhammad's emigration from Mecca to Medina in 622, his establishment of the *umma* (Muslim community), the publication of the Qur'an (Holy Book), the promulgation of the Sharia (Islamic law) and the commencement of the first Jehad (Holy War) in 624. The origin of current perceptions of Islam and Muslims, however, lies in more recent history. Unlike other religions, which have managed (or have been gradually compelled) to restrict their sphere of influence to the spiritual life and the faith which sustains it, Islam is an entirely holistic concept heavily influencing the religious–spiritual, cultural and political life of nations. Even in Turkey, nominally a secular state since 1924, when Ataturk suppressed Islam and abolished the caliphate (successor to the prophet Muhammad), Islam nevertheless has remained a potent influence on the body politic. 'Islam makes no division between secular and religious matters,' says Henley (1982). 'Daily life, food, dress, manners, education, politics and law are all religious issues' (p.17). 'Islam and politics are insepa-rable,' says Haynes (1993, p.67). Herein lies one of the most formidable obstacles in the way of non-Islamic respect for Muslims and their religion: the western notion that religion and politics should separate or, more specifically, that the former should have little or no influence on the latter. Such notions make little sense to many Muslims, whether they be the small band of Muhammad's followers 1500 years ago or, more recently, any one of the Islamist opposition groups challenging the legitimacy of governments in Egypt, Indonesia, Malaysia, and more than a dozen other states (Haynes 1993) These opposition groups clamour for the 'Islamization of their respec-tive societies' (p.44). They do not define 'Islamization', but we can be certain that their aim is to make Islam the dominant political, religious and cultural influence. Islam has been a highly politicised ideal since its inception, when it quickly 'developed as a religio-political community, albeit with different and rival Shia and Sunni interpretations' (Haynes 1993, p.45). Perhaps even more so today, Islam and politics remain inseparable.

Non-Muslim perceptions of Islam and Muslims

The 1500-year history of Islam (including the nearly calamitous split between Sunni and Shia Muslims, which still has a profound influence in contemporary world politics) is largely unknown in the Christian west. Islam's many 'golden eras,' its unparalleled contribution to the evolution of governments and societies and the advancement of education, law, art, literature, music, architecture and science and, not least, its current daily influence over more than a billion of the earth's inhabitants – all of this means little to today's non-Islamic world, dominated by communications media more dependent upon sound bites than objectivity and understanding. There has been no shortage of sound bites in the western media's portrayal of Islam since the 1967 Arab–Israeli war.

The demonising of Islam

In 1982 a young policewoman, Yvonne Fletcher, was shot dead in London by an assailant firing from the window of the embassy of another Islamic state, Libya. Libya and Colonel Ghadaffi had long been the scourge of western governments which were helpless in stemming that country's support of international terrorism. This outrage was made even worse by Colonel Ghadaffi's refusal to allow the Metropolitan police to conduct their inquiry within the embassy and interview all embassy staff. Diplomatic relations were severed and the British public had to endure the sight of each member of staff (including the murderer) calmly leaving the scene of the crime and boarding a Libyan airline for home and freedom. The 1980s was also the decade of hostage taking in Lebanon, worldwide hijacking of planes and ships with American or Israeli connections (usually culminating in the incineration of their passengers), the bombing of American embassies and military camps, assassination attempts on Israeli ambassadors, bomb outrages in the Paris metro, and the suicidal bombings of school buses and public markets in Jerusalem. All these events and their aftermath dominated western news broadcasts and were often interspersed with film of blood-spattered, Kalashnikov-wielding, foot-thumping Muslim men (e.g. Hizbullah in Lebanon, Algeria's Islamic Salvation Front and Palestine's Hamas), all threatening the world with another Islamic Jehad. The triumph of the Mujahadeen in Afghanistan in the early 1990s (ironically due to the support they had earlier received from western governments to help them defeat the Soviet Union) provided another powerful negative image of Islam: its subjugation of women. In an era when western women had made substantial strides towards emancipation in their own countries, the images of women subjected to the most extreme interpretation of Sharia (having not a whit to do with Islam or the Prophet Muhammad) further strengthened perceptions of Islam and Islamic culture as a wholly oppressive, terrorist force.

Muslims assert themselves in an anti-Muslim world

The reassertion of Islam and Islamic culture can be seen in numerous and diverse ways:

- the overt support of the Muslim struggle elsewhere (Muslims elsewhere generally perceived by non-Muslims as religious fanatics and/or terrorists)

- substantial increases in Muslim populations

- more prominent display of Islamic religious way of life (i.e. religion and culture)

- fervent adherence to ways of life (referred to as Islamic fundamentalism) which may be regarded as unacceptable by governments and public in the countries in which Muslims reside

- demands for a separate education system.

Each of these manifestations of assertiveness necessitate comment.

Supporting Islam

Throughout the turmoil of events in the Middle East and the related terrorism inflicted on western capitals, sizeable minority Islamic populations in western Europe and the USA appeared to support the militant Islamic groups responsible. They were willing to express this apparent support through marches and rallies, national debate and through fledgling radio, press and television outlets. This did not constitute support for terrorism or terrorists; rather, it was a universal Islamic support for some of the principal aims of groups such as Hamas and Hizbullah, including (a) a Palestinian state and (b) stemming the encroachment on Islamic values and way of life by totally incompatible western values and lifestyles. Today, the periodic upsurge in conflict between India and Pakistan over the disputed Himalayan state of Kashmir attracts 'British Muslims ... waiting to join the "holy war" against Indian forces' (*The Times*, 31 May 1999). The impression is that of a 'loose cannon' minority group in Britain, willing to go anywhere to fight any war on behalf of Islam, indifferent to the consequences for Britain's foreign policy and international relationships. Haynes (1993) tries to rectify this erroneous impression in his categorisation:

> Between those (the vast majority *of Muslims*) who would like to see a return to (often vaguely defined) 'Islamic values' but who would not resort to political violence to achieve their aims; a middle strata which may argue and lobby for Islamization without resorting to extra constitutional measures; and the small number of zealots or fanatics who believe that any means – including political violence – are justified by the end, the creation of an Islamic state. (Haynes 1993, p.45)

No such categorisation exists in the minds of most non-Muslim onlookers.

Increasing Muslim populations

Muslim populations in Europe have substantially increased during the past four decades (Husain and O'Brien 1996). The principal reason for the increase in the earlier part of this period was unrestricted immigration policies, dictated by the need for workers in virtually every sphere of labour. When restrictions were eventually applied to immigration, some countries, particularly Belgium, adopted a very liberal policy towards dependants joining their families. Muslim families are generally much larger than those within the host countries. For example, Quali and Rea (1995), quoted in Husain and O'Brien (1996), suggest that in Belgium the average number of children in Moroccan families (who constitute the largest number of Muslims in Belgium) is seven, in Turkish families four, and in Belgian families two. Husain and O'Brien demonstrate however, that even in countries which adopted illiberal policies towards migrants and their families, the Muslim populations to continued to increase substantially. These increases inevitably led to greater representation in business, politics, industry, trade unions, education, media and the arts and, eventually, Muslims being elected in national elections and invited to serve in governments. Muslim communities grew much larger and became more affluent, self-reliant and confident. Shops and businesses within these communities proliferated, run by people from the communities with distinctly Muslim names. Greater numbers also increased the unwillingness of Muslims to accept the endemic racism and cultural insensitivity to which they were subjected.

Overt expression of Islam

Muslims have traditionally been identified in Europe by the colour of their skin. Today, they are much more accurately identified (like Arooj and her sisters) through their visible and audible expression of their faith in Islam and their five times daily prayers to Allah. Such is the increase in their numbers, and the corresponding increase in the number of mosques (*masjid*) in which they worship, that the populations as a whole are more than ever aware of Muslims in their midst, and of the daily rituals of worship, fasting and alms giving in which they engage. The mosques also function as very effective focal points for various community enterprises and fundraising, occasionally as refuges for Muslim political refugees, and increasingly as 'a springboard for regional and national political alliances, and a training ground in polemics and adversary politics' (Werbner 1996, p.115). The principal focus of worship to Allah is through the Qur'an (more popularly known as the Koran). It is a holy scripture which is becoming increasingly familiar (if only by name) within literature, journalism, television and radio. Its contents are quoted to non-Muslims as the guidance or reference point for Muslim action or opinion. Muslims are generally not inhibited about being Muslim and living out their faith in Islam in nominally Christian countries. As repeatedly stressed by Prince Charles, they have in a sense become the model and inspiration of faith and spiritual discipline in a much less assertive and confident Christian world.

Aspects of Islamic religious and cultural practices unacceptable to non-Muslims

Some aspects of Muslim culture and religion are unacceptable to non-Muslims. *Halal* – the ritual slaughter of animals by throat cutting – is a source of much distress in countries where 'animal rights' have been given a high profile by activists. Arranged marriages, the 'apparent' isolation and 'subjugation' of Muslim women, the sending of daughters brought up in western countries back to the Indian subcontinent to live (and/or prepare for marriage) with extended families – all are commonly observed and narrowly perceived aspects of Muslim life which provoke criticism at best, and ridicule. Some may regard what they wrongly perceive not just as another manifestation of the assertiveness of Islamic culture but as an affront to their own culture.

Seeking an Islamic educational system

Probably the most powerful manifestation of the assertiveness of Islamic culture and religion is the successful campaign for the right to educate Muslim children in Islamic schools. Education is the primary means of assertion and influence for any minority group. A few Muslim communities now have their own schools. These will undoubtedly proliferate for all levels of education. The advantages are substantial. Such schools will help to consolidate and strengthen a sense of Muslim identity in an increasingly secular world. They will assist the survival of the many languages in which adherence to Islam is expressed and will sustain and promote numerous aspects of the diverse cultures which Islam has embraced. For individual Muslims and their families, an Islamic education will uphold family and moral values in the face of a relentlessly amoral and family fragmented social world.

Debate within Islam

One of the consequences of Islamic and Muslim assertiveness has been an 'upsurge in anti-Arab and anti-Muslim sentiment' in which 'racist stereotypes abound' (Haynes 1993, p.44). This has expressed itself in mockery, marginalisation and discrimination (the mockery of worship to Islam, as experienced by Arooj and her sisters in Chapter 2, is an abiding image in many western anti-Muslim protests outside the embassies of Muslim countries). Generally speaking, even the educated masses of western countries are unaware of the intense political debates within Islamic states. Western public opinion still invariably associates Muslims with international terrorism and Islam with extreme fundamentalism. Haynes goes to the heart of this misperception:

> 'Islamic rule', conventional wisdom would have it, is the slogan of the dictator who grabs power in the belief that he has a divine mandate to impose Islam on his people. He introduces 'Islamic law' comprising Islamic punishment for transgressors. Religious figures and Islamic political parties seek Government jobs, while women are declared of reduced social, political and economic status. Yet none of this is essentially Islamic. (Haynes 1993, p.67)

No one knows better than Muslim people themselves the extent to which many of today's leaders of Muslim countries have departed from the principles espoused by their spiritual head and founder. Islamic scholars have been prominent in exposing this development, and in promoting democratic government which takes account of popular demand and desires. Haynes (1993), referring to the work of a highly respected Islamic scholar, Ziauddin Sardar (1985), believes that such leaders 'should aim to create a politically and socially open society in which individuals may enjoy freedom of religion, of culture, and of social development'. Abd al-Rahman Azzam (1979) stresses the importance of the principles of *Shura* (consultations among the leaders of the *Umma*, community–society), while Muhammed Asad (1980) argues that justice, freedom and equality should be central tenets of any Islamic constitution. Sardar expresses his views with characteristic bluntness:

> It is an undeniable fact that, perhaps apart from Iran, traditional leaders in almost every Muslim country ... are among the most narrow-minded, bigoted, antiquated, thoroughly chauvinist and opportunistic groups in society. For them Islam is a personal property to be rented out and leased, hired and sold. (Sardar 1985, p.148)

Health and social services to Muslims

How have all these factors impacted upon the provision of health and social care to Muslim families? Many professionals may believe that such factors do not have any adverse impact upon the quality of service they provide. Regrettably, professionals are increasingly exposed as lacking insight and awareness of the nature and degree of prejudice they harbour against Islamic minorities and are most resistant to any processes of enlightenment about the origins of such prejudice (Husain and O'Brien 1999; Runnymede Trust 1997). There are four recent research projects carried out in different countries which support the contention that professionals are seriously adrift from their obligation to provide a culturally competent service to the Muslim community.

Young Pathan mothers living in Britain

Islam's threat to pregnant women!

Currer's (1991) research was based on interviews with 50 young Muslim women of the Pathan tribes, who had migrated from the North Western Frontier region of Pakistan and were now resident in inner city areas of Britain. She explored their perceptions of health services, particularly in relation to pregnancy and child rearing. A major area of concern for doctors and health visitors was the insistence of some of these Muslim women, when they were pregnant, to participate in the fasting for Ramadan. Currer draws attention to a headline in the *Birmingham Daily News* in 1987: 'Babies at risk from Ramadan'. Senior medical personnel enlisted the support of Muslim leaders to emphasise the fact that pregnant Muslim women were not required to keep the fast – the assumption being made by the media and medical personnel that 'a lot of Muslim women are ignorant of the rules. They don't realise that there is leeway'. Currer contested this assumption on the basis of her research. She was convinced that the women were neither ignorant nor irresponsible. They divulged to her that 'keeping the full month's fast at the appropriate time was a matter of religious pride and spiritual enrichment' (p.47). There were numerous other sound reasons too. Participating with one's family and extended family in any kind of deprivation (of food, etc.) is more meaningful and in fact less difficult than making such a sacrifice alone (pregnant women are duty-bound to carry out the Ramadan fast later, when they are also likely to continue to be responsible for preparing and serving the food). Similarly, another time outside of pregnancy may be much more prob-lematic because Muslim women cannot pray during menstruation ('praying' being the most important activity during the fasting). These women were therefore convinced that pregnancy offered them the best opportunity to carry out the fast in full.

Blaming the culture: not listening to the client

The *Birmingham Daily News* and the medical personnel to whom it spoke were obviously unaware of these factors. No doubt, however, rather than seeking enlightenment, most likely they would have reaffirmed the editor's view and the opinion of many of its readers: that the women were putting Islam before the welfare of their unborn children. Currer's work is instructive here too. The health of their children (decreed as much by holy scripture as by maternal instinct) was of the utmost importance to these Pathan Muslims. They had carefully made their own assessments of the risks involved in fasting. Some who had experienced difficulty previously agreed not to fast. Some would have ceased fasting if complications had arisen. They were all more than willing to listen to health visitors whose advice and opinions made sense to them, but they resented some health visitors' 'blanket condemnation of a practice which they [the health visitors] saw as unnecessary'. Currer writes: 'They saw health workers as ignorant of the importance to them of their religious observance, as well as underestimating their capacity to act responsi-bly' (p.47). As for the failure of some of the women to keep to antenatal appointments, Currer says that Pathan women have far more (culturally sig-nificant) responsibilities, such as caring for their existing children, fulfilling the demands of hospitality, or responding to the needs of extended family members (the Qur'an repeatedly stresses the importance of fulfilling family obligations). Currer's respondents offered another simple explanation: pregnancy was perceived as a normal and often shared experience (particularly within villages with large extended families). She writes: 'Because antenatal care was not seen as very important in the context of a concept of pregnancy which views this as a normal condition, clinic appointments might occupy a low place in women's priorities' (p.47).

Young Bangladeshi mothers living in Britain

Precisely the same observations were made in a much more recent piece of research. Katbamna's (2000) Bangladeshi Muslim mothers-to-be were 'generally inclined towards traditional childbirth practices and whenever possible they made every effort to avoid medical childbirth practices'. They 'did not worry unduly about obtaining medical confirmation of pregnancy, nor did they consider it necessary to attend antenatal clinics early in pregnancy, or attend antenatal classes' (p.130). Also identical in the two pieces of research was the reckoning. There was a price to pay for defying the medicalisation of their pregnancies and childbirths. Currer says the majority of her respondents eventually complied, believing 'they would receive poorer care during delivery if staff were angry because they had not done so' (p.48). Katbamna writes of the postnatal period:

> It was quite obvious from the women's accounts that they experienced the greatest pressure to reject their cultural ideology when they moved outside their community to obtain maternity care. Women were often worried about attracting derogatory comments from health professionals ... They were exposed to hostile comments from the nursing staff in the postnatal wards about traditional diets after childbirth. (Katbamna 2000, p.133)

The 'threat' to medical control from extended family and community

Pregnancies may indeed be normal, but they are not without their pain and ill health. Currer's respondents anticipated and accepted the pain and ill health of pregnancy: an attitude of mind encapsulated in the old Pathan proverb that 'the greater your wealth [of children] the worse your health'. They are no different from many women in other countries. Catholic women in Ireland, for example, have a hundred similar sayings and jokes on their 'free passage' to heaven as a consequence of their many pain-laden pregnancies. Such stoical

culture-based sentiment is unlikely to find resonance among today's professional health care workers, but it belies the fundamental discovery by Currer
(1991) that pregnant Pathan women, contrary to the impression of weakness
and helplessness which such an attitude conveys, lived out a concept of themselves as experts in the matter of pregnancy: an expertise and associated confidence gained through generations of experience and sharing, rather than
learning in an antenatal clinic. Precisely the same is observed among many of
Katbamna's respondents – the Bangladeshi women in particular – who were
more reliant on their families and traditional supports in pregnancy and childbirth and more determined to 'delay seeking medical advice' as a 'form of
resistance to medical control' (p.130). The common source of expertise for
both groups of women was their own Muslim families and communities.
Mothers and mothers-in-law were particularly significant. Western medical
personnel are often not aware of this fact; even if they are aware of it, they are
not likely to respect it. In her conclusion, Katbamna (2000) writes of the
'tendency on the part of health professionals to discredit the advisory role of
anyone except those who receive medical training in the West. In this context,
the literature makes the assumption that South Asian women, particularly
older women, pose the greatest threat to medical authority because many of
the traditional practices are promoted and supervised by older female relatives' (p.133).

    The respondents in Currer's and Katbamna's research were clearly not
victims of their Islamic culture, contrary to the perception commonly held
among health and social care professionals. While Islam and Muslim practices
were important to the women (and important in ways which the professionals
were often not aware of), they were nevertheless quite capable of recognising
and responding to priorities and interests that were neither culturally determined nor addressed within cultures. Currer interprets professionals' concentration upon culture to the exclusion of everything else, and the tendency to
seek explanations in culture (i.e. blaming) for all the clients' (awkward) behaviours, as a characteristic of racism.

Muslims in Wales and requirements of The Children Act

Colton, Drury and Williams (1995a, 1995b) carried out a major empirical
study on how social welfare practitioners and agencies in Wales were implementing Part III of The Children Act 1989. This included the obligation to
give consideration to the child's religious persuasion, racial origin, and cultural and lin-
guistic background (s.22(5)(c)). The research findings clearly demonstrate that

these obligations are not being fulfilled. Services to the Muslim community in Wales (in particular the Bangledeshi community) are explored in a training video produced on the basis of the findings (Mullan 1995). Ehsan Uh Haq, Director of the West Glamorgan Racial Equality Unit, gives a general overview of the shortcomings:

1. No consultations were held with Muslims and other minorities and no education programme/seminars were held to inform those affected about the Act.

2. Religious and cultural needs were not addressed. (Colton *et al.* 1995a and Husain and O'Brien 1996) draw attention to the fact that data on the religion of minority communities is non-existent in government and local government records. Because religion is so fundamental to the lives of Muslims, the lack of any data ensures that agencies have little grasp of the need to develop religiously sensitive policies and practices.

3. Social workers were deluding themselves that merely relying on the race equality unit to provide interpreters is all that is required to fulfil their obligations under the Act and to provide a culturally sensitive service.

4. There was a lack of contact and consultation between social workers and representatives or leaders within minorities.

5. There was a lack of knowledge on the part of social workers about the religious and cultural beliefs of minorities, and how these may impact upon the parents' perceptions of and relationships with professionals.

6. Social workers were not taking seriously and not trying hard enough to fulfil the responsibility of placing children in families of the same race and religion as that of (and requested by) their parents.

7. There was an acknowledgement of the statutory requirement in respect of minorities, but the oft-repeated excuse that government deprives local authorities of the funds necessary to fulfil the requirements.

Colton *et al.* (1995a) acknowledge the difficulties of managers operating within stringent budgetary impositions, but rightly point out that culturally sensitive services need not always be cost prohibitive. Echoing the sentiments of Ehsan Ul Haq, they argue for the need to learn 'how to approach ethnic communities so that they can train us' (p.93).

Services to Muslims in three European countries

Husain and O'Brien's (1996) research concentrates on three European countries, each with relatively large Muslim populations: the Moroccan community in Belgium; the Turkish community in Denmark; the South Asian community in England (with particular focus on Islington). Its specific objectives included: 'to outline best practice initiatives within the non-profit and statutory sectors for each country'; and 'to suggest possible ways of improving access for Muslim families and individuals' (p.3). Its principal focus is on the major statutory and voluntary agencies responsible for enabling the hundreds of thousands of Muslims and other cultural minorities to settle, integrate, learn the language, retrain and, most important of all, get work.

Statistics are provided from a number of sources to illustrate the general increase in Muslim populations. The impacts upon the existing majority populations are considerable. Research in Denmark, for example, reports that 37 per cent of 1600 Danish respondents said that they would not like Muslims as neighbours and 64 per cent said they did not want them as members of their immediate family. In a list of those groups considered least desirable, the respondents placed Muslims in fourth position, following Nazis, criminals and alcoholics (Gaasholt and Togeby 1995, quoted in Husain and O'Brien 1996).

Organisation and policy

Husain and O'Brien (1996) examine the organisational structure and policies underpinning services to minorities, and the degree of harmonisation and consistency between the various departments involved. These vary enormously within the three countries. In the borough of Islington, for example, there are many highly effective voluntary groups within the Muslim communities, but the links with statutory agencies are very weak: 'The lack of an efficient network between the two sectors appears to have created a wide gap of knowledge which makes it difficult for social workers to find services which are linguistically and culturally appropriate' (p.25). The research examines in some detail the proposition that Muslim service users should be allocated workers from similar cultural–nationality backgrounds, but concludes that there is a 'need to work together in untangling cultural complexities which may influence objective interpretation and in providing appropriate training for potential interpreters' (p.47).

Mutual perceptions in a changing world

Husain and O'Brien (1996) cover many other areas of complexity in the lives of Muslims coming to terms with the difficulties of integrating within majority cultures. These include the Muslim concept of family and family responsibilities, traditional male and female roles within families, gender issues, domestic violence, mental health, intergenerational differences, problems faced by young people, arranged marriages, under-age marriages, the elderly and respect for elders. These issues are discussed in the context of change within both Muslim minorities and non-Muslim majorities and, perhaps even more important, within the wider context of changing socio-economic conditions. The authors, for example, reflect on how difficult it must be (throughout western Europe) for Muslim fathers to maintain their 'breadwinner' role when there has been a virtual revolution in the job markets leading to 'high levels of male unemployment and new social norms which encourage women to work' (p.61). No minority can withstand the tremendous pressures – social, economic and cultural, direct and indirect, subtle and blatant – that they inevitably experience in highly sophisticated societies in which the rights of individuals are at the forefront of social and political agendas. The research makes clear that majority perspectives of many aspects of Muslim life are narrow and prejudicial, perceiving Muslims en masse as 'extremist, fanatic, fundamentalist, sexist and despotic'. As individuals, leaders and politicians among the white majorities campaign for (and succeed in getting) greater rights and freedoms for the whole populations. Muslims and the Muslim way of life is increasingly perceived as a major obstacle to individual freedom. Social workers in Copenhagen, for example, testify that when Danes see a Muslim woman they automatically assume that 'her husband has forced her to wear this ... And he hits her all the time ... She is suppressed ... So we have to help her' (p.65).

Husain and O'Brien present and explain many Qur'anic concepts regarding women and highlight how some of the rights granted to women within the Qur'an are conveniently ignored through misinterpretation in many predominantly Muslim countries. On the other hand, the perception of Muslim men as dominant and domineering, and the primary executors of sexist, oppressive Islamic law and scripture, seemingly pervades much of the thinking in statutory and non-statutory agencies that contributed to their research. One of the consequences is that many workers adopt the worst possible solution: avoiding Muslim men.

Intergenerational conflict necessitates more cultural sensitivity

Ironically, as Islam spreads throughout Europe, loyalty and adherence to Islam weakens within many Muslim families, as the children in particular are influenced by a non-Muslim world. Arranged marriages, for example, are increasingly critically exposed in western media. The non-Muslim educational systems which predominate in all three countries are instrumental in this process. Husain and O'Brien (1996) quote from a European Commission report which asserts that the families of minorities tend to adapt to the ways of majority families within one generation (European Commission 1994, p.77). This is a dubious proposition to apply sweepingly, but it suggests that the tensions and stresses within Muslim families and communities must be considerable. Values that have been cherished, relationships and roles that have endured for centuries and daily religious and spiritual exercises that are at the core of Islamic existence – all these are vulnerable if the generations upon which they depend, i.e. Muslim youth, are increasingly rejecting them. Husain and O'Brien, in their introduction and throughout, assert: 'There is a basic knowledge deficit about the religion of Islam at all levels of statutory social services provision in the three countries studied' (p.xii). Their research abounds in professionals' recorded statements which are alarming. These demonstrate gross cultural insensitivity to Muslim families and a blatant intolerance towards Muslims' religious-based thought and action.

Husain and O'Brien do, however, highlight some successes within the overall span of their remit. The Mission Locale in Brussels has achieved much greater success than elsewhere in establishing effective links between agencies serving minority groups. A location near London provided what they regarded as 'the best example of provision and training of interpreters'. It included the employment of a co-ordinator for interpretation and translation. For the grander objectives of enabling immigrants to settle, integrate, learn the language and retrain for employment, the Service Social des Etrangers d'Acceuil et de Formation in Belgium (SSEAF) was regarded as the model 'for removing dependency on the national welfare system' (p.87). Husain and O'Brien's principal recommendations include enlightening Muslims and non-Muslims alike about the 'heterogeneous richness of Muslim cultures and communities ... so as not to become ossified in essentialist definitions' (of 'Islam' and 'Muslim'); and improvements in organisational structure, policies and training specifically aimed towards enhancing cultural sensitivity in provision of services to Muslim people.

Causes of cultural incompetence in working with Muslims

Collectively, the findings in these four unrelated researches should be as much a matter of concern to politicians and community leaders as they would undoubtedly be to health and social care trainers. Clearly, many professionals have been influenced by the negative and hostile majority perceptions of Islam and Muslim, with the consequence that a crucially important component of culturally competent practice, namely an attitude and approach of openness and respect, was missing. Workers' unawareness of the cultural context of their clients' lives, and the consequential cultural insensitivity towards young Pathan and Bangladeshi mothers-to-be, are examples of the culturally incompetent attitude and approach. In the introduction, the point was made that our westernised attitudes to culture today are rooted in the confrontation with and the attempted annihilation of cultures in the past. Some professionals have undoubtedly uprooted and discarded such attitudes and provide excellent culturally competent services (we shall read more of them). But the following chapters will provide additional evidence of an anti-culture bias in much health and social care literature, practice and research. This bias is more easily exposed in health and social care responses to an Islamic culture which is expanding and thriving, which embraces a quarter of the world's population and probably even more of its languages, which manifests its power in a profound influence on both national politics and the global political order, which is intertwined with a religion commanding ultimate reverence and obedience from its adherents, and which decrees practices and rituals which health and social care professionals may find objectionable or abhorrent. There are concepts here, for example, religion, obedience and power, which may not fit easily among the convictions and principles of health and social care professionals. Chapter 9 will explore the specific challenges that religions in general often pose for workers, and describe numerous examples of culturally competent and incompetent practice in work among different faiths.

Summary and Conclusion

Islam embraces over a billion of the world's inhabitants. It has had a profound influence on the development of science and technology, art and literature, law and architecture. Adherence to Islam necessitates submitting to an array of guidelines and stipulations governing all activity, ideology, economic and political thinking, and human relationships. This 'holistic' impact and demand causes difficulty for those living in societies and under governments which rigidly uphold separation between religion and politics, and which continuously strive to promote individual freedom.

Islam and Muslims are perceived to be re-emerging as a significant force in the western world. This re-emergence is manifest in:

- active support for Muslims' struggles elsewhere

- substantial increases in Muslim populations and a corresponding increase in political representation and influence

- more visible and more audible expression of faith in Islam and adherence to Islamic values and principles

- greater assertiveness in carrying out Islamic practices which are generally regarded by the majority population as unacceptable

- successfully campaigning for separate education for Muslim children.

All these manifestations – or at least some of them – are likely to have contributed to a negative image of Muslims, which appears to be widely shared. Health and social care professionals are not immune to this imagery. Four separate pieces of research, in entirely different European locations, at different times, convincingly demonstrate that Muslim individuals and families have been in receipt of culturally incompetent services from numerous health, social care, education and employment agencies. The professionals themselves provide ample testimony of negative perceptions of and unfriendliness towards Muslims. The two most conspicuous characteristics underpinning culturally incompetent services to Muslims are:

- a lack of knowledge and understanding of Islamic culture and religion

- a lack of effort on the part of individual professionals and their agencies to do anything about it.

The consequence of this reality is that workers are often unaware of when and how they are likely to be culturally insensitive to Muslim people, and culturally incompetent in fulfilling their obligations to minorities generally.

CHAPTER 5

The Re-emergence of Culture
2. American Indians

Introduction

We have made a substantial leap forward in our current knowledge of the fate of the American Indians. Only a few decades ago, children throughout the world screeched in horror as the Apache killing machine (courtesy of Hollywood) descended from the hills and wreaked death and destruction on the poor God-fearing, good-living, white settlers, their young wives and angelic little offspring. Thirty minutes later, those same children yelled in triumph as the US army caught up with the 'murderers' and exacted a terrible revenge. We don't witness such nonsense any more. Nowadays, we see films and read books that tell us something very different. Colonialist governments and their settlers perpetrated genocide against American Indians over five centuries, and very nearly succeeded in wiping them out. The principal tool by which the genocidal policies were implemented was not, as many may think, mass murder (although there were no shortages of that particular attempted solution). The policy was much less crude and far more protracted: it was the forced removal of the Indians from the lands that were sacred to them. It signalled the beginning of the end of their cultures and the multiple expressions of cultures. As Indians today testify, their ancestors then merely 'died away', tens of thousands of them. This chapter will briefly touch on that history, concentrating upon the cultural diversity which existed when the colonists first arrived. It will elaborate on the core component of their cultures, their unique relationship with the land. A Cherokee Indian provides a modern-day perspective on what she calls the 'cultural genocide' perpetrated against her people, and describes her and her family's attempts to regain their lost cultural heritage. This development is occurring throughout the USA, within numerous Indian tribes, and the chapter will look at how the US government and health and social care agencies are responding. It will conclude by considering the work of Nadia Ferrara, an art therapist who has devoted much of her professional life to working with the Cree Indians. Her research and analysis of the emotional expression of the Crees provides a model of cultural competence for all health and social care professionals.

(Note: It is fashionable today to use the term 'Native American' rather than 'American Indian'. But Nagel's (1997) classic text makes it clear that the former is a concoction of a liberal white establishment, and is rejected as patronising by prominent Indian leaders.)

The scale of the demise

In the preface of Debo's (1995) *History of the Indians of the United States,* the author records a telling event. She has arranged to meet Oklahoma Creek Indians in their local church. It is a rural area she is unfamiliar with, and the directions she has been given are insufficient. She stops at a large, modern, well-equipped school. She sees some Indian children in the playground and is confident their teachers can tell her how to reach her destination. But not one of the teachers had ever heard of the church. She asks the Indian children in the playground. With the help of their teeter board, they quickly tell its precise location. It is on the top of a hill, only a quarter of a mile away. It is invisible from the school or from anywhere around, because it is surrounded by thick undergrowth and brush arbours. Yet it is and has been for generations an important community meeting place for the Indians. The author comments: 'The brush hid it from the schoolhouse, but there was a denser thicket in the minds of those teachers of Indian children obscuring their intellectual and spiritual view' (p.xii).

Similar observations can be made since the final victories over the Indians at the end of the last century: an ignorance and indifference to them and a determination to ensure they remained 'out of the way'. Of course when the colonisers first arrived, the Indians were not ignored. They were, over the next five centuries, nearly wiped out. In 1492, there was a population of between five and six million Indians. In 1900, the population had dwindled to 250,000 (Debo 1995; Nagel 1997). Such history has played no small part in the current resurgence of American Indian culture and identity.

Cultural diversity

Everyone knows that the USA today is the most culturally diverse nation in history. Before any colonist stepped on to its shores, however, it was already one of the most culturally diverse nations in history. There were nearly 1000 unique and distinct languages and cultures. There were more than 200 different languages spoken in California alone. Part of the resurgence of Indian culture aims to enlighten us at different levels. As well as being classi-fied according to their linguistic stock, Indians were also distinguished by their vastly different environments. A look at the map of cultural geography developed by American anthropologists (Haviland 1999) instantly tells one about the immense diversity in the ways of life of these native American tribes. On the 'Plains', for example, the buffalo-hunting Cheyenne (and the 30 other tribes with whom they shared the Plains) had a life that was totally dissimilar from that of the Western Shoshone tribe, in the west of the area designated as the Great Basin (comprising Nevada, Utah and portions of California, Oregon, Wyoming and Idaho). Even more dissimilar must have been the ways of life of the native tribes of the Yukon Sub Arctic, or those in the Central and Eastern Arctic.

Culture embodied in a mystical communion with the land

The decimation of American Indian tribes and cultures was the inevitable con-sequence of their forced removal from the land. It may be difficult for today's western urban mind to grasp the cultural significance of the relationship which the American Indians had with their environment. Debo (1995) speaks of Geronimo's mystical identification with the earth. He provides quotes from other revered Indian leaders. Garry of the Spokane tribe says, 'I was born by these waters. The earth here is my mother' (p.4). Tecumsah, probably the most famous American Indian chief in history, could not be bribed to 'sell off' the land. 'Sell a country,' he yelled contemptuously to a governor. 'Why not sell the air, the clouds and the great sea, as well as the earth? The earth is my mother, and on her bosom I will recline' (p.107). Harjo, in the old Creek town of Tulsa, said, 'The mountains and hills that you see are your backbone, and the gullies and the creeks which are between the hills and the mountains are your heart veins' (p.4). Debo (1995), Curtis (1907), Gill (1979) and Nagel (1997) all assert that the Indians were deeply religious and that religion and culture were entwined. The Indians' cultures evolved from their total integra-tion with the earth, with the perpetually changing skies, and with the animals which abounded around them. Debo speaks of the 'mystical communion' between the Indians and nature, and of their emerging feel for beauty 'that makes the modern Indian superbly gifted in the various art forms' (p.4). She writes: 'When the white man cut up this living entity with his surveying instruments, the Indian felt the horror of dismemberment' (p.4). Tens of thousands of Indians actually could not survive the loss of their culture, embodied in their mystical communion with the land. They simply died off. When the Choctaw tribe was banished from their Mississippi lands, an observer 'noticed that many of them reached out and touched the trunks of trees before they turned away on their journey' (Debo 1995, p.118). Another revered Indian leader, Pleasant Porter, speaking to the Board of Indian Commissioners in 1903, assured them that the 'dying off' was not due to any 'new disease', but was simply the 'want of hope'.

The fate of the Navajo is a reminder of what precisely was meant by this 'want of hope'. Curtis's (1907) first photograph in his famous twenty-volume collection is a poignant reflection of *The Vanishing Race – Navaho*, 'passing into the darkness of an unknown future' (Vol.1, p.36). A deeply spiritual people (Gill 1979) and residing in an environment (the desert) which was of little economic significance to the settlers and the government, they escaped relatively unscathed by the wars and upheavals visited upon the other tribes over four centuries; until 1863, that is, when the US army invaded the Navajo nation under a 'scorched earth' policy and forced 10,000 captives on a 300-mile march to a reserve in New Mexico, near Fort Summer, with the intention of converting them into sedentary farmers. No greater catastrophe could befall these people. The mountains that surrounded their desert homelands were regarded as sacred. Now they were in shackles in a camp so far away that they couldn't even see their mountains. The mountains were symbolically, spiritually and physically dominant in a belief system pervaded by emphasis upon harmony. The Diyin Dine'e (Holy People) of the Navajo nation constantly promoted harmony between them and their sacred landscapes. The ravages and suffering inflicted upon the Navajo in 1863–64 are even today attributed to a disharmony arising from the neglect of and a disrespect for the teachings of the Diyin Dine'e. 'As a result of this situation of disharmony, many of the prayers, songs, ceremonies, and even the healing herbs and medicines became ineffective' (Agency Network Program 1999).

The five great south eastern Indian tribes, the Creeks, the Cherokees, the Choctows, the Seminoles and the Chickasaws, were all compelled through various degrees of coercion to move to the state of Oklahoma, the eastern half of which the government had designated 'Indian territory'. (Today,

Oklahoma, according to the 1990 US census, has more than a quarter of a million Indians, 8% of the population.) The story of that migration, and of similar enforced removals involving many more tribes which were to continue throughout the nineteenth century, have become the stuff of legend for Indians today. The impact upon the Indian population provides chilling statistics: 24,000 Creek Indians forcibly removed from their homelands in 1836 were reduced to 13,537 by 1859 (Debo 1995); 4000 Cherokee Indians died on the infamous 'Trail of Tears' begun in 1838. (Shaver 1998). The Pawnees dwindled from a population of 10,000 in the early part of the nineteenth century to less than 700 at the beginning of the twentieth century (Lagace 1999). Debo writes: 'Geronimo was statistically correct when he said of the Apaches: "When they are taken from their homes they sicken and die"' (p.8).

One Indian's perspective

A modern perspective on this history is provided in Shaver's (1998) *The Cultural Deprivation of an Oklahoma Cherokee Family*. Shaver interprets the behaviour of the government and its various institutions towards the Indians as a deliberate and sustained policy of cultural genocide. The common assumption is that the government was merely serving its own political interests and facilitating the greed and plunder of big business in its forced removals of Indians from their lands. But Shaver credits them with a more fundamental objective: 'To deprive Indians of their culture (i.e. to ensure they will just sicken and die), developers knew that they must be separated from their land' (p.84). The process begun in the early nineteenth century continued in a different form in the middle of the twentieth century. 'Assimilation' was the means, effected by widespread removal of Indian children from their parents and sending them to religious boarding schools run by the Bureau of Indian Affairs. Here the children were forbidden to speak their language, to wear their traditional clothing, or to engage in any cultural activity associated with their tribe. More importantly, they were rewarded to the extent to which they did assimilate within this entirely different culture. Shaver asserts that 'Indians are federal dependants, bound by a multitude of laws, policies and practices that control their present lives' (p.85). She draws attention to the government sanctioned policies for identification of Indianness, the so-called 'certificate of degree of Indian blood' (CDIB). This administrative device (which echoes the race obsessions of apartheid South Africa) was an incentive to assimilate into white culture, to deny Indianness. The memories of the ravages of history convinced Indians that it was advantageous to deny their Indianness.

The Cherokees

Shaver concentrates on her own tribe, the Cherokees, and tells the story of her mother Lou Jane, who was born in the post-civil war period. Lou's earliest recollections are of the family's and the tribe's attempts to gather and hold meetings, only to be put on the run by 'white men riding in on horses'. All the children spoke Cherokee and English, but the schools and boarding houses to which the children were sent forbade Indian languages and any other expression of Indian culture (an early indication of welfare's role in the destruction of indigenous cultures; see Chapter 7). Lou's father deserted the family. The family was compelled to move in with relatives and at the time of the 1887 census taking chose to 'lower their quantum', i.e. identified themselves as having less than 25 per cent of Indian blood.

Lou Jane married an Irish emigrant, and moved into the town of Checotah. The final break with the land had been made. Restrictions on speaking Cherokee and on associating with other Cherokees greatly intensified in the town and within her new home. Shaver writes:

> 'Indian women were forced to assimilate ... To protect their children from public bias, to satisfy the wishes of the non-Indian husband, and in response to socio-cultural pressures from social and church groups, many Indian women changed their language, dress and religion, and carefully chose their social gatherings. (Shaver 1998, p.92)

Only as late as 1985 did Lou Jane make peace with her Cherokee cultural heritage. It was in Oklahoma during a Cherokee ceremony she was attending as an honoured guest. In the continent at large, the Indian cultural revival was well advanced. Shaver says: 'Her peace was a gift to her family.' She was in effect giving all the family members 'permission to find their heritage'. She adds: 'Whereas family members knew they were Indian, the knowing did not include living the culture (p.93)'. The family descendants – more than 100 of them – are attempting to do precisely that. Some are repurchasing their original land. Many have obtained their CDIBs, certifying their Indianness. They are a microcosm of a Cherokee cultural and national revival seeking to restore language and customs, achieve economic renewal and to take its rightful place within government and society. The tribe, says Shaver, 'has re-framed itself as the new Cherokee nation, skilful in survival in current times, but rooted in the bedrock of Cherokee beliefs'. As for her family, she writes: 'They have learnt what they lost, and in the learning they regained their culture ... They have defied the plan for cultural genocide by re-identifying themselves as an Oklahoma Cherokee family (p.95)'.

The census figures for 1970 and 1980 indicate an increase in the Cherokee population of 350 per cent, from 66,150 to 232,344. That figure increased to 364,072 in the 1990 census. This accounted for 25 per cent of the total increase of all Indians in the US census (Nagel 1997).

Re-identification as Indian

The resurgence of Indian cultures is the subject of Nagel's (1997) in-depth study. In the 1970 US census, there were 792,730 Indians; in 1980, 1,364,033 and in 1990, 1,878,285. This does not reflect population growth but, rather, re-identification by Indians. Nagel contends that the resurgence stemmed primarily from political activism and the establishment of the Red Power movement of the 1970s. This development triggered widespread support among Indians and whites alike. Its impact was felt at all levels of both federal and state governments. Significant individuals within the federal government, genuinely motivated by the interests of Indians (to say nothing of the spirit of the age), accelerated the resurgence through legislation and massive funding for programmes of economic revival and Indian education. In 1966, for example, the Navajo tribe gained full control of their own boarding school, Rough Rock, on their own reservation. It achieved prominence as a model of education and community participation which also ensured the maintenance of the Navajo way of life. Nagel (1997) and White (1990) both record many other manifestations of the re-identification, and include personal testimonies like these:

> I didn't know anything about my tribe. So much was taken from us. Now we have a tribal complex with tribal languages being taught. (Nagel 1997, p.195)

> There was a time when I just didn't want to be an Indian ... [And now] We are contributors. We have something to be proud of. People come from all over ... to see us, and they applaud. (White 1990, pp.136–137)

> I'm fifty-four and I'm just learning to be an Indian. (White 1990, p.269)

Political support

In 1968, shortly before he was assassinated, Bobby Kennedy chaired a special subcommittee to study Indian education. He visited Cherokee Indians in Oklahoma and declared that 'cultural differences are not a national burden, they are a national resource – the American vision of itself is of a nation of citizens determining their own destiny, of cultural differences flourishing in an atmosphere of mutual respect' (Debo 1995, p.415). In this atmosphere, Indian resurgence gathered pace in terms of education, politics, policies, population increases, economic development and tourism. More fundamentally, the resurgence was manifest in new-found determination to 'be' and to 'live' Indian, and to salvage and regenerate Indian languages, many of which were on the verge of extinction (White 1990). Slowly, yet inevitably, all professions awakened to this development. US health and social care professions participated. Steeped in the challenges which a country of such cultural diversity posed, they were already seeking to integrate concepts like cultural awareness, cultural sensitivity and insensitivity into their training and codes of practice. Many were aware of Indian overrepresentation in their caseloads – the inevitable and predictable results of decades of imposed, hopeless, cultureless existence.

Indian Health Service (IHS)

The Indian Health Service (IHS) is now the principal governmental health and care provider for American Indians. It is responsible for a health care system servicing 1.4 million Indians, who belong to 545 recognised tribes in 34 states. The health service includes 49 hospitals in 12 states, 180 health centres in 27 states, and 8 school health centres and 273 health stations in 18 states. It employs over 14,000 staff. The IHS has been instrumental in improving the health of Indians and reducing Indian mortality rates. More recently, the development and constant streamlining of the IHS has accelerated around the principal objective of decentralisation. The 1994 Indian Self-Determining Contract Reform Act facilitated the IHS surrendering responsibility and power and funding to the Indian populations and their leadership to enable them to run their own health services. This not only ensures the most culturally sensitive services (a long-standing objective), but maximum user participation, access and local accountability. In 1995, the IHS transferred $730 million to support health delivery programmes of tribal nations through self-determination contracts and self-government compacts.

The IHS has sponsored many health care programmes addressing the specific and unique needs of the Indian populations. The Traditional Medicine Initiative, for example, seeks to blend modern medicine practices and philosophy with the traditional healing practices of Indians. An attempt is currently being made to assist the IHS in strengthening ties between the locally recognised traditional healers and the established health system clinicians and chief medical officers. The Alcohol and Substance Abuse services, the Injury Prevention Initiative, the Elder Care Initiative and the Indian Women's Health Initiative are further examples of IHS programmes. These are most certainly not uncommon programmes in any sense, but the task which the IHS has set for itself is to find solutions which are culturally sensitive to the unique and culturally distinct populations which it serves.

The IHS and the Navajo

The Navajo tribes mentioned earlier eventually returned to their homelands. Today they number more than 200,000 and occupy a 25,000 square mile territory encompassing portions of the states of Utah, Arizona, New Mexico and Colorado. Their increase in population makes theirs the second largest of all Indian tribes, next to that of the Cherokees. The IHS policy towards the Navajo indicates an empathy and understanding at various levels of approach. There is the obvious awareness of history and of the significance of great events such as the 'long walk', and of its influence upon the collective and individual psyches. The Navajos are a intensely ceremonious tribe. Professionals are cautioned that first contact may see Navajo arrive at a clinic or hospital with their skins blackened, obviously the result of consultation with a traditional healer. The latter may be highly significant in the perceptions of the patient and consultation with them, including ceremonies initiated in the patient's own home; it may delay the patient implementing a therapy or taking a medicine prescribed by the clinic or hospital, all of this echoing, of course, the situation of some Asian Muslim women described in the previous chapter, whose faith in traditional healing may be much stronger than in British doctors and hospitals. The results of such consultation need to be known, as do the remedies offered and the restrictions decreed, in order that modern medical personnel do not offer something entirely contradictory. Professionals are taught that Navajo concepts of living and being, health and disease, are deeply rooted and intertwined with religion. Religious beliefs may vary. There are three main religions: ancient (traditional), Navajo American Church, and Christian Navajo. Beliefs within each may have significant bearing upon the acceptance and effectiveness of prescribed remedies. Traditional healers within the Navajos do not see the necessity of the conventional history-taking in medicine. They are reputed to 'know' what the problem is. At the more basic level, Navajos may not appreciate what to them is the uncommon practice of direct eye-to-eye contact (with a professional). Nor are they likely to feel comfortable with the typically American firm handshake. The Navajos will be content with a mere touching of hands (direct eye contact and the firm handshake are of course strongly advocated in the training of many professionals). Navajos do not indulge in such common courtesies as 'excuse me' and 'thank you'; nor may they be so readily receptive or appreciative of radiologists taking X-rays of various parts of their bodies. Incineration of body tissue such as toenails, scalp hair, or normal placenta may not be acceptable either. Instead, many Navajos will want to dispose of them ceremoniously in an appropriately religious manner. Basic necessary and common medical practices, therefore, often need to be prefaced by cultural exploration which enlightens the professional as to the precise cultural or religious objections which the Navajo patient may harbour.

Alaskan Native culture

These voyages of cultural discovery are being made by health and social care professionals throughout the USA and Canada. Research is being conducted, texts and papers are being written and the internet is being exploited with great enthusiasm. (My last keying in of the words 'American Indians' revealed the existence of more than 10,000 sites.) Many of these are informative: Williams (1997), for example, in a short paper on 'Nursing Across Cultures', culturally enlightens professionals working with native Alaskan tribes. Williams reminds her trainee nurses in Alaska that communication is like an iceberg: only 35 per cent is verbal and the remainder non-verbal. Non-verbal communication is subject to wildly contrasting interpretations. She quotes from Wolcoff (1989): the non-native interprets the nodding head as 'I under-stand what you are saying', while the Eskimo interprets it as: 'I hear what you are saying'. The arms held tightly to the body are often interpreted by the non-native as 'I am cold', while the Eskimo reads it as someone wanting to maintain their distance. Not having eye contact may be read by one as 'I am lying to you' and by the other as 'I respect you'. (The latter native interpreta-tion compels Wolcoff to advise professionals not to have eye contact with native Alaskans on initial contact).

Noland and Gallagher (1989) focus on the differences in communication patterns and language between Alaskan natives and non-natives, under three subheadings: presentation of self, distribution of talk and contents of talk. The differences are considerable but, more interestingly, the authors provide the extremely different perceptions which English speakers and Athabascan (Eskimo) speakers have of each other. The Athabascan speaker thinks the English speaker talks too much, always talks first, asks too many questions, always interrupts, doesn't give others a chance to talk, talks only about what they're interested in, and is not careful enough about what they say about others. The English speaker thinks the Athabascan does not speak, is too silent, avoids situations of talking, avoids direct questions, never starts a conversation, and is too indirect and too inexplicit. These are all correct observations on both their parts, but hopelessly wrong cultural interpretations which are certain to lead to cultural offence.

Williams (1997) contrasts the differing perceptions of time. The non-native perceives time as linear, with a beginning, middle and end (from birth to death, dawn to dusk, Monday to Friday, etc.). The native Alaskan perceives time as circular:

> Life is a circle that continues after death as people who live after you remember the good things you did in your life. The subsistence life style is oriented to the seasons – it is time to gather plants and berries, fish, hunt, and trap when the food is available. You pick berries until you have enough berries to last until the next time berries are plentiful. (Williams 1997, p.3)

There are numerous additional subject areas covered in the training, for example, language (key words and phrases), bereavement, suicide, native respect for the elderly (the latter again being contrasted sharply with the attitudes and behaviour towards the elderly in non-native 'developed' societies).

The Cree Indians of North West Canada

Professionals wishing to serve the native Alaskan community need to acquire knowledge in all these aspects of difference. The realisation on the part of any indigenous group that such an effort has been made, or admission by the professionals that they lack such knowledge and are willing to learn, are conducive to a satisfactory working relationship. Cultural competence, however, poses much greater challenges. It necessitates rigorous and honest scrutiny of existing knowledge research and practice. It may question the applicability of established assessment and diagnostic tools to all culturally distinct groups. It may challenge the conceptualisations (and implicit assumptions) within powerful and entrenched professions. This is precisely what Ferrara (1999) has done in her acclaimed research text, *Emotional Expression Among Cree Indians.*

The Cree reside on the opposite side of the American-Canadian continent, in the James Bay area of northern Quebec. They number approximately 9000 people. They have not endured anything like the same degree of decimation as southern tribes, though as late as 1975, when the Indian revival was gaining momentum, they lost their right to maintain their land and had to make way for a huge hydroelectric project. The Canadian government paid compensation and created self-government for each of their eight communities (a long-standing objective of the Cree). A century before, they gave way to Pentecostalism – more than half the population are Pentecostal – but much of their cultural heritage remains, particularly their relationship with the land and their reverence for animal life, both of which have ensured their survival over centuries.

'Psychological mindedness' and 'alexithymia'

Nadia Ferrara is an art therapist and psychotherapist who has spent more than a decade researching her work with Cree Indians. It is generally believed that within professions such as psychology, psychiatry and social work a successful participation and outcome is more likely if the patient is 'psychologically minded'. Ferrara quotes the definition of this concept provided by Appelbaum (1973): 'a person's ability to see relationships among thoughts, feelings and actions with the goal of learning the meanings and causes of his experiences and behaviour'. Ferrara writes that 'psychological mindedness implies the ability symbolically to express one's own feeling state' (1999, p.13). The principal thesis in her work is the strong relationship between psychological mindedness, culture and therapy. Patients lacking the quality of 'psychological mindedness' may suffer 'alexithymia', an inability to express emotion and/or resolve emotional conflict, and are therefore considered unsuitable for psychotherapy. Ferrara challenges many of the assumptions and the cultural constructs underlying these concepts. She suggests that ethnocentric biases may influence the construction and application of the concept of alexithymia. In the foreword to her book she writes: 'I am acknowledging cultural variability by attempting to gain insight rather than promoting culturally inappropriate stereotypes' (p.11).

Challenging the Cree stereotype

The Cree are particularly susceptible to being stereotyped. Often regarded as emotionally reticent and taciturn, they have been labelled as 'stone-faced' Indians, 'blocks of ice' who have a 'pronounced inability to express emotion'. This often precludes them from consideration for psychotherapy in a North

American/Canadian cosmopolitan culture in which the expression of emotion is crucial. Ferrara explores these perceptions of the Cree and the behaviours which elicit them. Unusual in art therapy and psychotherapy, she applies empirical research and sophisticated instruments of measurement to do so, acknowledging at the outset their limitations and their occasional cultural inappropriateness. But she nevertheless provides a fascinating insight into the Cree culture, and consequentially exposes the limitations within the mindsets of many of the professionals working with them. There is some irony in the fact that the general public are aware (chiefly through tourism and popular literature) of the creativity and artistry of many Indian tribes, and yet professionals in medicine, social work, psychiatry and psychotherapy lack awareness of the communicational and therapeutic potential in art during their work with these tribes. It is difficult to do justice to the merit of Ferrara's work, but some themes are particularly worthy of mention in the context of this chapter.

Functional and cultural aspects of emotional suppression

The perception of the Cree as 'stone faced' and/or 'blocks of ice' (emotionally) is misleading. Such apparent suppression of emotion is in reality a cultural and necessary feature of Cree life, a coping mechanism entirely compatible with centuries-old ways of living and surviving. However, the suppression is highly focused. Children are socialised to 'be reticent and not verbally expressive of their feelings'. As they get older 'both their verbal and emotional expression becomes muted'. They are 'encouraged to channel their feelings through other forms, such as hunting, dreams, and art and crafts. Thus, it is not that emotions are lacking or non-existent, but that they are expressed through various culturally appropriate channels that are not essentially verbal' (p.96).

Limitations of verbal expression

Conversation is the principal means by which experience is relayed from one individual to another. It is the crucial tool in therapy in many professions. Conversation is not so highly regarded in Cree culture. Using words to recreate experiences and images is problematic 'because the translation from inner experience into language takes away from the meaning of the experience ... giving words to images removes the special quality that is attributed to images alone' (p.68).

Animals and dreams in Cree culture

The expression of emotion through art often revolves around animals and dreams, both of which assume a significance in Cree culture which is seldom fully appreciated by those from other cultures. Ferrara writes about the 'Cree traditional ritual of dreamwork'. There is an attempt to recreate the visions of dreams 'through images which become sacred'. Ferrara's Cree respondents often produced drawings 'portraying images linked to their cultural ideology' and containing 'themes suggestive of their close relationship to animals and nature'. Ferrara states that 'animal life is highly respected and valued in Cree culture and animals are believed to be superior to humans as a class of living entities' (p.98) a fact of which the novelist Brian Moore (1985) was fully aware in his rigorously researched novel Black Robe.

Emotional expression in art

Contrary to the general view among professionals, emotions are easily evoked among the Cree through art and art therapy. There is a powerful and rich symbolism within Cree culture and emotional expression through art is 'an inherent cultural experience' (p.62). Ferrara illustrates the point through two cases. Nine-year-old Luke was diagnosed as non-psychologically minded, in other words, unable to converse about and identify his own emotional state. In art therapy, however, he demonstrates that he is quite capable of expressing and understanding his emotional state. Tom is a 37-year-old deaf and mute Cree. His upbringing with these disabilities, the death of his father (who taught him the skills of hunting) and his mother's cancer, combined to devastate him. He resorted to violence, drunkenness and isolationism. Tom would be assessed unsuitable for therapy in numerous disciplines. Ferrara enables Tom to begin the process of constructive expression of emotion through art. He emerges as skilled in drawing as he is in hunting. He uses his artwork 'as a means to re-connect with his cultural identity' and is eventually 're-introduced to his community as a self-discovered artist' (p.65).

The need for cross-cultural analysis

In her conclusions, Ferrara questions the validity of the concepts of 'psychological mindedness' and 'alexithymia' when they are applied within a specific cultural framework which bears no relation or reference to other cultures. She argues for the necessity of cross-cultural analysis and an understanding of the organisation, expression and communication of emotion within differing cultures. She believes that culture determines to varying extents the nature and extent of all expression, and that caring professionals must strive to learn how. She has done so admirably and states that the research has 'enhanced my culturally sensitive framework in both my clinical and research endeavours. My experience has cultivated a more in-depth understanding of assessment, methodology and measurement processes, especially how cultural dynamics are played out in these processes' (p.110).

The work of Ferrara and of many health and social care professionals mentioned here represents excellence in the pursuit and achievement of cultural competence in working with minority groups. They point the way forward in numerous respects: breaking away from the 'professional' ethnocentric traditions of the past; exploring and exposing the limitations of conventional theories and assessment tools of the present; and, crucially, approaching their work with minority cultures with sincerity, openness and humility.

Summary and conclusion

The history of the American Indians is primarily a recording of the near annihilation of a thousand different indigenous peoples and their widely varying and distinct cultures. Their relationship with the land was the single most powerful factor in their lives, determining and permeating throughout all aspects of their cultures, particularly their religions and their languages. The forced removal of Indians from their lands therefore constituted a genocidal act, making the demise of countless tribes inevitable. Since the 1960s, a remarkable resurgence of Indian self-identity and culture has taken place. As with many cultural groups reasserting themselves, they are partially motivated by a growing consciousness of the culture they have lost, and an acute awareness of the scale of barbarism perpetrated against them. From a population of a quarter of a million at the turn of the century, the most recent census figures reveal two million Americans identifying themselves as Indian. There are widespread attempts within Indian tribes, particularly the larger ones, to revive their cultural heritage in all its diverse forms. The US government has responded in its policies underpinning education, health and social services to the Indian people.

The Indian Health Service (IHS) is the principal health-care system servicing 1.4 million Indians belonging to 545 recognised tribes in 34 states. The IHS has been instrumental in reducing the higher than average mortality rate among Indians. It provides volumes of literature and research material on many Indian tribes. It promotes cultural competence in all public health and social care agencies. The chapter has looked at some examples of cultural competence, in work with the Navajo, for example, the native Alaskans, and the Cree. It has concentrated on work with the latter by an art therapist and psychotherapist, Nagel Ferrara. Her research exposes the cultural biases and consequential inadequacies in assessment and treatment provided for culturally distinct groups. Her skills and techniques in assessment and therapeutic practice display a cultural competence worthy of the accolades bestowed upon her. Such practice is a model for health and social care professionals providing services to any cultural minority group.

CHAPTER 6

The Re-emergence of Culture
3. Australian Aborigines

Introduction

In 1988, Australia celebrated its bicentennial year. Not all Australians felt like celebrating. On the concrete walls surrounding the Australian parliament building in Canberra, someone had daubed 'White Australia has a black history'. This referred to Australia's treatment of its indigenous population. The Aborigines experienced much the same treatment as the American Indians. Indeed, the impact was greater because their numbers were much smaller and their means of resistance far less. In another sense too their fate was sealed. Whereas in the USA some whites recognised and respected the sophistication of numerous aspects of Indian culture, in Australia the Aboriginal culture and way of life was generally regarded as 'Stone Age' and certainly unworthy of preservation.

The way back for the Aborigines also has similarities with the experiences of American Indians. Leadership within their communities, effective political action, challenging institutional discrimination and inequalities in the courts and on the streets, evoking sympathy and support within the population as a whole and, not least, landmark court rulings, all played a part. From a point of near extinction, the Aborigines are now reasserting themselves. Their struggle for justice and equality has led to numerous government inquiries, laws, policies and professional practices, all of which seek to reverse the course of their terrible history. The reversal process is slow and they are still the victims of widespread abuses in education, employment, housing, health and criminal justice (for example, the suicide rate of Aboriginal youth held in police custody remains one of the highest in the world). But they have survived nevertheless and today they are represented in virtually every aspect of Australian life. Aspects of culture have also survived and they are increasingly expressing their cultural identity through their unique religions, languages, music and art, and through their relationship with the lands which have been partially restored to them.

This chapter will concentrate upon the laws, policies and practice which aimed to do precisely the opposite: to destroy Aboriginal culture and assimilate Aborigines within the white European settler population. As with American Indians, Aborigines were increasingly prevented from living and expressing the most important components of their culture, for example, their communion with the land, their religions and languages, their social and family life, and their religiously inspired and sophisticated system of values. What successive Australian governments did to the Aborigines is often termed racism. No doubt there were racists in abundance and rampant racist discrimination. But as the testimony of Australia's present day politicians and Aboriginal leaders in this chapter will demonstrate, stamping out the expression of culture was the chosen method of securing the ultimate goal of obliterating the indigenous population.

The chapter will begin by looking at one of these components of Aboriginal culture – religion. The objective here is twofold: to give some indication of its complexity and relevance to the Aboriginal way of life, and to enable readers to reflect on the colonists' perception that it represented the lowliest and most primitive life style. Second, the Australian government's 1997 Human Rights and Equal Opportunities report 'Bringing Them Home' (Commonwealth of Australia 1997) will be considered. This is probably the most damning self-indictment by any government for its treatment of indigenous populations. Third, the process of guilt and atonement in which white Australia is now engaged will be explored. Finally, the chapter will trace the development of progress in the way in which some social care professions now respond to Australia's indigenous population. Child care and child protection workers in particular were already implementing many of the recommendations that would be made in the Bringing Them Home report. The impact of the report overall will be considered.

Aboriginal religion

The cultures of indigenous populations are universally perceived by colonisers and settlers as primitive, inferior and harmful. The principal reason for this error is the perpetual tendency of the latter to perceive the former through the conceptual frameworks of their own cultures. In the case of religion, the inevitable tendency on the part of Christian and Muslim colonisers has been to view the multiple and entirely different religions which they encountered through frameworks derived from Islam and Christianity. It was not until well into the twentieth century that anthropologists discovered that Australian 'Aboriginal societies were, traditionally, religious societies'; that their beliefs and rituals were of a profoundly religious nature and that Aboriginal religion itself was 'intimately associated with social living, with relations between the sexes, with the natural environment and with food collecting and hunting' (Berndt 1974, p.13). Hitherto, Aboriginal beliefs and rituals had been regarded by the colonisers as nothing more than magic, superstition and sorcery. Another misperception saw Aborigines as one distinct group with one religion and one language (just as many in the west mistakenly view the whole of Southern Asia's population). There were in fact 500 distinct Aboriginal tribes and 300 distinct languages.

During the past two decades popular literature, current affairs and constant publicity surrounding the Aboriginal struggle for justice and equality have all enlightened people about the unique Aboriginal relationship with the land. But this relationship, crucial and sacred as it was, is only one strand of a complex threefold relationship between the Aboriginal and (a) human beings; (b) nature as a whole (not just the land); (c) gods, spirits and other supernatural beings. The dominant themes in Aboriginal religion revolve around the life crises (in which the opportunity for rebirth is much valued) and fertility and procreation. Many of the rituals and symbolic expression emphasise and celebrate life and living. Berndt (1974) quotes from Stanner (1965): 'The whole religious corpus vibrated with an expressed aspiration for life. Vitality, fertility, and growth ... Aboriginal religion was probably one of the least material minded, and most life minded of any of which we have knowledge' (p.217).

'The Dreaming'

'The Dreaming' is a fundamental concept in Aboriginal religion (Elkin 1933). It represents a co-ordinated system of belief and action, the significance and relevance of which is demonstrated in a range of important matters in Aboriginal life and culture. Existing tribal laws and customs can be traced back to 'the Dreaming', a time when amazing beings are thought to have lived, eternal beings whose souls live on for ever. They instituted tribal laws, customs and rights, through which today's Aboriginals can have direct contact with them. Elkin writes: 'The ancient time of the heroes is the 'dream time', but not the passing dream of the night, but the eternal dream time of spiritual reality to which historical significance is attached' (p.166). It is a fundamental religious duty on the part of Aborigines to live within the ethical framework and the institutions and various forms which the spiritual beings created. This is made easier by knowing and sensing both the physical and spiritual presence of these beings, being aware of their human as well as their supernatural attributes. They are alive today, as they always have been, and as they will continue to be.

'Totemism'

'Totemism' in Aboriginal religious belief focuses upon the shape-changing power of the mythic beings who created the universe. Aborigines associate themselves with the earthly form (totem) that these mythic beings took on. These would have included the form of animal, bird or insect, or some earthly feature or element (a rock, river, tree). Rock and cave paintings (Stourton 1996) are said to be sites in which the mythical creatures settled, sometimes metamorphosing into the animal form which the painting depicts. Each of these animal species then became a reflection of the spirit of the particular mythical being, containing 'its essential Dreaming essence. The spirit character is perpetuated in its continued presence on Earth' through the existence of whichever species or earthly feature they have adapted (Berndt 1974, p.9). In Chatwin's (1988) *The Songlines*, Arkady tells the author that if an Aboriginal says that he has a wallaby 'dreaming', he is in effect saying that his totem and the totem of his clan is a wallaby one. A bee totem figures prominently in Wells's award-winning (1971) novel, *Men of the Honey Bee*. Totemism, writes Elkin (1933), quoted in Berndt (1974): 'is a view of nature and life, of the universe and man, which colours and influences the Aborigines' social groupings and mythologies, inspires their rituals and links them to the past. It unites them with nature's activities and species in a bond of mutual life-giving, and imparts confidence amidst the vicissitudes of life' (p.165).

In other words, totemism is a core aspect of identity in Aboriginal society, providing individuals with an unmistakable and all-pervading sense of who they are, their origins, their religion and religious duty, their rituals (often used to evoke the ancestral spirit being) and, probably most important of all, their location and purpose on this earth and their relationship with everything in it. The sense of identity may be further strengthened and validated by the *tjurunga*, a sacred board or stone on which is carved easily identifiable markings denoting all those aspects of identity, including the totemic ancestral spirit being, from which one has descended – an Aboriginal's 'holy of holies,' says Chatwin of the *tjuringa* in *The Songlines*, 'or, if you like, his soul'. Little wonder then that Elkin speaks of 'confidence amidst the vicissitudes of life'. Confidence in any life invariably stems from one's sense of identity.

The 'Songlines'

Probably the most incredible (and for some the most beautiful) concept in Aboriginal culture and religion is that of the songlines. The religious duty of the Aborigine is ritually to travel the land, singing the ancestor's songs, singing the world into being afresh (Chatwin 1988). In the Dreaming, the ancestral mythical beings travelled across the land and sang the world into existence. Every tree, river, creek, gully, rock, mountain and waterhole was created through song. As well as leaving the 'tangible expression of their spiritual essence' in each of these (sacred) sites, they also left the songline denoting the space between the sites. The songs may have a basic recognisable musical structure and conventional verse form, but they are likely to contain much sacred and complex symbolism and many indecipherable sacred words, requiring translation and explanation. A whole series of song cycles developed, which today may be sung in a ritualistic re-enactment of the process of creation. The songlines (or dreaming tracks) therefore functioned in part as the equivalent of the modern map and compass: 'an interlocking network of "lines" or "ways through"' writes Chatwin (1988, p.62). Each individual was thoroughly familiar with their own ancestral being and their songlines, and the sacred sites which they had sung into existence. They could travel the country, guided by the song cycle and the sites associated with their particular ancestral spirit. They could go through different tribal areas and linguistically defined territories, knowing that as long as they kept to the track of the mythological songlines they would inevitably encounter another who shared the same ancestral heritage (Dreaming). Berndt writes: 'Almost everywhere, throughout the continent, "tribal" territory is or was criss-crossed with a network of mythical tracks or "pathways" along which such beings are believed to have travelled (*singing the world into existence*). The whole Western desert is crossed by the tracks of mythic beings extending in every direction' (1974, p.9). The songlines of these mythical beings, and the topographical sites they create, were the only meaningful boundaries and landmarks for the Aborigines. Each of them inherited a section of the total song cycle and the portion of land which their particular songline (or verses) had created. This was not ownership in the western sense, however, more custodianship and discipleship. 'A man's verses were his title deeds to territory,' writes Chatwin.

'He could lend them to others; he could borrow other verses in return. The one thing he couldn't do was sell or get rid of them' (1988, p.64). The contemporary importance of the songlines may now be gauged by the extent to which developers consult with Aboriginal elders, in order to avoid the sacrilegious defilement of sites which occurred over two centuries. Only in Australia have the songlines assumed an important legal role; they have actually been used in courtrooms as evidence of early settlement in the Aborigines' struggle for the return of their land (Haviland 1999).

Social aspects of religion and life

There is an intensely social aspect to Aboriginal life and religion. 'Religion is relevant to all members of an Aboriginal society' (Berndt 1974, p.19). The symbolic, systematic and protracted rituals through which semi-nomadic tribes hunted for food and practised their religion necessitated social cohesion and collaboration of a high order. Reference has already been made to the religious, non-material nature of Aboriginal life. The extent of this is clearly demonstrated in the divisions of spoil after a successful hunt:

> When an animal is killed ... the meat is divided among the hunters' families and other relatives. Each person in the camp gets a share, the size depending upon the nature of the person's kinship ties to the hunters. The least desirable parts may be kept by the hunters themselves. When one hunter kills a kangaroo ... the left hind leg goes to the brother of the hunter, the tail to his father's brother's son, the loins and fat to his father-in-law, the forelegs to his father's younger sister, the head to his wife, and the entrails and the blood to the hunter. The hunter and his family seem to fare badly in this arrangement, but they have their turn when another man makes a kill. (Haviland 1999, p.205)

Haviland refers to this practice as *generalized reciprocity* which, however apt the term may be in an essay on distribution and exchange in ancient societies, is inadequate in conveying the social and religious value system underpinning Aboriginal life. It also says nothing at all about the selfless, non-material and enduring philosophy of such life. 'Aborigines in general,' says Flynn, the ex-priest in Chatwin's *The Songlines*, 'had the idea that all "goods" were potentially malign, and would work against their possessors unless they were forever in motion' (p.63).

A 'bizarre' culture in a distant land?

It is neither necessary nor important for western health and social care professionals to learn about Aboriginal religion (unless of course they wish to work
with Australia's indigenous population). But can they respect it? Can they
sense something of the profundity of meaning it has for Aboriginals? Bruce
Chatwin certainly could, and his predecessor too, the novelist and anthropologist A.E. Wells (1971). The questions need to be asked in respect of all
religions, and of all the other core components of cultures. Cultural competence is largely based upon knowledge and understanding. But respect,
attitude and approach are even more important than knowledge. Cultures
vary enormously. Their core components may appear (as did Aboriginal
religion) as magic or superstition, fantasy or nonsense, irrelevant or ridiculous.
Such perceptions of Aboriginal religion and of other components of their
culture generated one of the many motives to destroy that culture in its
entirety. The remainder of this chapter will reflect on:

- the principal means by which the attempted destruction was carried
  out

- the impact of Aboriginal resurgence on social care agencies in
  particular.

Break up the families and confiscate the land

In 1995 Michael Lavarch, the Australian Attorney General, requested the
Human Rights and Equal Opportunity Commission to inquire into the 'past
laws, practices and policies which resulted in the separation of Aboriginal and
Torres Strait Islander children from their families by compulsion, duress or
undue influence, and the effects of those laws, practices, and policies' (Commonwealth of Australia 1997). The result was the publication of a 700-page
report, entitled *Bringing Them Home*. Seldom if ever has a government
produced such a devastating critique of its perceptions and treatment of its
indigenous people and no nation (not even post-apartheid, post-truth and rec-
onciliation South Africa) has been so profoundly affected in terms of its collective expression of guilt, and its willingness to seek atonement. One of the
inquiry's conclusions was as follows:

> Between one in three and one in ten indigenous children were forcibly
> removed from their families in the period 1910–1970. During that
> period, not one family escaped the effects of forcible removal. Most

families have been affected, in one or more generations, by the forcible removal of one or more children. (Commonwealth of Australia 1997)

One does not have to read too far into the report before realising that the forced separation of Aboriginal children was the principal attack strategy in weakening the core pillar (i.e. the family) of Aboriginal cultural life (Thorpe 1994). Aboriginal culture was as incomprehensible to the colonisers as its religious component was an obstacle to a ruthless acquisition and exploitation of the land: thus the promulgation of the doctrine of Terra Nullius, a declaration that the Aborigines had no rights or claim to the land on which they and their ancestors had lived for 50,000 years. An MP in the Victorian parliament debating the report remarked: 'Let there be no doubt that the doctrine of terra nullius was the catalyst for some of the most inhumane, savage and illegal treatment meted out to indigenous Australians' (Hansard 1997). Even without the savagery, terra nullius was certain to kill off the Aborigines.

State legislatures

Aboriginal history during the eighteenth and nineteenth centuries in particular is peppered with massacres carried out by the colonisers. Legislation became an effective weapon in the attack upon Aboriginal culture (Commonwealth of Australia 1997; Thorpe 1994). Each of the state jurisdictions in Australia enacted laws which aimed towards the elimination of Aboriginal culture. If they were ever judged to be ineffective, they were replaced by more ruthless laws. The principal driving force underpinning new legislation was invariably the conviction 'that there was nothing of value in Indigenous culture' (Commonwealth of Australia 1997, p.7). Legislation inevitably led to the establishment of organisations, societies and institutions which would formulate and implement the necessary and specifically cultural–genocidal policies derived from the laws. The most prominent of these bodies, ironically, would be welfare institutions, the police, educational departments and the Christian churches.

Making the perception a reality

The report reveals a shocking abuse of language in the attempted annihilation of Aboriginal culture and identity. 'Annihilation', the indisputable aim, is repeatedly lost in the welter of more rational and scientific concepts such as 'biological absorption', 'miscegnation', 'social assimilation' and 're-socialisation'. With regard to Aborigines born to indigenous and non-indigenous parents, the offensive terms 'half-blood', 'half-caste', 'quadroon' and 'octo-roon' were commonly used. The authorities believed at one point that the further Aborigines went down the line of 'mixed-ness' the better: 'once half-castes were sufficiently white in colour, they would become like white people' (p.73). (Note that the issue here is not race but way of life and culture; black people can never look like white people, but if they can live like white people, think, speak and behave like white people, discard all the remaining remnants of their Aboriginal culture and identity, then they may become acceptable.) Some of the more 'committed' purists such as James Isdell, an officially designated local 'protector' of Aboriginal peoples in Western Australia, thought the process needed to be considerably speedier than that: 'I would not hesitate for one moment to separate any half-caste from its aborig-inal mother, no matter how frantic her momentary grief might be at the time. They soon forget their offspring' (quote from Choo 1990, p.11). The latter part of this utterance is more relevant than the cruelty of the first part. It exposes an ignorance of the centrality of fertility, procreation and child rearing in Aboriginal culture. A more intelligent presentation of the latter (i.e. Aboriginal child rearing) is provided by Healy, Hassan and McKenna (1985), emphasising the prolonged physical intimacy between Aboriginal mothers and their children, the security and love children receive as opposed to disci-pline, and the later sharing of parental duty within extended family and tribe members. Thorpe's (1994) child protection research in Western Australia led him to discover the widespread poverty, squalor and deprivations inflicted upon the Aborigines – an inevitable consequence of the oppressive and coercive legislation, yet somehow 'remnants' of their idealised 'mode of child rearing appear to have survived the holocaust' (p.164).

Denigrating Aboriginal culture

All the usual methods of law enforcement and the implementation of policies aimed towards the destruction of culture were adopted: dispersal of communi-ties; banning all cultural activities; preventing Aborigines from using any of the myriad indigenous languages then in use. Concurrent with the states' intensifying projection of the image of a worthless Stone Age Aboriginal culture was a concerted attempt to inculcate the worst possible self-identity among the tens of thousands of Aboriginal children forcibly removed. This was done in a number of ways; for example, the alternative carers, foster parents, residential teachers and workers and Christian missionaries assidu-ously reminded the children 'how fortunate' they were in being 'rescued' from their own 'dirty, lazy, immoral, unintelligent, and decrepit people'. The authorities of the time were incapable of realising that their laws and policies were certain to inflict a material poverty and deprivation upon Aborigines, which would ensure they appeared as though they were indeed dirty, lazy, immoral and decrepit (similar to the actions and thought processes in South Africa's apartheid policy). A state of Victoria politician would later state: 'These people [the 'carers'] did not understand Aboriginal culture, and did not want to understand, because they thought Aboriginal culture was less worthy than their own' (Hansard 1997).

Vulnerability and resistance

The means by which the children were severed from their parents (cruel even by the standards of the time) constituted an additional and valuable weapon in the unspoken war against Aboriginal culture, probably in a way that the authorities could not have realised. It is a well-known fact in child care that many children who are witness to violence perpetrated in their name assume that they are the cause of the violence. This can be devastating to their sense of personal integrity and to their sense of identity. No doubt some Aboriginal children, recalling the painful memories of their parents begging the authorities not to take them, held themselves responsible for their parents' sufferings. Such children were extremely vulnerable to a process of inculcation that would have offered them the opportunity to lose their former selves and to repress the cruelty surrounding their removal. Some authority figures however had a much more realistic and apprehensive image of Aboriginal culture and were constantly promoting greater vigilance. Ida Standley, a matron in the Northern Territory, warning of the dangers of any future contact between Aboriginal children severed from their parents, made this remark: 'What it takes us five years to build up is undone by the black influence in five minutes' (Commonwealth of Australia 1997, p.62).

'A wilcha bed, the stars, the embers of the fire and the closeness of my family'

Even the goodness of Aboriginal life was perversely projected as badness: 'The reliance of community members upon each other to care for their children in times of difficulty was regarded not as a strength but as an indication of neglect' (Commonwealth of Austalia 1997, p.59). Many of the personal testimonies are enlightening on this point. Fiona, for example, having described the authorities arriving in the darkness writes:

We went to the United Aborigines Mission in Oodnadatta. We got there in the dark and then we didn't see our mother again. She just kind of disappeared into the darkness. There was no time given us to say goodbye to our mothers.

From there we had to learn to eat new food, have our heads shaved … Then we had to learn to sleep in a house. We'd only ever slept in our wilchas, and always had the stars there and the embers of the fire and the closeness of the family. And all of a sudden we had high beds and that was very frightening.

I guess the most traumatic thing for me is … that you forbade us to speak our own language and we had no communication with our own family.

I realised later how much I'd missed of my culture and how much I'd been devastated … I can't communicate with my family, can't hold a conversation. I can't go up to my uncle and ask him anything because we don't have that language.

Once that language was taken away, we lost a part of our very soul. It meant our culture was gone, our family was gone, everything that was dear to us was gone. (Commonwealth of Australia 1997, p.92)

The beginning of the end of the long nightmare

There are many significant milestones in the fight for justice for Aborigines and in the re-emergence of Aboriginal culture and identity. These include the 1975 Racial Discrimination Act and the Australian government's acquisition of powers in 1967 to legislate on Aboriginal affairs. (As in every other colonial situation, central government was deemed far more sensitive than some of the state legislatures.) The most important milestone, however, is the Mabo judgment of 1992, when the Australian supreme court overturned the iniquitous Terra Nullius doctrine. Twelve years earlier, Eddie Mabo, an Aboriginal from the Murray Islands, was refused permission to return to his homeland to carry out some oral history research with his people. He had always believed the islands belonged to the indigenous native islanders. He later led a campaign to gain legal recognition of the Murray Islanders' claim to traditional title. The Queensland state government (which then had jurisdiction over the Murray Islands) countered with emergency legislation which stated that any rights the islanders ever had were 'hereby extinguished without compensation'. This was successfully contested on the grounds that it contravened the Racial Discrimination Act and Mabo proceeded with his case to the Supreme Court, which eventually made the historical ruling in his favour: that he did own land not because of any title which the Crown may bestow upon him, but because his family and his ancestors had owned the land according to the native traditions of the islands in which they lived. The judgment was as important in terms of culture and identity of the Aboriginal people as it was in terms of human rights. It sent shudders through the boardrooms of Australia's business communities, particularly its mining companies, which had for two centuries ignored any protests the Aborigines made about the violation of the sacred Dreamtime places dotted throughout the continent.

National Sorry Day

On 26 May 1999, the first anniversary of the tabling of the *Bringing Them Home* report, a 'National Sorry Day' gave Australians the opportunity to respond to the acknowledgement of the wrongs perpetrated against the Aboriginal peoples. Some indication of the extent of guilt felt throughout Australia and the need for atonement can be gauged by the earlier responses of its politicians. J.G. Kennett, for example, Prime Minister of the state of Victoria, opened the Apology to Aboriginal People debate of 17 September (Hansard 1997) by expressing his abhorrence of past practices in the management of Aboriginal affairs and child welfare systems. He reaffirmed his government's commitment to helping maintain Australia as a culturally diverse, open and tolerant society. J.M. Brumby, the opposition leader, reminded the house that the forced removal of Aboriginal children continued well into the 1970s:

> They were taken on the basis of having indigenous people adopt European culture and behaviour to the exclusion of their families and cultural backgrounds. The assimilation policy assumed that over time indigenous people would simply die out and would be so mixed with the European population that they became indistinguishable ... Indigenous children, particularly those of mixed heritage, were removed in the hope that Aboriginal and Torres Strait Islander identities would totally disappear. (Hansard 1997, p.5)

Brumby said that the aim of the laws and the policies was 'destroying the culture of the Aboriginal people'. He quotes Sir Ronald Wilson's use of the word 'genocide' in the *Bringing Them Home* report (Commonwealth of Australia 1997), describing these events, and explains: 'One is left in no doubt whatever that the program of forced separation was intended to kill off, to destroy, the culture' (Hansard 1997, p.6).

Another politician, Dr. R.L. Dean, quotes the contribution made by Link Up, one of the many emerging organisations enabling ·Aborigines to re-establish their identities:

> We may go home, but we cannot relive our childhoods. We may reunite with our mothers, fathers, sisters, brothers, aunties and communities, but we cannot relive the 20, 30, 40 years that we spent without their love and care … We can go home to ourselves as Aborigines, but this does not erase the attacks inflicted on our hearts, minds, bodies, and souls by caretakers who thought their mission was to eliminate us as Aborigines. (Hansard 1997, p.15)

Throughout the debate, Victoria's politicians continually referred to the harsh statistics which the report provided (e.g. the number of Aboriginal juveniles incarcerated within the juvenile justice system was 20 times higher than the rate for all other groups put together), and recalled their own comparatively privileged upbringings for which they now carried a burden of guilt. With bitter irony, they attacked their legislative predecessors who laid the foundations for the policies of forced removal that would evolve. 'Perish the thought,' said P.J. Ryan, 'that we should ever again enact legislation with the direct intent of destroying the very fabric of family life which today we hold so precious' (Hansard 1997, p.9). Ms L.J. Kosky scorned the so-called charitable impulse of many involved in the removals:

> It was anything but charity … it was about the superiority of white Australia and the denigration of Aboriginal culture and values. It was an attempt to wipe out the Aboriginal race, not through direct genocide, but through the destruction of their culture and lineage. It amounted to the same thing. (Hansard 1997, p.19).

The developing childcare context of the 'Bringing Them Home' report

The *Bringing Them Home* report and its recommendations impacted upon every agency of local and national government and upon all voluntary welfare agencies. It should be stressed, however, that many individuals and organisations, embracing both the indigenous and non-indigenous populations, had long before set in motion the processes that would make such a report and its recommendations inevitable. Great strides had already been made in the

1980s and early 1990s. In 1981, nearly 100 Aboriginal-community run children's services amalgamated to form the Secretariat of National Aboriginal and Islander Child Care (SNAICC). The submissions of SNAICC were much in evidence throughout the inquiry. In 1994, a conference in Darwin attended by representatives from every state began the process of bringing to light precisely what had been done to the indigenous population and to formulate strategies for the survivors. Civil actions by Aborigines in New South Wales and the Northern Territory soon followed (and continue to this day). Another landmark court ruling, this time going against the Aborigines, was made in August 2000, when the Northern Territory Federal Court ruled that the government did not have to pay punitive damages to two adult Aborigines, who had sought compensation for psychological trauma, emotional stress and cultural isolation as a consequence of being removed from their families; the judgment is likely to go to appeal (*The Times*, 12 August 2000).

Thorpe's (1994) action research on child protection in Western Australia gives indications that some front-line child protection workers were already practising in a way much more compatible with the future recommendations of the *Bringing Them Home* report than with the stipulations of their own agencies. For example, their 'unofficial' regular use of the Aboriginal kinship networks to keep children out of care constituted what Thorpe refers to as 'an invisible but culturally sensitive form of social work practice' (p.165). Amazingly, as late as 1987, the workers' agency, the Department for Community Services, produced a guide for child protection workers which did not even mention Aboriginal children; this despite the facts emerging from Thorpe's research (known by every child protection worker in the area) about the gross over-representation of Aboriginal children on workers' caseloads. Thorpe says that many workers and managers 'spotted this ... extraordinary omission' and proceeded to rectify the situation. Their first action was prolonged consultation with Aboriginal representatives, which led, 18 months later, to the publication *Enhancing Child Welfare in Aboriginal Communities* (Aziz 1989). This contained, among other things, 11 criteria for enabling workers to 'determine child abuse and neglect in Aboriginal communities'. Thorpe gives numerous examples of culturally competent practice in terms of both assessment and support of Aboriginal families, and concludes: 'These criteria give an excellent illustration of a child welfare agency's capacity to adapt to the realities of diverse child rearing practices, as they are encountered by social workers' (Thorpe 1994, p.168).

Adoption of the Aboriginal Child Placement Principle

SNAICC formulated the Aboriginal Child Placement Principle and success-fully lobbied for it to be incorporated into the childcare legislation of numerous states. The *Bringing Them Home* report fully endorsed the principle. It declares that Aboriginal children who have to be placed outside their home, or who are being adopted, should be placed:

- with a member of the parent's Aboriginal family
- where such a person is not reasonably available, with a member of the Aboriginal community
- where such a person is not reasonably available, with a person approved by an authorised Aboriginal agency as suitable.

The state of Victoria enthusiastically applied the principle in its 1989 Children and Young Persons Act (s.119). Its practices in respect of Aboriginal children placed in or out of family care were commended in the *Bringing Them Home* report as a model which should be universally adopted. The Principle makes it highly unlikely that Aboriginal families will ever experience the same again, by ensuring their people, both lay and professional, are primarily responsible for decision making in respect of Aboriginal children, and for the provision of the services which the children may need. If indigenous carers are not available, the report recommends:

- family reunion should remain a primary objective
- continuous contact with the child's indigenous family, community and culture must be ensured
- the carer must live in proximity to the child's indigenous family and community (recommendation 51d).

National Library Oral History Project

The federal government has ensured that further revelations and debate about what was done to its indigenous peoples will continue into future generations. The government has funded Australia's National Library Oral History Project, dedicated to collecting and preserving the stories of indigenous peoples and others, including missionaries, police, welfare workers and administrators involved in the process of child removals. Academic institutions will play an important role in this project and are already well prepared, through their own Aboriginal education and research centres, to contribute to the debate.

Typical is the Koori Centre in the University of Sydney, providing programmes, services and facilities to encourage and support the involvement of Aboriginal and Torres Strait Islander people in all aspects of tertiary education. Just as important as ensuring an adequate distribution of educational resources is the challenging of perceptions of Aboriginal culture and society as a whole. The challenge is well articulated by the feminist Aboriginal activist and poet, Oodgeroo Noonucul (1984):

> Until our culture is recognised for its richness and complexity, and given this recognition by education authorities, we will always have to live with the derogatory stereotype that lowers the self esteem of our children and causes them to feel that the education system has no relevance to them whatsoever (Noonucul 1984, p.285, quoted in Smallwood 1995).

Summary and Conclusion

Aboriginal culture and identity is re-emerging after centuries of attempted genocide perpetrated by successive Australian governments. 'Genocide' is an emotive term, but the Australian government's own commissioned report *Bringing Them Home* (Commonwealth of Australia 1997) provides a lengthy argument justifying its use in describing what was done to the Aborigines. As the testimony of both white and Aboriginal leaders confirms, the principal means of destroying the indigenous population was the prevention of Aboriginal cultural expression and the sustained denigration of Aboriginal cultural identity. There was an additional reason for adopting these particular means: the wholesale expression of Aboriginal culture was the major obstacle to the settlers' exploitation and domination.

The chapter began by identifying the religiosity of Aboriginal culture. It quoted from both anthropological research and popular literature to demonstrate the profundity of meaning and relevance which Aboriginal religion had in everyday life. It posed the question: can we respect those components of someone's culture that may well appear to us as bizarre or nonsensical? Could we, as health and social care professionals, foster pride and respect within Aborigines (or any other minority) for their own religion and for the numerous other components of their culture?

The *Bringing Them Home* report has abundant evidence of the opposite: contempt and denigration towards every aspect of Aboriginal culture. The statistics on forced removal, social and economic deprivation and criminal justice are chilling. The report has led ordinary Australians to support a National Sorry Day. Most politicians from all parties have responded with honesty and humility. Health, education and social care agencies are responding too, and this chapter considered some of the developments in childcare and child protection work in particular, where many of the childcare principles recommended by *Bringing Them Home* were already being implemented.

There can be no turning back for Australia's Aborigines, but it will take generations for them to shed the effects of a terrible and brutal past, and effectively to combat the existing widespread discrimination in education, employment, health and social care still directed towards them. Just as the American Indians did, Australia's Aboriginal population teaches us two contrasting truths:

- the crucial significance of culture in people's lives

- the relative ease with which every government agency can be enlisted in the prevention of expression of that culture.

In Chapter 7, we look more closely at the role of health and social care agencies in the treatment of indigenous and minority cultures generally, in the present as well as the past.

Part II

Obstacles and Challenges
to Cultural Competence

CHAPTER 7

Cultural Awareness within the Caring Professions

Introduction

Managers and trainers within health and social care professions are aware of the importance of a multicultural perspective in the delivery of services. Such awareness is a consequence of:

- political pressure
- legislation
- complaints about discrimination and/or cultural bias
- consultation with the representatives of minority cultural groups
- current literature and research.

Awareness, however, does not constitute action. We have seen evidence in Chapter 4 of cultural insensitivity in professionals' actions towards minority cultural groups. It is necessary to explore some of the reasons for this. The chapter will highlight the fact that there is no tradition of cultural sensitivity or cultural competence in health and social care professions, neither in their literature nor their practice. Worse still, those professions were partly instrumental in the destruction of indigenous cultures in many British and French colonies. We shall look in more detail at that particular role, but the chapter is generally concerned with culturally incompetent practice in the present. It will review current literature and practice in each of the high profile professions such as general practice, nursing and midwifery, social work, psychiatry, child protection, counselling and psychotherapy. There are indications of an increasing awareness of culture, particularly in the field of child protection work, but generally the literature clearly demonstrates that formidable obstacles to the goal of cultural competence remain.

The role of 'caring professionals' in cultural genocide

In the personal testimonies of indigenous peoples, past and present, there are painful memories of contact with professionals from health and social care agencies (Commonwealth of Australia 1997; Debo 1995; Nagel 1997; Survival International 1999). These professionals include generic and specialist social workers, welfare workers, midwives, nurses, juvenile justice workers, child protection workers, residential workers, doctors, health visitors, paediatricians, psychiatrists, psychologists, teachers in mainstream education or in specialist schools, foster parents and adoptive parents, church missionaries, police, magistrates and judges.

Health personnel

The *Bringing Them Home* report (Commonwealth of Australia 1997) clearly indicates that nurses, midwives and doctors played a pivotal role in the severance of newborn Aboriginal children from their mothers. High-ranking senior doctors often instigated and directed the policies designed for the elimination of the Aborigines. For example, Dr Cecil Cook in the Northern Territory and Dr W.E. Roth in Queensland were both appointed Chief Protectors of Aboriginal Affairs (surely the most ironic titles); Cook also served as the State's Chief Medical Officer (Commonwealth of Australia 1997).

Survival International's (1999) current campaign on behalf of the Canadian French-speaking Innu reveals health personnel unwittingly repeating the destruction of indigenous culture. First, there is the same lack of awareness that culture and the environment are crucial variables in the health of an individual. As Andrew and Sarsfield (1984) put it: 'The Innu are sick and dying because of a well documented syndrome of collective ill-health brought on by the enforced dependency and attempted acculturation of an entire people' (quoted in Survival International 1999, p.1)) Second, the process of acculturation begins with an imposed sedentary existence, in which the indigenous people are compelled to live in drab, unhygienic, and uniform settlements. Religious orders of the Catholic Church provide education and boarding institutions, with the occasional exposure to brutal regimes and physical and sexual abuse. Well-meaning and influential medical personnel establish hospitals and clinics for the Innu, and the authorities will ensure health visitors and nurses visit their children, but the cumulative effect of such 'benevolence' is merely to remove the Innu further from their nomadic ways of hunting, fishing and trapping, and from a community existence evolved from their surrounding ecology. The consequences for the Innu are predictable. The Utshimassits Innus in Labrador, for example, have the highest rates of suicide in the world. More than 50 per cent of all Innu deaths during the last two decades were of people under 30 years of age; the corresponding figure for the whole of Canada was 5 per cent. The Innu child is between three and seven times more likely than the average Canadian child to die before the age of five (Survival International 1999). Some present-day Canadian medical personnel apply the same derogatory labelling and 'analysis' as was applied to Australia's Aborigines in explaining their poor health, for example, ignorance, inability to cope with change, irresponsibility, laziness, poor child rearing, poor diet, drunkenness, etc. This colonialist legacy is one that has to be confronted by today's trainers of health and social care workers in Canada (Rogers 1995).

Social workers

Australia's *Bringing Them Home* report (Commonwealth of Australia 1997) revealed that social workers and police were primarily responsible for the severance of newborn Aborigines from their parents and their transport to alternative (white) care. If the newborns were not immediately removed, then coercion and threat would be applied in the weeks which followed to make mothers 'consent' to adoption. If this did not happen, there would be ample opportunity later, when Aboriginal infants and toddlers, suffering chronic health problems mainly caused by malnutrition and forced settlement, would be admitted to a local hospital. Co-ordination between doctors, nurses, social workers and police would then ensure that the children did not return to their parents. 'Some Protectors and Inspectors resorted to kidnap,' says the *Bringing Them Home* report, 'taking the children from school, or tricking them into their cars.'

Just as ironic as the title of 'chief protector' was that given to many of the departments in which social workers operated. Departments of 'child welfare', 'social welfare' and the 'Aboriginal Welfare Board' all played an important role in the task of eliminating Aborigines. There are more personal testimonies about social workers than any other health and social care group. They are remembered as cruel and indifferent to the Aboriginal mothers running after them, frantically begging them not to take their children. The safeguard of judicial scrutiny in respect of Aboriginal children and families was removed in most states. Later it was reinstated, but if parents contested removal the welfare workers would use the time-honoured tactic of testifying in court that the parents were bad, negligent, poverty-stricken, unemployed, alcoholic, sick and unfit to care for their children. Seldom did courts disagree. Part Three of the report, 80 pages long, is largely devoted to the testimonies of Aborigines as children. It makes extremely painful reading. The Australian Association of Social Workers admitted its share of responsibility, apologised and stated:

> The Association acknowledges that social workers were involved in the forced separation of Aborigines and Torres Strait Islander children from their families in every state and territory in Australia during this century. (Commonwealth of Australia 1997: Submission 721, pp.1–2)

The church, church welfare and church child care

The role of the Christian churches and their numerous welfare organisations in the forced removal of Aboriginal children and the destruction of Aboriginal culture is of particular interest because many of the caring professions, particularly social work and nursing, have their origins in Christian-inspired charitable enterprises. The extent of their culpability may be gauged by the fact that *Bringing Them Home* contains no less than three full pages of acknowledgements and profuse apologies from the hierarchies of the Roman Catholic, Anglican, Baptist and Uniting Churches (Commonwealth of Australia 1997). The report details countless incidents of brutality perpetrated against Aboriginal children by clergy, nuns and social workers employed by the churches. There was also evidence of a pervasive racism, but it is likely that they attached more importance to the condition of the soul than to the colour of the skin. For this reason, religion-inspired white welfare workers were more assiduous and determined in their attempts to undermine the culture and identity of Aboriginal children. There is not the slightest evidence anywhere in the report of workers' awareness of anything good about Aboriginal culture and identity. It was universally perceived as something bad which needed to be eliminated, because its many manifestations were a major obstacle to conversion and assimilation.

An identical crime in the interests of empire

In Britain the authorities began planning for another great enterprise, wholly compatible with the destruction of the Aboriginal race and culture. Australia was grossly underpopulated. The rate of emigration from Europe was too slow. The authorities and church leaders decided that the process of populating and Christianising Australia could be greatly accelerated by shipping tens of thousands of British children who were being cared for by many of the long-established British Protestant and Catholic church-based charitable and welfare organisations. Barnardos, the Children's Society and numerous orders in the Catholic church all enthusiastically participated in the enterprise. Bean and Melville's (1989) research exposed this scandal and exploded the myth that the vast majority of these children were orphaned and languishing in residential care with no prospect of adoption. Many, in fact, were meant to be in care only briefly because their (mostly) single-parent mothers had been persuaded by clergy and welfare workers that 'care' was preferable to the inevitable poverty, stigma and shame of single parenthood. Once the mothers had 'got on their feet' they expected the children to be returned to them. But many mothers were repeatedly refused access to their children and denied knowledge of their whereabouts.

The role of the welfare branches of the Christian churches in the cultural genocide in Australia is now universally acknowledged – hence the official and profuse apologies. But what about the role of their colleagues in Britain, helping to accelerate and intensify that process? What were the social and welfare workers doing to the culture and identity of the children they shipped to Australia? What precisely was it like for the children who suddenly found themselves severed from their mothers, from their residential homes, from siblings and friends, schools and little possessions which they may have had? These children too had a culture and an identity, maybe not as distinct or as rounded as the Aboriginal children they were meant to supplant, but nevertheless important to them. We know from subsequent child development research that the children were of an age to have already experienced 'a considerable cultural formation' by the time they were removed (Hoksbergen 1997). To be shipped to the other side of the globe without one's parent(s) and to be placed (as many of them were) with unfit, untrained, abusive foster parents, whose very first command was that the child must be called by another name and never talk about his or her past – this constituted an attack upon the children's sense of culture and identity. Goffman's (1961) area of interest was the incarcerated psychiatric patient, but his words are just as applicable to the hapless 'children of the empire' the title of Bean and Melville's work: 'the ultimate purpose being to deprive the new inmate of the links with the past, and destroy his or her personal identity' (Goffman, 1961, p.19). The Australian childcare writers Goddard and Carew (1993) wrote specifically about the children: their past 'was a door to be closed, rather than a rich seam of culture and identity to be treasured' (p.23).

Ireland

The industrial schools

Perhaps the most sustained, concentrated assault upon a nation's children and their cultural heritage, by state, church, education and welfare authorities combined, occurred in Ireland in its so-called industrial schools. These schools 'catered' for children found begging, destitute, not attending school, guilty of indictable offences, or lacking proper guardianship (meaning primarily moral guardianship – a young widow's sexual relationship with a man was enough to warrant instant removal of her children). This period in Irish childcare history has been researched and publicised by Raftery (1999) and Raftery and O'Sullivan (1999). The statistics are staggering for a country of less than three million people: 105,000 children were incarcerated in the schools between 1868 and 1969. Up to 8000 children were detained at any one time. Countless abuses took place in the schools – physical, emotional, psychological and sexual abuses. Precisely therefore as occurred in Australia at the same time and perpetrated by the same professions and religious orders, tens of thousands of Irish children were experiencing something almost identical. The analysis of these events invariably interprets them in terms of class, poverty and the abuse of power by a church oligarchy; but reading the personal testimonies of the children themselves, it is undeniable that cultural identity (without the workers even realising it) was the main objective of attack:

> When I went in there, the first thing that happened was they took away my name and gave me a number. Mine was 12847. Everything I owned in the school from that time on was numbered 12847. It was on my boots. It was on my bib. It was on my blankets. It was on my towel. It was on my brain. (Raftery and O'Sullivan 1999, p.269)

Few children had the resilience and coping strategies to survive the experiences unscathed and many carried the emotional and psychological scars well into their teenage and adult years, in addition to the predictable identity crises.

How could it be otherwise?

Little is known of the backgrounds and training of health and social care workers and of members of religious orders functioning in a 'welfare' capacity during those years. But we can be certain that they knew little about childcare and child development and nothing about cultural competence. Substantial improvement has been made in respect of the former, but what about the latter? What improvements are there in literature, training and practice today? Are the experiences of yesterday, in far-off places, merely aberrations of history, involving only heartless bureaucrats and 'welfare' misfits masquerading as professionals? The current-day experiences of the Innu tribes in Canada and the campaign on their behalf by the prestigious Survival International would suggest not (Survival International 1999). Let us then consider each of the most prominent health and social care professions separately, briefly looking at the relevant histories and, more importantly, reflecting at length on their current literature, research and practice in the context of 'culture' and the treatment of cultural minorities.

Doctors and medicine

The literature of medicine and the current scandals engulfing the medical profession suggest that doctors have not yet wakened to the challenge of cultural competence. Kavanagh and Kennedy (1992) comment: 'There are few books and journals in the average medical library ... that acknowledge [cultural] diversity' (p.5). Qureshi's (1989) opening statement in *Transcultural Medicine* might seem a little exaggerated: 'English general practitioners and health professionals tend to regard everyone as English, and to assume that all patients have similar needs' (p.vii). Yet more up-to-date standard modern texts for British GPs (e.g. Fabb and Marshall 1996; Hall, Dwyer and Lewis 1999; Irvine and Irvine 1996; Jones and Menzies 1999) suggest that Qureshi may not be far off the mark. There is not even the briefest mention of culture or cultural diversity in any of these textbooks.

The medical profession has, historically, been closely involved in political atrocities against minorities. It played the dominant role in the eugenics experimentation directed against select groups in 27 US states in the 1920s, in Germany throughout the 1930s and 1940s and in Sweden over the last three decades. The Indian government depended heavily upon sections of the medical profession durings its compulsory sterilisation programe in the 1970s. The groups which were targeted in these countries included people with learning difficulties, people wrongly (but conveniently) judged to be mentally ill, emotionally unstable, inadequate, inferior, unmanageable, uncontrollable, promiscuous, dangerous, multiparous and too poor, and needless to say, Jews and black people. Everyone knows of the roles of some doctors in the hideous medical experimentation during World War II; few may be aware that such experimentation continued in the USA until 1972:

> In Tuskegee lives an old man, a hardworking churchgoing cotton farmer who signed up in the 1930s along with 600 other black men, for a government 'medical study' that promised free health, free meals, and eventually free burial. No one told him that the study was in reality an examination of 'the effects of untreated syphilis in the negro male' and for forty years, his horrible, potentially fatal disease went untreated, even when a cheap and simple penicillin cure became available. 'They were subjects, not patients. Clinical material, not sick people,' the director of the programme blithely explained. The Tuskegee syphilis study was not stopped and exposed until 1972, and it took another quarter century before Bill Clinton offered a formal apology for this astounding act of official racism. (*The Times*, 20 May 2000)

Removing children's organs: mere insensitivity or cultural incompetence?

In May 2000, the British government issued a damning report on medical trials carried out in a North Staffordshire hospital between 1989 and 1993, in which 28 premature babies died and 15 were left brain-damaged (*The Times*, 9 May 2000). Parents were appalled at the suggestion that they had knowingly signed consent forms, or that they were aware of the experimentation status of the trials. The events in Staffordshire were the latest in a series of scandals that were to convulse the medical profession. In 1997–8, it was revealed that incompetent surgeons at the Bristol Royal Infirmary had been operating over many years on children with serious heart defects. Hospital management knew of the scandal long before it was exposed, and did nothing. Many of the children died. In 1999, it was revealed that the organs of children had been systematically removed without their parents knowing about it. Alder Hey hospital in Liverpool admitted removing the hearts of 2089 dead children and had recently discovered 'hundreds of other organs' removed at the same time (*The Times*, 4 December 1999). In May 2000, mortuary workers at a Nottingham hospital revealed that they had been ordered by consultants to 'throw babies' brains and hearts into rubbish sacks for incineration as well as the vital organs of adults' (*The Times*, 5 June 2000). This order followed the publication of guidelines by the Royal College of Pathologists (in response to

CULTURAL AWARENESS WITHIN THE CARING PROFESSIONS   105

the previous scandals). The consultant in charge was suspended by the minister of health. Since the discovery at Alder Hey hospital, numerous other 'research stores' have been revealed, within Britain and elsewhere. Our Lady's Hospital for Sick Children, based in the sprawling council estates of Dublin, confirmed that the practice of storing organs removed without parents' knowledge had been going on for more than five years (*Irish Times*, 13 December 1999).

These are only a fraction of the exposures about medicine and doctors during the last decade. The profession has been accused by the public, press and government alike of a shockingly endemic arrogance and insensitivity. What has not been generally recognised is that it also constitutes the worst excesses of cultural incompetence. An important manifestation of cultural incompetence is to attack one's sense of identity. Writers and researchers have consistently agreed that one's culture is the most potent moulder of one's identity (Chapter 3) Dozens of women have been traumatized and multilated by incompetent gynacologists; many of the women victims of the surgeons involved have invariably described their experiences as an attack upon their sense of identity and self; some claimed that the psychological disintegration they experienced was worse than the physical butchery perpetrated against them.

Doctors who experiment with human life and/or remove organs without relatives knowing are unlikely to have any intelligent conception of the meaning of culture. Nor are such doctors likely to feel any obligation stemming from an awareness of the cultural aspects of bereavement and grieving and the cultural importance of the rituals associated with burials or other forms of final departure (Pincus 1974). They would have no respect for the values within virtually all cultures, from the dawn of civilization, that dictate reverence for corpses generally and for the bodies of family members in particular, most particularly of children. Even Neanderthals respected their corpses 40,000 years ago (Bray and Trump 1982). The usually efficient, scientific, objectivity-based medical training of such doctors – with no cultural dimension – would preclude them from understanding the anguish and disgust expressed by many affected parents, or that that anguish and disgust was as much culture-based as it was the expression of the emotional wounding inflicted upon them.

With regard to doctors' cultural incompetence towards minorities, there is evidence and personal testimony to suggest that training is largely defective (Ahmad, Baker and Kernohan 1991; Currer 1991; Henley and Schott 1999;

Hopkins and Bahl 1993). A number of recent texts specifically addressed to the medical professions attempt to do something about this (Helman 1997; Hewison and Wyke 1991, Kelleher and Hillier 1996; Papadopoulos, Tiki and Taylor 1998), and one uses an apt metaphor to convey the depth of the problem. Hewison and Wyke (1991) believe that the medical professions are 'attempting, in the manner of King Canute, to order back the tide' (p.5). Papadopoulos *et al.* speak directly: 'We strongly believe that health care education in general ... is failing in any significant way to prepare students to develop knowledge, skills and attitudes relevant to caring for clients from diverse cultures' (p.vii).

Nursing, health visiting and midwifery

Nursing, health visiting and midwifery are all making strenuous efforts to incorporate cultural awareness within their training curricula. Their tradition in literature, research and practice is no different from that of the other health and caring professions – a neglect of all matters pertaining to culture and the challenges of cultural diversity. In Britain the legislation which underpinned their work, chiefly the Nurses, Midwives and Health Visitors Act 1979, was just as culturally backward as numerous other statutory instruments governing the work of the caring professionals. That Act has only recently been amended to make reference to the health care needs of culturally diverse groups. The publication of texts such as Leininger's (1978) anthropologically based primer on transcultural nursing in the USA and Mares, Henley and Baxter's (1985) book on health care in multiracial Britain are the forerunners of a spate of texts and articles aimed at rectifying the situation. Correspondingly, studies and directives from the Department of Health (e.g. *The Patient's Charter: Raising the Standard* 1991; *Health of the Nation Strategy* 1992c; *Ethnicity and Health* 1993) all address the health needs of differing ethnic communities and how best health professionals can meet those needs.

Gerrish, Husband and MacKenzie (1996) researched training for nurses and midwives. Their aim was to determine the extent to which pre-registration training programmes were equipping practitioners with the necessary competencies for health care provision to cultural minorities. A chapter is devoted to the latter (i.e. personal testimonies by individuals, many of whom were subject to gross cultural insensitivity and different forms of racism). The authors make every effort to highlight the opposite: culturally sensitive practice, but they also reveal that some ethnic minority groups refused to participate in the research 'given their experience of the apparent irrelevance for practice of previous research' (p.37). Kelleher (1996) suggests that such resistance to health-related research is quite common among minority groups.

The attention given to cultural diversity and cultural competence in the provision of nursing and midwifery services varied substantially (as one might expect given the geographical distribution of these training centres). A small number of colleges ignored the issues altogether. The concepts of ethnicity, culture and race 'were usually not neglected', but the health-related topics of health beliefs, ethnic minorities' health needs and ethnic minorities' access to health services received 'scant attention in a significant number of programmes' (Kelleher 1996, p.56). Minority users' perceptions that research into health-related matters is an 'irrelevance' is ironically mirrored in the responses from trainers and practitioners. The authors write: 'We must record that some of the returned questionnaires were unambiguous in their willingness to declare ethnicity as an irrelevance to them, or, expressed more bluntly, a blatant hostility to being expected to address the issue' (p.61). One staff member revealingly says: 'It's not one of the things that I want to get up and shout to the world about' (p.91). The research gives due recognition to the few training establishments seriously attempting to confront the challenges and the 'small cohort of senior managers' and grass-roots staff 'dedicated to an equitable health service for all'. Their ultimate message, however, is that 'nursing and midwifery education has barely begun to address the problem'.

Social work

Lorenz's (1999) theoretical exposition provides one reason for social work's anti-culture stance: it had long sought to avoid the labelling, categorising, and differentiating which some may associate with cultural diversity: 'to make a contribution to the integration of society ... social work strove to rise above the level of the culturally particular and reach a level of universalism as the hallmark of its professional autonomy' (p.27). Freeman and Rustin (1999) suggest that some countries' efforts to create welfare states (in which social work would inevitably have a role) have included a denial of culture. They believe that the universalism of the welfare state, including its 'bureaucracy and its rationality, appears as an elaborate, sustained attempt to do without culture' (p.15).

Payne's (1997) widely read *Social Work Theory* provides a rather hesitant and uncertain definition of culture: 'a difficult concept. It implies a relatively unchanging, dominating collection of social values, and assumes that members of an identified group will always accept all of these' (p.244). This may partly explain why a text of considerable volume, dwelling upon even the most obscure, least known and least used social work theories, says very little about culture. What it does say, however, in the opening pages, is significant. Payne rejects certain arguments against western social work theory, which include the arguments that such theories (a) may be incompatible with some of the core components of indigenous cultures, for example, their values and religion; (b) do not provide explanation for the problems and issues faced by indigenous non-western peoples; (c) ignore the fact that they were used extensively in the processes of assimilation and/or annihilation of indigenous culture. Payne does not seem to be aware of the central role played by social workers and other health and social care professionals in the destruction of Aboriginal culture. A New Zealand based social work professor, (Fulcher 2000) rejects Payne's defence of theories which 'have been used to maintain structural disadvantages in many indigenous communities, as graphically illustrated through the early application of psychological theories in New Zealand that identified "deficits in the Maori character structure"' (Stewart 1997, quoted in Fulcher 2000, p.329).

Psychiatry

Psychiatry has been negligent of culture until relatively recently. Many standard psychiatric texts, used over decades within psychiatry and related disciplines such as mental health social work and community psychiatric nursing, lacked any cultural dimension. The profession has been criticised for its 'ethnocentric view' which has led to widespread and inappropriate diagnoses 'with little regard for the cultures of non-Western people' (Pilgrim and Rogers 1993, p.55). The charge of cultural incompetence and cultural insensitivity has arisen not just from psychiatric literature, but more importantly from the realisation that disproportionate numbers of culturally distinct minority groups (particularly African-Caribbean people) are being referred to psychiatric services, admitted to psychiatric hospitals and diagnosed schizophrenic (Carpenter and Brocklington 1980; Hemsi 1967; Rwgellera 1977). African-Caribbean people are additionally grossly overrepresented in referrals to psychiatric services through the police, courts and prisons (Bhui et al. 1998. They are two and a half times more likely than white people to be detained under s.136 of the 1983 Mental Health Act (Pilgrim and Rogers 1993). Various reasons are advanced for this state of affairs: the widespread sense of alienation felt by minorities, social deprivation, poor housing, financial difficulties, lack of education and racism. Cultural incompetence in psychiatry, however, stems from a more sinister source: psychiatric theory was rooted in assumptions about genetic inferiority and race. The theories of the German psychiatrist Kraepelin, for example, were central in the eugenics programme adopted by Nazi Germany, Sweden and numerous states in the USA and these theories 'dominated post- as well as pre-War Western Psychiatry' (Pilgrim and Rogers 1993).

The profession has made progress in attempting to escape these shackles of the past. Fernando (1988, 1991, 1995) is one of the profession's severest critics and a leading reformer in mental health writing on issues of race, ethnicity and culture. Abas *et al.* (1998) regard culture as a crucial variable in determining the quality and effectiveness of approach to various culturally distinct groups: hence the title of their paper: 'Culturally Sensitive Questionnaires ...'. Chandler and Lalonde's (1998) research demonstrates that cultural continuity provides a bulwark against suicide among adolescents and young adults – high risk suicide groups in most cultures. Their research appears in a recent edition of *Transcultural Psychiatry*, in itself an indication of the profession's commitment to understanding culture and its implications for professional practice (Guéllar and Pariagua 2000; Herrera, Lawson and Sramek 1999; Kaye 1999). Transcultural psychiatry has given rise to worldwide networking and research on culture and details are freely available on the internet.

Counselling and psychotherapy

Counselling and psychotherapy have expanded more than any other caring profession in the twentieth century. The greatest expansion occurred in the USA, where Sigmund Freud and Carl Rogers were dominant influences. The Americanisation of counselling and psychotherapy is the single most important factor in its early development as a culturally incompetent profession. There is some irony in this fact, since the USA was and is the most culturally diverse nation. But as McLeod (1993) points out, the cultural context in which the expansion took place was one which trumpeted individuality, nourished a 'distrust of experts and authority figures', emphasised 'individuals' needs rather than shared social goals', had a 'lack of interest in the past' and 'greatly valued independence and autonomy' (p.16). These are of course, potentially alien if not hostile tenets to the core aspects of many cultures and cultural identities. Cultural identity can only exist in relation to an acute sense of sharing and culture is meaningless without a past. McLeod (1993) acknowledges:

> The field of cross-cultural counselling has received relatively little attention. Many counselling agencies and individual counsellors in private practice have so many clients applying from their majority cultural group that there is little incentive for them to develop expertise in cross-cultural work. (McLeod 1993, p.118)

Lago and Thompson (1996) and Paniagua (1994) represent major leaps forward in the promotion and teaching of culturally sensitive counselling on both sides of the Atlantic. The latter concentrates on work with Hispanic, African-American, American Indian and Asian American clients. Lago and Thompson's opening chapters expand on the contemporary critiques of counselling and psychotherapy for their traditional neglect of culture and conclude that professionals must acquire a 'range, depth and subtlety of understanding' that is necessary for counselling culturally different clients. The challenge for counsellors today, they believe, begins with the question: what impact does our own cultural heritage have upon our attitudes and perceptions of those from another culture? Cultural heritage embraces our own cultural identity, beliefs and value systems, each of which play a part in shaping perceptions and responses to clients.

Culture in child care and child protection

Many health and social care professionals seek to ensure the care and protection of children, as evidenced in the diversity of contributions to the literature. Writers in this field include anthropologists, paediatricians, obstetricians, social workers, health visitors, nurses, forensic scientists, epidemiologists, psychiatrists, teachers and psychologists. Within the mountainous library of childcare and child protection publications, the cultural aspects of children's lives have long been neglected. Many mainstream family and childcare child protection texts make little reference to culture. Hill and Aldgate's (1996) text is excellent in most respects and actually originated with the 1989 Children Act, yet the only reference to culture is a warning that 'a stance of cultural pluralism may oversimplify complex issues' (p.115). Pringle's (1998) wide-ranging European perspective on child care is much more preoccupied with oppression than 'culture' – the word culture doesn't even make it to the index. The most significant publication on child protection during the last decade was *Messages From Research* (Dartington 1995), which summarised the findings of 20 major pieces of research into differing aspects of child abuse work. Not one of these explored the cultural aspects of any the cases dealt with, or whether or not child protection workers were aware of their statutory obligation in respect of culture. Parton's (1996) critique of the research included the following: 'Child abuse ... can only be understood in the cultural and organisational contexts in which it is not simply constructed but constituted' (p.7).

Brissett-Chapman's (1997) review of the literature persuades her that there is: 'too little interest and related capacity in the child welfare field for elucidating the complexity associated with effectively managing cultural distinctions presented by children and families (p.50). McPhatter (1997) prefaces her criticisms of cultural incompetence in family and childcare work and the dearth of training literature on cultural competence with statistics demonstrating the over-representation of minority culture children in the care and fostering systems throughout the USA (much the same as in Britain, Europe and Australia): 'Child welfare practitioners often assume that competence with racially, culturally, ethnically distinct groups can be achieved through short-term – and often one-shot – workshops or classes. This assumption reflects a short-sighted, simplistic view of a complex process' (p.259). There are indications, however, of an increasing consciousness of culture, particularly in child protection literature. One manifestation of this consciousness is positive, the other negative. We shall briefly consider both.

An increasing awareness of the cultural aspects of child abuse

Jill Korbin is undoubtedly the leading authority on the cultural aspects of child abuse (1977, 1979, 1980, 1981, 1987, 1990, 1994, 1997). As an anthropologist, she was well placed to expose the weaknesses of the child-abuse knowledge basis in working with cultural minorities since it was based 'almost entirely on research and clinical experience in Western nations' (Korbin 1981, p.1). She now has a substantial group of followers who have researched child abuse and the perceptions of child abuse in virtually every country in the world. Regrettably, her remarkable contribution is yet to be fully appreciated through inclusion in the reading lists of many family and childcare and child protection courses.

Keats (1997) *Culture and the Child* is the first text focusing entirely on the influence of culture in the development of children. Its opening chapters differentiate culture from ethnicity and it provides valuable knowledge and insights into the development and cultural differentness of children in many countries. Canino and Spurloch (1994) concentrate on cultural influences on adolescents, though most of their chapters have general application and contribute to the principal goal of learning how to make culturally competent assessments. Hong and Hong (1991) enlighten child protection workers about differing parental perceptions of 'child abuse' and agency intervention among the Chinese, Hispanic and white American peoples. Aspects of the difference in Chinese perceptions can be traced to 'filial piety and familism' – two prominent traits in Chinese culture enshrined in the folklore tales *Twenty-four Cases of Filial Piety* (see also Bakken 1993). The authors plead for cultural sensitivity in child abuse investigations within cultural minorities in particular. Ahn (1994) reflects upon the consequences of cultural insensitivity in child abuse investigations generally. Thorpe's (1994) research on the same subject reveals that much of the legacy of social workers' abuses of Australian Aboriginal families and children remains. Seen through 'Eurocentric 'child protection' eyes, Aboriginal child rearing practices become 'pathologized'. He provides a vivid account of a worker making a grossly culturally incompetent interpretation of a child's behaviour and concludes that 'child protection cannot claim to be any different from those apparatus of the state which discriminate' (p.162).

Blaming culture in child abuse literature

Additional studies and research in the field of child protection have stressed the crucial importance of culture in understanding the following:

1. child maltreatment in Greek families (Agathonos-Georgopoulou and Browne 1997);

2. the perceptions of child maltreatment and parenting styles in a Pacific Island community (Collier *et al.* 1999);

3. the views and experiences of child abuse workers in China (Hesketh, Shu Hong, Lynch 2000);

4. the attitudes of Kuwaiti parents towards the physical punishment of their children (Qasem *et al.* 1998);

5. the beliefs of Mexican mothers in the 'positive' effects of punishment (Corral-Verdugo *et al.* 1995);

6. the impact of the loss of cultural values upon family fragmentation and the consequences for child welfare in Nigeria (Odujinrin 1995).

Not all these publications convey respect for culture in general or minority cultures in particularly. Some authors attribute dangerous beliefs to particular cultures. Disciplining children through physical punishment is one such belief. Mexican, Kuwaiti, Greek, Pacific Island and Chinese parents are more inclined to use physical punishment and condone its use by others, according to the above research. Such beliefs are often regarded in child abuse literature as cultural traits, without reference to socio-economic and political contexts which may exercise a greater influence.

Blaming culture in children's rights literature

Children's rights literature often ignores culture, or perceives it as an obstacle (Dalrymple and Hough 1995; Flekkøy and Kaufman 1997; Fox Harding 1996; Franklin 1995; John 1996a, 1996b, 1997; Marshall 1997; Masson and Oakley 1998; Milner and Carolin 1998; Thompson 1997; Waller 1998). Many of these publications expose a multitude of denials of rights perpetrated against children by governments, policies, laws, and societies worldwide. They introduce the concept of adultism and argue for the need to develop a *culture of advocacy* to combat it. But few of them acknowledge a child's right to maintain his or her cultural heritage, and there is insufficient emphasis on statutory obligation to provide accommodation and care conducive to that maintenance. Keats's (1997) work on the crucial role of culture in children's identity formation makes little impact in this literature. Instead, the authors are increasingly immersed in and taking sides about the complexities of cultural conflict between parents and children (Patel, Naik and Humphries 1998). The most common form of conflict occurs when adolescent children such as Lavely Noor (*The Times*, 30 June 2000), who have been assimilated into the British culture where they have spent their formative years, attempt to resist aspects of the culture of their parents (for example, language, religion, customs, etc.). Shocking consequences then sometimes occur, including abductions, forced marriages, beatings and even murders (BBC1 1998; Prentice 2000; *The Times*, 29 May 1999).

Children's rights literature often projects these extremities as the norm and, worse, attributes them to the culture of the families concerned. Such trends in the literature are not likely to contribute to the goal of cultural competence; nor are they likely to make the worker's task of reaching out to cultural minority parents easier (stressed by Ahn 1994; Hong and Hong 1991). All cruelties and denial of rights endured by children must be exposed and the perpetrators apprehended. Few family and childcare social workers would oppose the establishment of a genuine children's rights charter. But there is a danger, apparent in the literature, of the children's rights movement becoming increasingly *culturally insensitive* in the process.

Cultural relativism

Some child abuse inquiry reports, for example, Jasmine Beckford (Blom-Cooper 1985) and Tyra Henry (Lambeth 1987) concluded that 'culture' and aspects of culture had impinged upon events leading to the deaths of the children. It was suggested that the workers involved were too optimistic in their assessments of family carers, that abusive behaviours were interpreted as aspects of culture and that the workers, predominantly from white middle-class culture, believed they had no right to criticise the supposedly cultural (child-abusing) practices of others. This gave rise to the concepts of *cultural relativism* (Charmer and Parton 1991; Dingwell, Ekelaar and Murray 1993) and the *rule of optimism*. Ahmad (1996), O'Hagan (1999) and Corby (1993) critically reflect upon the implications of cultural relativism, one of which gave the erroneous impression that these cultures condoned and/or encouraged abusive behaviour, and that child protection workers stood by regarding such behaviours as immune from criticism. A similar attitude has been noted in mental health work: 'identifying the problem as being situated in the person's own culture, viewing it as pathological' (Pilgrim and Rogers 1993, p.51) and recently a spokesperson's focus on 'cultural value judgements' provided a convenient deflection from professionals' incompetence in the Anna Climbie case (The Guardian, 13 January 2001). O'Hagan (1999) writes of cultural relativism:

> It merely provides one explanation for incompetence … Instead of an exposure of the behaviours which have been wrongfully interpreted as culture, and the ineffectual response to such behaviours, cultural relativism speaks of those interpretations as if they are fact. The interpretations are then used as a framework upon which to construct a theory (i.e. cultural relativism). (O'Hagan 1999, p.278)

Female genital mutilation

Another belief attributed to culture is the 'need' for female genital mutilation, invariably perpetrated against children. 'Torture, not culture' is the verdict of the black feminist writer Alice Walker (Robson 1993), whose novel *Possessing the Secret of Joy* challenges the practice head-on. The most extensive review of the literature on the subject has been carried out by Barstow (1999), who has traced the practice back to the ancient Egyptians. It had absolutely nothing to do with culture then, but seems to have been highly significant in the politics of the pharaohs, used as a method of directing and controlling inheritance rights and 'ensuring the legitimacy of all claims to kingship' (p.502). It has wrongly been attributed to the religions of culture, notably Islam (the Qur'an) and Christianity (the Bible). Barstow nails the most common, culturally attributed excuse for female genital mutilation, that is, the 'male preoccupation with the faithfulness of his wife', which he refers to as 'a classic example of [male] projection'.

Perceiving culture as protecting children

Rather than blaming culture, Odujinrin's (1995) Nigerian research revealed that its many components and influences served as a bulwark against child abuse. The increasing fragmentation of Nigerian societies and families and the loosening (or severing) of cultural ties poses a major threat to the welfare of Nigeria's children. Robin *et al.* (1997) also see this connection. They suggest that their findings of high rates of sexual abuse and psychiatric disorders among children in a south-western American Indian tribe correspond 'with an accelerated deterioration of the social structures and cultural traditions in this population' (p.783). Few child protection workers have taken this kind of research as seriously as those in New Zealand: like child protection workers everywhere, their first question is always whether the child is safe. But the equally important supplementary question follows: 'Does that include cultural safety?' Other questions include: 'How is this child connected to the cultural traditions (of the carers)?' 'Where are the people in this child's life who might offer the longest term security and cultural safety' (Fulcher 2000, p.335).

On balance...?

These profiles of the various health and social care professions began with doctors and medicine and ended with child protection work in New Zealand. Those two profiles in particular represent the extremes of cultural competence and incompetence, cultural sensitivity towards minorities and cultural insensitivity, respect and openness towards different cultures or the tendency to blame. There are many shades of each of these extremes in the profiles overall. The more pervasive impression, however, is a negative one. We can again state categorically that there is no tradition of cultural sensitivity and cultural competence in health and social care professions. Furthermore, their own current writers and researchers: (a) expose much ignorance and indifference towards culture; (b) provide many examples of gross cultural insensitivity towards particular cultural minorities; (c) clearly indicate a great deal of potential for culturally incompetent practice.

Summary and Conclusion

This chapter has postulated that the health and social care professions have a poor tradition of cultural sensitivity and cultural competence. The reasons for this postulation include the following:

1. Issues such as *cultural diversity, cultural sensitivity* and *cultural competence* had no place in the training of caring professionals. It is only recently that such training has been imposed upon trainers, with predictably variable results.

2. Literature and research within health and social literature has until recently ignored the challenges posed by cultural diversity, and meeting the social and health care needs of cultural minorities.

3. The 'caring' professions have contributed significantly towards the destruction of indigenous cultures in many countries.

Current literature in each of the professions consolidates the argument that a tradition of cultural competence has still not yet been established. There is no evidence, for example, that doctors are being seriously challenged to consider a cultural dimension in their training and working practices.

The nursing profession gives every indication of a growing awareness of cultural issues, but recent literature and research suggests that formidable obstacles lie in the way of translating this awareness into culturally competent practice.

Psychiatry has made progress in the field of transcultural psychiatric practice, but many of its roots lie in discriminatory theories and much of its practice produces racist results. Counselling and psychotherapy have recently produced some excellent texts promoting cultural competence. But the professions remain predominantly casework driven, involving primarily white counsellors and therapists with little awareness of cultural diversity and no compulsion to be culturally sensitive.

Social work clearly has no roots in cultural sensitivity or cultural competence. Even today its literature adopts a distinctly anti-cultural stance, compatible with its monocultural theories and practices, in pursuit of its 'loftier' goals of integration, assimilation and universality. The multiprofessional field of family and child care and child protection shows encouraging signs of a cultural perspective, but there remains, within, a substantial anti-culture and/or blame culture tradition. Cultural competence is best exemplified in the New Zealand child protection services, which promote the novel concept of the 'cultural safety of children' (Fulcher 2000) and fully assess the cultural contexts of the children for whom services are provided.

CHAPTER 8

Perceptions of Culture
Within Anti-racist and
Anti-discriminatory Practice

Introduction

Recently I was taking a class for experienced health and social care managers and trainers studying for an advanced award. The subject was culture and cultural sensitivity and I was exploring with them the various contributions of different theories and disciplines towards defining culture. I made the point that social work had in fact contributed very little to an understanding of culture and nothing at all towards defining it. This led to a lively discussion, during which a number of course members expressed the view that social work had made a contribution through its adoption of and adherence to anti-racist and anti-discriminatory practice (ARADP). No one could tell me precisely how ARADP had contributed towards understanding culture generally, nor how it had enhanced their own understanding of the different cultures with which they came into contact in their daily work.

I want to explore this issue further. It seems to me that health and social care workers in the 1970s did become increasingly aware of diversity, not in terms of culture, but rather nationality and colour. They later became very pre-occupied with the specific challenge of racism and consequently became committed to combating racism through the development of anti-racist and anti-discriminatory practice. This chapter will first look at the development of ARADP and raise questions about the narrowness of its focus and the extremities of some of its literature. Second, it will identify a distinctly anti-culture theme in anti-racist literature in particular. Third, it will look at Macey and Moxon's (1996) critique of anti-racist writing, which played no small part in the demise of ARADP in the 1990s.

Fourth, it will attempt to clarify the meaning of a term which actually subsumes culture in much ARADP literature, that is, *ethnicity*. It will refer to literature and research and indeed to the etymology of ethnicity, to argue that it should neither subsume culture, nor be used as a substitute for 'culture'. The preoccupation with race and the (mis)use of the concept of ethnicity are the final two formidable strands of an enduring anti-culture tradition within health and social care literature, practice and training.

The emergence of ARADP

In the 1960s and 1970s, the quality of services provided to minorities began to emerge as a matter of concern in the literature of some health and social care professions. It was an inevitable development, following the eruption of riots in many of the cities of Europe and the USA, the emergence of the US Black Power movement and the rush of government-commissioned reports leading to landmark legislation in both continents. Civil rights legislation and the Race Relations Act of 1976 were inevitable responses to the increasing and justifiable disaffection of economically and politically oppressed minority communities, and concentrated the minds of many writers and researchers. Within social work in particular, there was a proliferation of publications on racist issues, beginning in the late 1970s, and reaching its peak around 1991, when the profession's main body published *'One Small Step Towards Racial Justice: The Teaching of Anti-Racism in Diploma in Social Work programmes'* (CCETSW 1991). Significantly, however, these efforts said little about culture, cultural sensitivity or cultural competence. Their principal goal was to enable workers to seek out racism and adopt anti-racist practice. Racism and anti-racism became the dominant themes in the peculiarly named concept of 'anti-racist and anti-discriminatory practice' (Ahmed 1987; Editorial 1988; Devore and Schlesinger 1981; Naik 1991; Whitehouse 1983). The concept was peculiar for a number of reasons. First, it regarded racism as the most common and worst form of discrimination (thus the careful and prominent positioning of 'anti-racist' in the title). Second, it was interested only in the racism experienced by certain sections of the community, defined by colour. Third, it identified those certain sections as 'the black community'. Racism meant discrimination and persecution of black people. Humphreys, Atkar and Baldwin (1999) use the term 'black' 'as a political term for people who suffer from racism and powerlessness' (p.294). For Blakemore and Boneham (1994) 'blackness refers to status in a minority group disadvantaged by racial discrimination, that is, discrimination prompted by physical differences such as skin colour' (p.5).

The debilitating obsession with race

Some indication of the intensity and narrowness of this focus in ARADP literature can be gained from Robinson's (1999) paper on racial identity attitudes in the interactions between 'black' people and social workers (predominantly white). Racism and racial awareness are the all-pervasive themes, irrespective of whatever other problem may exist. For the (white) worker, there are five stages of the development and transformation of racial identity:

- contact (lack of racial awareness)

- disintegration ('acknowledging one's whiteness and understanding the benefits of being white in a racist society')

- reintegration (basically a racist identity; the individual believes that 'white privilege should be protected and preserved')

- pseudoindependence (the individual begins to 'question the assumption that blacks are innately inferior to white people')

- autonomy ('the individual abandons personal, cultural and institutional racial practices and has a more flexible world view') (Robinson 1999, pp.318–319).

For the black client, the five stages of development and transformation of racial identity are:

- pre-encounter (devaluing his or her ascribed racial grouping)

- encounter attitudes (the awakening process, usually as a result of some racist incident)

- immersion-emersion ('learning and experiencing the meaning and value of one's racial group')

- internalisation (achieving pride in one's racial group or identity)

- internalisation–commitment (the individual 'finds activities and commitments to express his or her new identity') (Robinson 1999, p.317).

A successful outcome of these interactions, Robinson believes, depends upon whichever stage of development of racial identity both worker and client are at. There are numerous permutations and 'a progressive relationship exists when the social worker's racial identity status is at least one level above the client's (obviously because most of the stages of development of white racial identity are fundamentally racist, and it is not until the fourth stage that some critical self-questioning takes place).

Anti-racism – ignoring the rest?

This preoccupation with race and racism actually hinders rather than helps in training health and social care professionals to be more culturally aware, culturally sensitive and culturally competent. It precludes serious consideration of other forms of discrimination provoked by numerous aspects of the culture and identities of all people. Racism is not the most common form of discrimination in Britain as a whole. The abuse of women in general, for example, and single parents and their children in particular, is much more widespread (O'Hagan and Dillenburger 1995). In Northern Ireland, sectarianism over the past quarter of a century has perpetrated atrocities of such vileness that the public cannot even learn all the facts of the matter. Hundreds of entirely innocent individuals, Protestant and Catholic, playing no role in either side of the conflict, have been picked up on the streets, tortured and butchered, and their bodies made identifiable only through dental records. Sectarianism and many other forms of discrimination have been ignored for decades in social work's anti-racist, anti-discriminatory crusade, casting doubt on its consistency and core values as well as on its credibility. Discrimination perpetrated because of differences in language, sexual orientation, age, dress and diet, etc. have also received scant attention in ARADP literature.

Anti-racist: anti-culture

The most significant feature of anti-racist literature, however, was its emerging attitude towards culture:

> The important point is that for black clients, the centrality of racism needs to be more explicitly acknowledged in the assessment process and cultural explanations need to be considered in the context of racism. (Ahmed 1987, p.6)

This distinctly anti-culture stance actually began to appear in the titles of ARADP literature: *The Trouble with Culture* (Ahmad 1996); *Cultural Racism* (Ahmed 1994); *Racist Culture* (Goldberg 1993); *Cultural Racism in Work with Asian Women and Girls* (Ahmed 1986). Conspicuously, none of these anti-culture writings are preceded with any intelligent definitions of culture. Ahmad (1996) justifies his title by conveniently creating a concept that is wonderfully easy to attack:

> Stripped of its dynamic, social, economic, gender and historical context, culture becomes a rigid and constraining concept which is seen somehow to mechanistically determine people's behaviours and actions rather than providing a flexible source for living, for according meaning to what one feels, experiences and acts to change. (Ahmad 1996, p.191)

Of course it is not culture which Ahmad is talking about: culture, 'stripped of the various contexts' simply does not exist. Had he been thinking from the baseline of any one of the countless definitions of culture (see Chapter 3) he would have realised this. Had he been aware of any of the disciplines which have contributed most to our understanding of culture, he would also know that the 'dynamic context' is the crucial, determining context of culture (Bhate and Bhate 1996; Moore 1997).

Another ARADP proponent, Thompson (1993), gives the briefest definition of culture: 'shared ways of seeing, thinking and doing' (p.139). His distrust of culture (he speaks of its 'dangerousness') possibly stems from a preoccupation with what he perceives as a predominant white culture, racist, sexist and ageist, a prejudicial 'discriminatory and oppressive culture base manifesting itself in and through individual thought and action' (p.20). He quotes Ahmed (1987) approvingly and also Fernando (1988):

> An emphasis on culture, however well intentioned, may lead to a racist -approach in practice ... the promotion of cultural sensitivity without challenging racism may result in the reinforcement of racism by masking it and thereby inducing complacency. (Fernando 1988, p.167)

In a later work, Fernando (1991) asserts more directly that 'culture is used to conceal racism' (p.22). Kelleher (1996) gives another reason for anti-racists' negative attitude to culture, specifically in the field of medical research: anti-racist writers claim that researchers focus on the culture of minority groups only to 'show the negative aspects of that culture in relation to health' or merely to 'describe exotic elements in it' (p.74). This is part of a process of the construction of minorities as 'Other', emphasising aspects of lifestyle 'which differ from what is assumed to be a 'normal' English lifestyle' (p.74). In mental health there is the implicit linking of madness with the Other: 'the different and irrational non-European black person' (p.74).

ARADP writers are on much stronger ground here. We have seen in the previous chapter how the concept of *cultural relativism* has led to a perception that some cultures promote child abusive practices. But this is an erroneous perception, having nothing to do with culture. Again, the root cause of such confusions is the lack of adequate definition of culture.

Lorenz's (1999) analysis of the role of culture in the development of social work in Germany contains this revealing generalisation:

> Once a plurality of cultural universes has become theoretically accepted, often to the point of an uncritical fascination with the exotic 'otherness', it renders itself powerless to fight the inequalities that can be masked as cultural differences, and which a multicultural approach appears even to sanction. (Lorenz 1999, p.39)

This creates an incredible image of tens of thousands of caring professionals naively caught up in the colour and vitality ('the exotic' is the term mostly used) of multiculturalism, thereby conveniently rendering themselves blind and uncritical to whatever divisions, injustices and discrimination exist underneath. He later writes of the current German situation: 'Exciting and imaginative projects have developed for and with minority ethnic groups, but the issue of racism remains hidden' (p.39). It is difficult to think of any other country which has been subjected to both internal and external scrutiny as much as Germany (for both historical and political reasons) in attempting to ensure that issues of racism do not remain hidden. The anti-cultural sentiment, however, is the most significant part of Lorenz's quote: multiculturalism is seen as sanctioning the inequalities and injustices which stem from racist attitudes. Culture itself is seen by all these writers as something which conveniently conceals or masks racism.

The demise of ARADP

ARADP is now seldom referred to in the literature, having been replaced by the more acceptable terms *anti-oppressive* and *anti-discriminatory practice* (Dalrymple and Burke 1995; Millan 1996; Macey and Moxon 1996). There are at least two reasons for this. First, the special status given to racist discrimination within ARADP is no longer universally accepted and the neglect of other forms of discrimination is seen as offensive. Second, Macey and Moxon's (1996) critique demonstrated that much of the anti-racist literature is 'theoretically inadequate, being informed by neither sociological, political nor economic theory or research' (p.297). Macey and Moxon highlight its narrow focus which, in a general welfare context of high unemployment, poverty and inequality, may have the effect of actually exacerbating existing tensions (many differing groups such as recent European refugees may feel as much oppressed as those upon whom anti-racist literature exclusively concentrates). Anti-racist literature, they believe, owes more to fashion than to theoretical or analytical rigour. Its 'conceptual confusion and its analytical inadequacy' in both literature and practice have become exposed. It has projected a simplistic explanation of racism as being merely the outcome of power plus prejudice. This then assumes a single cause and type of racism and 'dangerously implies that there is a single solution to the phenomenon' (p.302).

Macey and Moxon (1996) concentrate on anti-racism's irrational fixation on and misuse of the term 'black' and its compulsive need to emphasise the black–white categorical distinctions (exemplified by Robinson 1999); thereby ignoring 'the host of other aspects of the self which constitute a person, any of which may take precedence over skin colour in particular situations' (p.307). Arooj and her sisters in Chapter 2 come to mind here, and Kelleher (1996) makes an identical point. Macey and Moxon shed much sociological light on the debate, 'after more than a decade in which to challenge the analytical adequacy of the term 'black' was to be declared racist'. They expose the naivety of social work's governing council, CCETSW which, despite the research that demonstrates that Irish people are more likely to be sectioned under mental health legislation than Asians, could still state the following in one of its most prominent mental health, anti-racist publications:

> The word black is used to refer to African-Caribbean and Asian people. While the authors recognise the needs of other groups in relation to mental health care, it has been decided that, on the basis of the representations of these two groups within the psychiatric services and the particular experiences of the authors, all case examples and discussion relate to African-Caribbean and Asian experiences and needs. (CCETSW 1991, quoted in Macey and Moxon 1996, p.303)

Macey and Moxon believe this kind of insensitivity and racist exclusivity is 'rooted in racist stereotyping and thinking'; that the fixation with the term 'black' has been rejected by many African, African-Caribbean and Asian people 'who object to the homogenization of different histories, cultures and religions' (p.304). In effect, it downgrades, ignores or denies the countless instances and many different types of cultural insensitivity perpetrated against all minority groups, including African-Caribbean and Asian peoples.

ARADP and statutory obligations

A concept in demise does not warrant undue attention unless its unhelpful influences are still manifest. ARADP has contributed substantially to the current anti-culture stance of much health and social care literature and practice and has done little to help family and childcare professionals to fulfil the statutory obligations in relation to cultural background and racial origins (Children Act 1989, s.22(5)(c)). Many of its quotations above may encourage professionals to disregard culture, or at best relegate consideration of culture to a context of racism. This is not what is meant by the obligation to 'give due consideration to the child's cultural background'. Nor is the parallel obligation to 'give due consideration to the child's racial origins' likely to be fulfilled by a preoccupation with racism and a conviction that all black peoples are victims.

Current legislation governing the work of health and social care professionals requires them to know and learn about the racial origins and cultural background, not for the purpose of perceiving and/or approaching their clients as victims but, on the contrary, to understand why such origins and background are highly significant to clients. It obliges professionals to enable their clients to continue fostering pride in their cultural and racial heritage. A literature which concentrates on all 'black' people as victims, on racism rather than race (or racial origins), and which perceives one's own (white) culture through a pervasive negativity at best, and more commonly an hostility, is not likely to help workers fulfil these statutory obligations.

Race, culture and ethnicity

A need for clarity

Ethnicity, culture and *race* are terms increasingly used by health and social care practitioners. In much of the current anti-racist, anti-oppressive and anti-discriminatory writings, authors substitute culture with ethnicity. In some writings, ethnicity actually subsumes culture (e.g. Fernando 1991). For others, the terms may (confusingly) be used simultaneously (e.g. Beevers 1981; Blakemore and Boneham 1994; Kelleher 1996). There is a need for some clarity.

Race

Race is the least complicated term of the three. Its distinctive contemporary meaning originated in the perceptions of Europeans keen to produce race classifications conducive to the social, political and economic domination which they inflicted on the peoples they conquered. We have seen however (Chapter 3) that most of the prominent pioneering anthropologists dismissed the concept as a basis for the study of culture and human development, and also the racist assumptions about moral and genetic inferiority and superiority associated with it. In marked contrast to anti-racist literature, in which the concepts of race and racism dominate, other related disciplines undermine the viability of 'race'. For example, the strong anti-race tradition of anthropology continues in Montagu's (1974) best-selling text *Man's Most Dangerous Myth: The Fallacy of Race*. Montagu believes that the concept of race 'is the witchcraft of our time. These conceptions of "race"are compounded of impure wishful thinking and represent naught but muddied myth – the tragic myth of our tragic era' (pp.3, 5).

Sociology has been no kinder to the concept. Over 70 years ago, Robert Park (1934, 1939), the most influential sociologist of his generation, from his vantage point in the midst of the US 'race' melting pot, was forecasting the inevitable demise of race in the irreversible onward march of trade, immigration and intermarriage. Generally, sociologists regard race merely as a social construction, albeit one of major significance in human perception – perceptions which in themselves often have far-reaching social and political consequences. Yet the term race is widely avoided in current sociological literature. For example, Gidden's (1993) classic text (800 pp.) barely gives it a mention, and then primarily for the purpose of dismissing it: 'Human population groups are not distinct, but form a continuum ... these facts lead many biologists, anthropologists and sociologists to believe that the concept of race should be dropped altogether' (p.255). Collier (1998), a researcher in modern human communications, expresses similar views and echoes the work of Park. She implies that the concept of race will become even more subject to ridicule and dismissal given the accelerating interactions and interdependency of peoples and nations in an increasingly shrinking world.

Ethnicity: seeking consistency

Fernando (1988, 1991, 1995) believes that it is difficult to disentangle race, ethnicity and culture, but he makes clear that he regards culture as less significant than ethnicity: 'concepts of race and culture are being combined and absorbed into that of ethnicity'. He believes the reason to be that ethnicity 'is seen as a term that avoids the pejorative meaning attributed to the word race and the limitations implicit in using the term culture' (p.12). Such 'limitations' are not explained.

Cornell and Hartmann (1998) consistently draw attention to the fact that ethnicity 'often has its origins in assertion, in the claims groups make about themselves' (p.30). They declare that ethnicity is linked to power and that ethnic activities are often bound up in power relations. They claim that ethnic identities often originate in struggle and conflict, but may also emerge in the group's search for meaning 'that can make them feel a part of some manageable community of sentiment and cultural heritage' (p.30).

Thompson (1993) gives much prominence to ethnicity. He uses Storkey's (1991) definition, in which the term becomes synonymous with cultural identity. Ethnicity is, according to Storkey: 'all the characteristics which go to make up cultural identity: origins, physical appearance, language, family structure, religious beliefs, politics, food, art, music, literature, attitudes towards the body, gender roles, clothing, education' (pp.109–110).

Blakemore and Boneham (1994) confuse when they write that culture is the 'umbrella' term and yet, in the same paragraph, 'but it is preferable to use ethnicity as the broader concept which includes culture' (p.7).

Hall's (1992) attitude is ambiguous. He sees it functioning in the same way that anti-racists perceive 'culture', yet he defends it passionately:

> The fact that this grounding of ethnicity in difference was deployed in the discourse of racism, as a means of disavowing the realities of racism and repression, does not mean that we can permit the term to be permanently colonised ... we are all ethnically located and our ethnic identities are crucial to our sense of who we are. (Hall 1992, p.9)

Glazer and Moynihan (1975) refer to ethnicity as a 'new term' which is still very much 'on the move' in terms of both meaning and status. It has certainly 'moved' substantially from its original meaning.

The origins of ethnicity

The word ethnic, from which ethnicity has derived, originated in the Greek *ethnikós*, which meant nation, a unity of persons of common blood or descent. *Ethnikós* became *ethnicus* in Latin and its meaning was transformed. It then meant 'those who were not Christian or Jewish', such as 'heathens' and 'pagans' (*Oxford Library of Words and Phrases* 1986). Cornell and Hartmann (1998) write: '"*Ethnic*" clearly referred to others, to those who were not "us"' (p.16). They correctly make a similar assertion about race: 'Race has been first and foremost a way of describing "others", of making clear that "they" are not "us"' (p.27). It is reasonable to assume that in those ancient times the labelling of individuals, groups, communities and nations with the term *ethnicus* (just as labelling someone today with 'ethnic') could have serious consequences. This Latin, pejorative, potentially discriminatory meaning has been sustained for 2000 years and right throughout most of the twentieth century, as the following random examples from Burchfield (1972) will testify:

- The Jews are an ethnic group, although one which has little regard for spatial considerations.

- The Irish had their origins largely in the peasant stratum. The Jews were of the burgher class. These differences in the ethnics' social class backgrounds ...

- The ethnics have conspicuously succeeded in getting ahead in the Yankee City social hierarchy.

- The former ethnics, a polite term for Jews, Italians, and other lesser breeds just inside the law ... (This example is taken from the *Times Literary Supplement*, 17 November 1961).

- The groups who, by reason of rural or small town location, ethnicity or other parochialism, feel threatened by the better educated, upper middle class people.

Ethnic, ethnocentrism and ethnic cleansing

Discriminatory and racist as these examples are, they are nevertheless using the term ethnic in the same sense in which it has been used since Biblical times: the identification of a group ('them', not 'us') not based primarily on a positive attribute(s), or quality or language of that group, but more fundamentally based on a negative(s). More crucially, the group identified is not the dominant group making the differentiation in the first instance. This more authoritative meaning supports the explanations and interpretations made by Cornell and Hartmann (1998) and by Glazer and Moynihan (1974), namely that the modern-day concept of ethnicity emerged from the struggles of specific groups of peoples, negatively perceived, oppressed and discriminated against, who eventually triumphed through the assertiveness and collective power of an identity which observers refer to as an ethnic identity. The conflict origin of ethnicity and the emerging characteristics of assertiveness and collective power are conducive to the condition and attitude named ethnocentrism, another derivative of ethnic. This is defined as:

> the tendency to view one's own ethnic group and its social standards as the basis for evaluative judgements concerning the practices of others with the implication that one views one's own standards as superior. (*Penguin Dictionary of Psychology*, Reber, 1985)

According to Cornell and Hartmann (1998), ethnocentrism is 'a common aspect of ethnic identity' (p.30), the view that its people and its way of life are superior to that of other groups. Another derivative of ethnic (and just as ancient) is *ethnize*. The modern-day equivalent of ethnize is most probably to carry out *ethnic cleansing*. This is a term understood by everyone and particularly by the victims of ethnic cleansing. The genocide of Rwanda, the rape of East Timor, the disintegration of Yugoslavia and the consequential wars fought out by its constituent parts, culminating in the Kosovan catastrophe – all these horrors have made ethnic cleansing one of the most common terms in current usage. Its essential core within that common use retains the meaning of the original word ethnic – 'them', not 'us' – and implies a consequential barbarity on the part of 'us' against 'them'.

These etymological and historical facts add to the mystery of why ethnicity is so commonly used today in the literature of the caring professions. Historically and etymologically, the word has such pejorative connotations that its newly created status borders on the incredible. One wonders what part, if any, the members of 'ethnic' groups had in this etymological redemption. A logical development in the process is to refer to members within the group as 'ethnics', but Thompson (1993), although favouring the terms ethnicity and ethnic, condemns as racist the use of the term 'ethnics' in reference to members of minority groups (he makes no such criticism if the term is applied to members of the majority). This raises the question of how ethnicity and all its associated terms are perceived by the whole populations of the groups to which they are applied. Apparently no one among care professionals, health researchers and social work writers, who are those predominantly using the word ethnicity and its related terms, has asked members of any of the diverse minority groups in any country what they think and feel about such terms when applied to them. Fortunately, there is an accumulated body of research which suggests some answers. It concentrates on the analysis of national census reports and household surveys. One of the most recent (Aspinall 1997) provides a fascinating insight into the difficulties which have arisen out of 'ethnicity' classifications.

Perceptions of ethnicity in census- and health-related research

Aspinall's (1997) paper researched the statistics of the 1991 Census in Britain and concluded that the term 'ethnic group' was inadequate as a classification for submissions to respondents. Significant numbers of respondents had difficulty in answering questions about their 'ethnicity'. Consequently, there were enormous variations determined by location and context. In the 1991 British Census there were seven designated categories of ethnic groups: White, Black African, Black Caribbean, Indian, Pakistani, Bangladeshi and Chinese. Three-quarters of a million people eschewed these categories and described themselves otherwise in the free text fields which the forms provided (allowing the respondent to self-identify in whatever terminology they chose to use).

Similarly, Aspinall (1997) claims that when a London health authority issued questionnaires (SE Thames RHA 1993), 17 per cent of respondents apparently found the ethnicity classifications unsatisfactory and provided their own descriptions. In the USA the problem is magnified. In the 1990 Census, for example, 9.8 million (20% of minority groups) chose not to write in the designated ethnic areas but in the 'Other race' free text field (actually 3% more than the remaining minority population of 6.8 million). Aspinall provides examples of self-descriptions made by respondents in a Welsh health authority, indicative of their perception of the inadequacies of the ethnic classifications used. Respondents chose instead to describe themselves as: 'European (I am not a colour)'; 'Part African, Part Welsh'; 'Maltese'; 'Caribbean-Indian'; 'White-Muslim'; 'Spanish descended Latin American'; 'Kashmiri'; 'White Father, Half Nigerian mother', etc.

The Census Validation Survey (CVS) is a follow-up process by which the government is able to check the accuracy of the data collected in the Census. During the last occasion it was used (following the 1991 Census) it reported a gross error rate (the proportion of times the response on the Census form was not the same as that given in the CVS interview) of 13.2 per cent in respect of the ethnic groups designations on the forms, with the exception of the white category.

Aspinall's research reveals many more inconsistencies and numerous hypotheses are offered to account for them. One particular hypothesis, however, is glaringly missing: that respondents may not like the word ethnic and like even less to be identified as a member of an ethnic group. It is perplexing that citizens are required to label themselves within the framework of a concept (i.e. ethnicity) which they may not believe in, they may dislike or detest, and which has been constructed without any reference to them. Research is needed to answer such questions, but Aspinall's work is enough in itself to suggest the mere possibility that the sight and sound of the word ethnic is as unappealing (maybe repellent) to the substantial minority of respondents who choose to ignore it, as its ancient meaning would surely be to the unwitting researchers attempting to impose it. It is regrettable that those preparing for the 2001 Census have seemingly learnt nothing from Aspinall's research; precisely the same 'ethnic' based questions, only many more, are going to be asked (*The Times*, 11 January 2000). A similar unacceptably high margin of error rate in the findings relating to ethnicity is guaranteed to occur.

Ethnicity and culture

Ethnicity should not become synonymous with culture. Even less should it be permitted to subsume culture. The reasons why are summarised as follows:

1. 'Ethnicity' and related terms such as 'ethnic', 'ethnics' and 'ethnocentrism' have their origins in an identification process potentially and actually discriminatory. At the core of this process is a 'them' and 'us' mentality easily conducive to discrimination. Parsons (1952) writes: 'Ethnic groups are traditionally mutually exclusive' (p.57). Culture has no similar origins. Its original meaning was – a universal activity in which all human beings needed to participate to survive, i.e. make the land productive.

2. Ethnicity today is associated with struggle and conflict between oppressed peoples and the social, political and economic forces which generate that oppression. The most destructive of these forces is racism. When so-called ethnic groups are struggling against oppression they also need to strive for *power* and *assertiveness*, which sociologists and political scientists recognise as core features of ethnic groups. Ethnocentrism is another feature of ethnicity, more likely to manifest itself when an ethnic group has emerged victorious from the struggle and conflict in which it has engaged. Culture has no such history or meaning. It embraces many aspects of living that have nothing to do with struggle or conflict and the core themes of many cultures have a universality and spirituality distinctly lacking in the concept, ethnicity.

3. 'Ethnic' and 'ethnicity' have an 'image' and/or a 'public relations' problem (as evidenced in the extent to which the words are ignored or

replaced by respondents to whom they are aimed). Many people, referred to as 'ethnic' by census reports, government departments and health and social sciences researchers, provide clear evidence that they resent the word and resist attempts to be labelled as such. No one is absolutely certain about the reason for this resentment. It may be awareness of the original meaning of the word ethnic; resistance to the assertiveness and exclusiveness associated with ethnicity; or an imagined association with the daily reported ethnic cleansing in different parts of the world. It could also be that the word ethnic has certain onomatopoeic qualities, echoing or suggesting any of these connotations.

Summary and conclusion

Anti-racist and anti-discriminatory practice (ARADP) has been perceived by many as a comprehensive concept which teaches cultural sensitivity and cultural competence. The reality is that ARADP is a markedly narrow and insular concept, with the numerous writers who promote it revealing a distinctly hostile attitude to culture. The definitions and understanding of culture within ARADP writing are erroneous and limiting, and anti-racist writing in particular has been exposed as 'theoretically inadequate, being informed by neither sociological, political nor economic theory or research' (Macey and Moxon 1996, p.297). The most serious deficit in anti-racist and anti-discriminatory literature is that it contributes nothing towards enabling care professionals to fulfil their statutory obligations in relation to culture and cultural sensitivity. On the contrary, its negativity and hostility to culture make it difficult for those who adhere to it to understand and appreciate the value which clients give to their culture.

The literature of the caring professions generally has increasingly followed anti-racist literature's preference for the concept of ethnicity to that of culture. This tendency seems to betray an ignorance of the long-standing meaning of ethnic – namely, a label applied to groups of people different in some way from the majority or ruling group, a 'them' and 'us' situation, with much discriminatory potential. The derivatives of ethnic, for example, *ethnize*, ethnocentric and ethnic cleansing are universally recognised as pejorative terms and the latter in particular has become synonymous with some of the worst barbarisms in human history. Yet no one among the researchers, writers, theoreticians and practitioners within health and social care professions seems to realise that their clients, patients and research respondents may actually not like to be addressed as ethnic or ethnics, or categorised within a framework of ethnicity. There is substantial evidence within research on the British and US Census findings that this is precisely how respondents from diverse minority cultures feel; a significant number of them do not answer the questions on their ethnicity as they are compelled to do, thus rendering the results hopelessly inaccurate.

CHAPTER 9

Culture and Religion

Introduction

Religion, religious beliefs and spirituality can pose a major challenge for health and social care professionals. This chapter will examine the origins and nature of that challenge. Definitions of religion and the related terms, spirituality and faith, will be provided. Individuals from both majorities and minorities may regard religion as the core aspect of their culture. They fervently adhere to their religious beliefs and duties and are highly sensitive to how others regard them. The first objective in this chapter therefore is to elicit some of the thoughts and feelings underpinning such adherence: why precisely is religion important for so many people? There are perfectly understandable reasons why some professionals may not have positive perceptions of religion. These need to be identified and acknowledged, and their influences upon professionals' attitude and perception explored.

New Zealand provides a unique example of a government whose health, social care and law enforcement agencies recognise and respect the religious legacy and beliefs of its indigenous Maori people. We shall look at how ancient Maori religious concepts and principles are being used to underpin a service (Family Group Conference) that is of interest to family and childcare workers around the world. At the core of this discussion is the crucial question: how do the literally millions of devoutly religious individuals from both majority and minority cultures obtain culturally competent services from professionals who are increasingly indifferent to religion or, worse, irreligious and anti-religious? The premise of the chapter is that any negativity or indifference towards the religious beliefs and/or spirituality of clients constitutes cultural insensitivity; this guarantees cultural incompetence in outcome and failure to fulfil statutory obligation in practice.

Definitions of religion

If many of those receiving services from health and social care professionals believe that religion is very important to them, it is necessary to look at some definitions which might tell us why. This is particularly so if professionals declare no interest in or allegiance to a religion of any kind. There are two other related terms which need clarification, 'spirituality' and 'faith', both of which frequently appear in definitions of religion.

Haynes (1993) provides the most elaborate definition and explanation of religion. He sees religion as a 'multifaceted concept with three distinct yet interrelated meanings'. First, it refers to organised religious establishments (which include priests, bishops and administrative officials) and also diverse groups sponsored by religious organisations. Second, it has a spiritual dimension, pertaining to models of social and individual behaviour, and to the ideas of transcendence and the supernatural, 'a system of language and practice that organises the world in terms of what is deemed sacred'. Third, it is about ultimacy: it 'relates people to the ultimate conditions of their existence' (Haynes 1993, p.28).

Much briefer definitions include: Hargrove's (1989) 'Religion is a human phenomenon that unites cultural, social and personality systems into a meaningful whole' (p.29); Seden's (1995) 'a belief system' and 'the expression of that belief', revolving around and including the worship of 'a supernatural power' (p.10); Canda's (1998) 'an institutionally patterned system of beliefs, values and rituals' (p.88); finally, Fromm's (1967) 'any system of thought and action shared by a group which gives the individual a frame of orientation and an object of devotion' (quoted in Seden 1995).

'Spirituality' sometimes assumes greater significance than religion. It is possible, after all, to have a spiritual dimension within one's life and yet have no allegiance to an organised religion. But many will contend that their spirituality derives from their religion, and from the values it decrees and promotes. It is wrong to think of spirituality as an experience uniquely individualistic. Wayne's use of the word 'social' in the above definition is crucial to the understanding of spirituality, as is Canda's (1998) 'the basic human drive for meaning, purpose and *moral relatedness among people.* In the Christian Bible, the Jewish Torah and Islam's Holy Qur'an, the word 'spirit' is strongly associated with communion and fellowship, with belonging and togetherness: 'The Spirit of the Lord filleth the world,' says the Book of Wisdom (i, 7), which one writer interpreted as 'to be touched and energised by His life-giving Spirit, is to be delivered from isolation and to know that human beings were made to live in relationship' (*The Times*, 10 June 2000).

Similarly, the word 'faith' is often assumed to mean something personal and private, the individual's pursuit of knowledge and belief about the world, his or her place in it and life hereafter. But Johnathan Sachs, Britain's Chief Rabbi, sees religious faith somewhat differently, as a covenant between a whole body of people and their divine power (whatever that may be). He cites the covenant between God and the people of Israel on Mount Sinai as the classic example of faith and faithfulness (Sachs 2000).

However one thinks about religion and the attempts to define it, there can be no disputing the fact that it is of crucial significance in the lives of many people and probably more particularly so for those from minority cultures, living in culturally alien and often hostile irreligious or sectarian environments. Wolffe's (1993) edited collection provides testimony to the enormous growth of religious diversity in Britain among minority cultures in the second half of the twentieth century.

How people may value their religion

Religion (as with language) has traditionally been subordinated to the issues of 'ethnicity', racism and sexism within health and social care literature and research. In an increasingly secular and irreligious world, those who regard their religion as much more important than their race or their gender (e.g. Arooj and her sisters) may have difficulty in finding professionals who can either accept or understand that. They may also be puzzled at the fact that the national census necessitates them declaring their 'ethnicity' (a question which as we have seen in the previous chapter may cause them difficulty and which many resent), yet makes no reference to their religion, about which they would have no ambiguity at all. Health and social care professionals increasingly come into contact with patients and clients who are devoutly religious and believe that their religion is the core component of their culture. It is important for the professionals to understand 'the way in which an individual's spirituality is shaped by and expressed through diverse institutional religious forms' (Canda 1998, p.88). Some patients and clients may even regard religion as a separate more important entity, distinct from culture, yet the most crucial component in moulding culture. Macdonald writes: 'In many families, religion is important in its own right, not as an element of culture. Here religious belief forms the foundation stone of family life and the culture that develops and grows outward from it' (McDonald 1991, p.112). Henley and Schott (1999) make the point that religion often provides people with the beliefs and values that underpin their daily living. Numerous writers and researchers have learnt the reasons why religion is considered vitally important for many individuals (e.g. Dosanjh and Ghuman 1997; Hillier and Rahman 1996; Patel, Naik and Humphries 1998, O'Hagan 1999; Seden 1995):

1. The beliefs and spirituality emanating from particular religions are, for many individuals and their societies, the core components of their cultural identity. One immediately thinks of Islam and Muslims in this regard, but it applies equally to New Zealand's indigenous Maori population and, to a lesser extent, Ireland's Catholic population (Churm 1999; Fulcher 1999). 'For most Punjabi families,' write Dosanjh and Ghuman, 'religion is the key element upon which their personal identities are nurtured and formed' (1997, p.300).

2. Individuals derive self-esteem and confidence from their religion and religious beliefs (Amin 1998; Henley and Schott 1999; Thakur 1998).

3. Religion provides rituals and ceremonies which help strengthen the bonds of family and other social groups within societies; this is of fundamental importance within cultural minorities who feel themselves alienated or threatened within dominant majority cultures.

4. Organised, established religion provides crucial supports for the individual and community in times of illness, bereavement, tragedy and national calamities.

5. Organised, established religions help combat the racism, sectarianism and bigotry endured primarily by minorities.

6. Religion can be the principal means by which a culture (and its other aspects such as language, music, dance, etc.) is maintained and consolidated during times of repression or when oppressors attempt to assimilate or eradicate one's culture.

7. Religion offers a spiritual meaning and purpose in life, increasingly disregarded or rejected by the dominant non-religious or irreligious majorities.

8. The value base of many individuals within minority cultures stems directly from their religious faith and upbringing; these values embrace respect for others, charity, sacrifice and social responsibility. (There is

some irony in the fact that health and social care professionals attach great importance to values, yet in an increasingly secular materialistic world are seemingly unaware of the religious origins of most people's value systems.)

9. Organised religion and churches provide a valued role for women in particular. Many professionals may think that they do the opposite, that is, oppress women and act as bastions of sexism. But, as Elaine Foster (1992) points out in respect of African-Caribbean churches in Britain (she may also have included the Catholic church worldwide), these churches are dominated numerically, socially and spiritually by women: 'Women have created the context in which the social, spiritual and emotional needs of the (black) congregation, and at times the wider black community, are taken care of (Amin 1998, p.54).

10. Many religions foster spiritual growth. They encourage their adherents frequently and regularly to engage in critical self-examination. This predominantly revolves around their impact upon the world, their actions and interactions – for good or ill – with others. Such exercises are also in effect facilitating emotional, social and psychological growth.

Cumulatively, these opinions and perceptions of the benefits of religion should compel all health and social care professionals at least to respect it. But there is ample justification for believing that, for many professionals, this is a difficult task.

Obstacles and objections to respect for religion

The role of Christianity in colonialism and destruction of indigenous cultures

Health and social care professionals are generally well aware of the fact that Christianity and the established Christian churches played a significant role in colonialist expansion and in the destruction of indigenous cultures (see Chapters 4, 5, 6). Haynes (1993) writes: 'Just like in 16th century Latin America, Christian missions in sub-Saharan Africa were integrally involved in European expansion that went far beyond the preaching of the gospel' (p.57). Yet professionals are also aware that church welfare and educational activities provided the foundations and greatly accelerated the development of professions such as social work, child care, residential work, etc. (Forsythe 1995). This is an uncomfortable irony. Today's training of health and social care workers emphasises the scourge of racism (Dominelli 1988; Thompson 1993). Racism is invariably traced back to colonialism (CCETSW 1991; Dwivedi and Varma 1996). The Christian churches zealously promoted colonialism (and its inherent racism) for their own particular ends (Bean and Melville 1989); the Dutch Reformed Church actively promoted the racism of South African's apartheid. These historical facts are not likely to generate respect for Christianity in particular or religion in general among many of today's professionals.

Scientific rationalism

The training of health and social care professionals is based primarily upon the social and physical sciences, in which there is little or no understanding or appreciation of the meaning and value of religion in people's lives. Professions such as social work, psychotherapy, child development, psychology and psychiatry have been inevitably drawn towards the scientific rationalism underpinning the much more prestigious profession of medicine. There is scant regard for religion or religious considerations in medicine. One of the consequences of this development is immediately apparent in the leading journals of some professions; historically, they would have given ample space to issues like ethics, values, principles and conscience, etc. Such issues now often give way to a relentlessly stultifying barrage of statistics, in which not only are the cultural and religious contexts neglected, but also the individual respondents of the research have little significance other than a numerical one. Guerin's (1998) 'social contingency analysis of religious behaviours' goes one better. Religion is reduced to a 'very common form of organising or shaping the behaviours of groups of people to perform low-probability but socially functional behaviours' (p.57). Guerin believes his analysis displaces the truth of any religious claim and that the 'events to be studied are the social consequences of talking about religious matters or praying, not the existence of what is talked about or prayed to' (p.69). Contrary to the benefits that many adherents to religion may identify, Guerin believes that 'religions typically act to increase anxiety rather than reduce it' (p.53).

Religion exercises far too much authority and control

Religions may exercise a powerful influence over many aspects of individuals' lives (particularly women's), giving the strong impression of authority and control (Sinha 1998; Thompson 1993). This is at variance with long-established principles of self-determination, which have been assiduously promoted in social care literature over many decades (Biestik 1961; Braye and Preston-Shoot 1995; Sanzenbach 1989). Seden puts it bluntly: 'Historically and currently, religions have been used as a tool of political oppression ... and to keep the poor content with their position in society' (1995). Guerin (1998) asserts that 'there is no difference in principle between religious and non-religious social control' (p.53).

Religion: a sexist institution

Religion (as with language) has traditionally been subordinated to the issues of 'ethnicity', racism and sexism within health and social care literature and research. In an increasingly secular and irreligious world, those who regard their religion as much more important than their race or gender may have difficulty in finding professionals who can either accept or understand that. Gender is of particular interest because of a significant western perception that religions such as Hinduism and Islam are the bastions of sexism. Sinha's (1998) research on *The Cultural Adjustment of Asian Lone Mothers Living in London* is prefaced by a chapter concentrating upon the oppressive features of these religions and the cultures in which they predominate:

> Husbands have authority of their wives who should regard them as their master ... one of the principal religious duties of Hindu parents is the marrying off of one's daughter ... marriage is confirmed as a business deal ... women must renounce all their sexual impulses as well as their loyalties to their parents when they get married ... women have to be guarded excessively and their virginity protected, and this makes them an almost intolerable burden on their families. (Sinha 1998)

There are some fifteen pages of this sustained theme of oppression, with little or no counter-balance of gain, privilege, status or benefit which any Hindu or Muslim woman may feel in their allegiance to Hinduism or Islam.

A more balanced view is provided by Brah (1992), who mimics these excesses of Indian families and their women victims: 'ruthlessly oppressed creatures who must be saved from their degradation' (p.69). Both Brah (1992) and Ahmed (1992) trace such attitudes back to the so-called 'civilising missions' of colonialism. Ahmed speaks of one of Lord Cromer's arguments for Britain remaining in Egypt: 'to ensure an [English] liberalising impact upon the lot of Muslim women, while the British Raj in India, according to Brah, believed it had the task of offsetting the impacts of inferior, barbaric, superstitious, and emotional Indian culture!' (Ahmad 1996, p.195). With regard to Islam in particular (as the 'oppressor of women') Henley reminds us:

> The Holy Qur'an raised the status of women ... and gave women a legal status as independent human beings, with special emphasis on their economic rights ... It is laid down in the Qur'an and the traditions of the Prophet Muhammad that women have the right to equal education, to earn and possess money, to inherit, and to control and dispose of their money or property without reference to their husbands or fathers ... to run a business of her own without consulting her husband. (Henley 1982, pp.36–37)

Henley also notes wryly that it took 12 centuries for western, non-Muslim women to be granted the same right under British legislation, the Married Women's Property Rights.

Authors insufficiently stress that it is not religion or religious teachings which inevitably lead to the oppression of women, but other aspects of societal, economic and tribal life. Take arranged marriages, for example, pejoratively referred to by Sinha above. Here is the view of a victim of such an 'arrangement' who actually runs a support group for other victims:

> All the main religions of the world teach their followers a type of positive morality. Islam embraces all manners of peoples regarding race, class and gender, accepting them as equal before Allah/God – the same God as that between Christians and Jews. Islam advocates justice and equality for all peoples and for both genders. It is not the Islamic religion which is at fault, but the misinformed, male-orientated interpretation of it, which socially and economically benefits men and disadvantages women. Religious ethics are contaminated by a male political and economical agenda, which turns women into dependants and, as a result, denies them equality, respect and control of their lives and the opportunity to contribute meaningfully to society. (Anonymous 1998, p.54)

Religious fundamentalism, cults and catastrophes

There is good reason to believe that health and social care professionals are increasingly sceptical about religions in general, and that their training 'is hopelessly infused with the doctrines of secular humanism' (Sanzenbach 1989, p.85). Their attitudes to religious fundamentalists and diverse cults are likely to be more severe, particularly if they have been involved in caring for people who have been the victims of such cults. Cults have increased dramatically. There are more than 5000 websites provided by the leaders of cults, their supporters, critics, or those researching them. Children are commonly rescued from individual fundamentalist parents whose constraints upon them go well beyond legal boundaries and often constitute psychological abuse (O'Hagan 1993). Whole families are often the victims of cults whose leaders have seemingly had no qualms about confining their followers to mass funeral pyres and extermination camps. Such incidents have increased alarmingly in recent years, occurring in the most diverse and unconnected locations (Guyana, Texas, Switzerland, France, Japan, Los Angeles). The most recent cult to hit the headlines was that of the Uganda-based 'movement for the restoration of the ten commandments of God'. Its leaders saw fit to imprison in a barn more than a thousand of its followers (a third of whom were children) and to immolate them by fire.

The cataclysmic ends to these cults are very disturbing events for the public worldwide. It is not surprising that for professionals who may already be sceptical, suspicious, distrustful or hostile towards religion, they evoke some sense of vindication or even moral outrage. These cults are after all the most excessive forms of oppression and repression against victims who are predominantly uneducated and poor. (If they are not poor when they join, they inevitably become so, as the cult leaders invariably demand surrender of all material possessions.) Another feature of cults is that they retain much of the core ritual and devotion of the established churches which their congregations have deserted. The Uganda-based cult, for example, originated and was sustained around devotion to the Blessed Virgin Mary, had an ex-Catholic priest in the triumvirate which ran it, and the majority of its members were Catholic rural peasants. Such associations may contribute to an even greater tendency on the part of professionals to ignore or avoid the religious faith of their clients, and to remain unaware of how this may impact upon the problem at hand and, more importantly, upon the effectiveness of the treatment prescribed.

Religion: the clergy and child abuse

Previous chapters have given some indication of the extent of emotional, physical, psychological and sexual abuse perpetrated by religious clergy against children (Commonwealth of Australia 1997; Raftery and O'Sullivan 1999; Walker 1992) Since those chapters were written, barely a week has passed without further revelation of shocking abuses, convictions and apologies from church authorities. In a radio broadcast on Sunday 21 May 2000 (BBC Radio 4) a discussion took place on the extent of abuse perpetrated against indigenous tribes by the Anglican clergy and schools in Canada's British Columbia. The discussion then focused on the likely prospect of the Church of England going bankrupt after making the necessary reparations to the victims (all now severely damaged, malfunctioning adults). Similar scenarios emerge with the Catholic Church in England, the USA and Ireland.

Another indicator of the growth of this particular phenonomen is the fact that for a decade or more academics and researchers have made the child victims of clergy the main focus of interest, but are now increasingly focusing upon the characteristics of the clergy perpetrators themselves. It is reasonable to presume that these revelations have adversely impacted on professionals' perceptions of religion and the clergy. (Many may not wish to acknowledge the fact that the number of 'childcare' professionals involved in child abuse is also depressingly high – probably higher because they have actually had responsibility for the day-to-day care of their victims.)

As with the impact of fundamentalism and suicidal or murderous cults, child abuse perpetrated by clergy is likely to reinforce existing negativity towards religion and further desensitise professionals in their approach and attitude towards devout individuals of strong religious faith, in particular those whose spiritual allegiance is with the established churches which have harboured the most persistent abusers among their clergy. The Catholic and Anglican Churches have been conspicuous in this regard and a Channel 4 (2000) Dispatches programme on *The Fight for a Child* gave clear indications of social services' discriminatory attitudes towards practising Christians seeking to foster and adopt children.

Religion: an object of ridicule and scorn

For centuries, the middle classes and the intelligentsia have made religion the object of ridicule and scorn; names which immediately come to mind include Voltaire, Rousseau, Swift, Huxley and Russell.   This basically healthy tradition of satire has continued and intensified, with popes, ayatollahs, rabbis and bishops considered fair game, and health and social services professionals enjoying the fun as much as anyone else. But something quite different has happened over the last half century. It is not just that the satire is more percep-tive and (viciously) penetrating, but that the authors actually seek out what religion's ordinary adherents regard as the most sacred and most revered aspect of their worship and faith, knowing full well that the mockery then devised will have the most shocking, lasting and ultimately profitable effect.

Christ's crucifixion is a case in point – for most practising Christians a central profundity of meaning and emotion, spiritual resolution and regeneration that is unlikely either to be understood or accepted by non-Christians. 'Humourists', 'satirists', 'dramatists' and 'actors' have increasingly portrayed the crucifixion for laughs and made fortunes. The suggestion that ordinary Christians might be deeply offended by such a portrayal makes no impact, but merely provokes further laughs.

The whole matter of the degree of offence which writers and their amused audiences might cause to religious adherents was to be dramatically changed by Rushdie's (1988) *Satanic Verses*. His work provoked outrage among Muslims and led to riots, international crises and even death. Rushdie himself was under sentence of death (*fatwa*), decreed by Iran's Ayatollah Khomeni and has only recently emerged from a ten-year-long nightmare in which round-the-clock protection and countless homes had to be provided for him. But the issue still reverberates and raises many questions that need further exploration and comment.

Cultural competence training and Satanic Verses

Many lengthy and tortuous debates about *Satanic Verses* and its impact have taken place. Weeks' (1995) article is particularly illuminating in its concentration upon the dilemma which the whole issue posed for the left of British politics: free speech versus the rights of minorities not to be treated in this way (which is in effect an extension of colonialism's contempt for the culture and religion of minorities). He quotes Keith Vaz in *The Independent*: 'To goad and mock religions is to rob them of their roots and sensitivities' (29 July 1989). Whatever opinion one adopts towards the *Satanic Verses* however, there can be no denying that reactions to the book must have enlightened health and social care professionals who provide services for religious minorities (particularly those professionals who adhere to no religion). Prior to publication of the book, it was simply inconceivable to many such professionals that ordinary individuals within cultural–religious minorities could experience such depths of pain, anger and humiliation as a consequence of what someone may have written about their religion, or some revered aspect of that religion.

A counter-argument and explanation was forcefully put at the time: that such individuals were merely the hapless tools of Muslim mullahs and opportunist Muslim politicians, who otherwise probably would not have concerned themselves about *Satanic Verses*. But this is a nonsense. Laris Forouki is a Muslim woman living in Belfast where she works in a university bookshop.

She has no political affiliations. There are not many Muslims in Belfast and she was interviewed by local television at the time of the furore. She said that Rushdie's book was the equivalent of someone piercing her heart with a dagger. This may have been as incomprehensible to viewers as the riots which the publication provoked, but the raw emotion of her voice and the pain in her face certainly conveyed genuineness. I have since spoken to her, a decade after the event, and she feels precisely the same about the book as she did then.

Publicly respectful, privately contemptuous

Health and social care professionals may choose to live a schizophrenic existence in this matter: feigning interest in and respect for the client's religious beliefs and practices and yet in their private lives indulging in thoughts and actions supporting those who cause great offence to the religious sensibilities of the client. I made this point once to a group of Northern Ireland senior professionals. Their cynicism and disrespect for culture in general and religion in particular (understandably rooted in their disgust with the sectarian murders and mutilations of hundreds of innocent Catholics and Protestants, including their own relatives and friends) was obvious in their responses. Yet some of them believed they could actually function effectively in these opposite ways: in the daytime ostensibly adhering to their statutory and professional obligations to respect all the religions of all their clients; in the evening retreating into a mindset that could elicit opinions and feelings about specific religions and sacred, revered aspects of those religions every bit as wounding as anything Rushdie had written.

Smyth and Campbell (1996) have written of the 'silence and denial' which operates among Northern Ireland's professionals in respect of religion generally and sectarianism in particular. There is no more effective environment for fostering such a duality of living. In an age of partnership, when trainers of health and care workers depend so much upon input from agencies providing the services, it is highly unlikely that practitioners who harbour a profound distaste of or even indifference to religion will stress the importance of religion and respect for the religious faiths of the people they serve. Until professionals, and managers in particular, regain the capacity of empathy, are able to believe, understand and feel the depth of pain and humiliation that irreligious and anti-religious attitudes and behaviour may inflict upon religious minorities, the goal of achieving a consistently culturally competent service will remain illusive.

Manifestations of insensitivity towards religion

Here then we have seven potential contributors to a negative, insensitive approach to religion and to those espousing a spirituality derived from and sustained by allegiance with some institutional religious form. There is no research available confirming the potency of any of these contributors, but readers will have the opportunity in Chapter 15 to test out their relevance through the provision of frameworks specifically aimed towards self-exploration in respect of many of the issues which have arisen here. There is ample research and anecdotal evidence to suggest that negativity and insensitivity towards religion is widespread. Few childcare professionals, for example, would contest Seden's (1995) argument that the religion of children in care amounts to nothing more a 'nominal tick on a form', or express any surprise with Amin's (1998) social worker who, when asked what was the child's religion, 'replied after a long pause by saying: "I don't think I've ever known that"' (p.27); or disagree with Henley and Schott's (2000) conviction (based on a lifetime's writing and research on health care matters) that health professionals often make note of the patient's religion and then discard it, thereby denying themselves the opportunity to learn about the spiritual life and needs of that patient; or, finally, be surprised that Colton and Roberts' (1997) Islamic patients looked in vain for prayer mats and a private space in which to pray. In Gerrish, Husband and MacKenzie's (1996) research on nursing in a multi-ethnic society, the words 'religion' and 'religious' do not even appear in the index, yet, ironically, there are two instructive examples of sensitivity and insensitivity to Jewish hospital patients, the former in respect of kosher food and the latter in respect of her wish to have her baby boy circumcised. The latter said, 'I was called barbaric and received other degrading comments from the nurses.' She attempts to explain circumcision: 'it is part of our religious needs' (p.42). The authors, in an otherwise excellent text, do not seem to realise the significance of this particular respondent's experiences, nor precisely what it is implying about the workers. It is not just that their treatment of the patient is grossly culturally insensitive, but that they know nothing of the significance of circumcision in Jewish religion, nor of the context and atmosphere in which it is carried out. More crucially, they are obviously unaware of how their comments greatly exacerbate the stresses and strains normally associated with the joyousness of the birth of a Jewish child:

> The social worker needs to understand that, for the Jewish family, circumcision is seen as both necessary and normal. At the same time it can be a very emotionally charged event, especially for the new mother. Apart from the ordinary demands a new baby brings, she may have to entertain

relatives and in-laws at her home, or organise sleeping arrangements and catering … In vulnerable families tensions are bound to surface at such times. Poorer families may be under additional financial strain. (Wood 1998, p.76)

Looked at in this context, we can see that the culturally insensitive remark about circumcision may have far worse consequences for both mother and child than mere acute emotional pain. This lack of awareness is one of the consequences of relegating religion far below other aspects of culture, as the vast majority of health and social care authors do. For many minority patients and clients, their cultural and world view is often dominated by and dictated to by their religious faith and their adherence to the regulations and rituals of established church forms. The values and beliefs derived from their faith and allegiance are woven into the fabric of their daily lives.

Religion and The Children Act 1989

All of the experiences described above would be at variance with the following:

- the requirements of The Children Act 1989

- earlier childcare legislation (e.g. Child Care Act 1980; Boarding Out Regulations 1991)

- the Patient's Charter (DoH 1991) requiring medical staff to respect and to respond to the 'religious and cultural beliefs' of patients

- virtually all the 'equality', 'equal opportunity' and 'anti-discriminatory' guidelines produced by public and voluntary health and social care agencies.

'Due consideration' in the Children Act (meaning a serious positive attitude) 'must be given to their religious persuasion' and looked-after children should have the opportunity, insofar as it is possible, to be brought up by parents/carers of the same religion, or by parents/carers committed to bringing up the child in its own religion. This is a major challenge for many childcare professionals. Apart from the probability of a secular, humanist approach to these matters, in which the significance of religion in the client's life may not be recognised, childcare workers are likely to be more concerned about 'race' and/or nationality in making decisions about placements and carers.

Sumpton (1993) tells of the unfortunate consequences of such a preoccupation: the ten-year-old Indian Muslim child placed with Sikh parents. The latter knew nothing of the Muslim importance of halal meat, nor of the Muslim strictures on eating pork. The child knew nothing of the Sikh conviction about the sacredness of cows. In addition to these serious incompatibilities, the naming systems were different and confusing to the child, as well as the clothing. While both child and family could manage to speak in English, the family's language was Punjabi and the child's Urdu. Not unexpectedly, the placement ended in failure.

Using religion to enhance services

There is now evidence in health and social care literature to suggest that western-based, western-trained health and social care professionals are perceiving religion in a new light, acknowledging it as a potential source of help in their efforts. Counselling literature leads the way (Aldridge 2000; Johnson and Ridley 1992; Lyle 1994; Swinton 2000; Willows and Swinton 2000), though much of this literature is confined to seeking the 'integration of an explicitly Christian approach to counselling' (McLeod 1993, p.120). Asian and African-Caribbean professionals (Lago and Thompson 1996) are increasingly making a vital contribution to counselling (Syme 1994), but they focus much more on race and racism than they do upon the various religions of minorities. In training and practice, two impressive efforts to enhance knowledge and awareness of the influence of religion in the lives of clients stand out, in two entirely different locations.

Chalma, Mexico

Dennis Poole is an American professor of social work. His students when qualified will be serving populations in which many rural Mexican migrants predominate. These migrants are a religious people and each year join millions of Mexicans in visiting a shrine, the Santuario de Señor de Chalma, to give thanks, to fulfil vows and to seek divine intervention for illnesses and other difficulties. Social work students from around the USA join Poole and his own students in making the same pilgrimage each year. They are engaged, he says, in a two-week 'cultural immersion course'. They live with Mexican families, learn Spanish, visit health and social service providers and tour important cultural sites. Poole emphasises that he is a learner too:

In the case of Chalma, we have come to observe first hand the central role of religion in Mexican culture, especially among rural Mexicans, who have a high migratory tradition to the United States ... Mountain water collects in a deep basin beside the Santuario de Señor de Chalmo. Pilgrims believe this water is holy and miraculous. Last year more than half of my students – 20 in all – placed their hands or feet in the basin. (Poole 1998, p.163)

Poole is well aware of how others may perceive his students' efforts: in college life generally they avoid sharing spiritual issues because 'faculty and students might ridicule them' (p.164). He regrets this and asks: 'How can social workers provide culturally competent services in, say, matters of death and dying, without having first examined their own spiritual views on these matters, not to mention those of their clients?' (p.164). As for the Mexican migrants, 'We recognise the need for greater competence in our efforts to serve this population.'

New Zealand: cultural influences regained

In Chapter 6, the religiosity of Australia's indigenous Aboriginals was explored. The purpose was to highlight the complexity and social and environmental significance of their religious beliefs and rituals, and to remind ourselves that this was all interpreted by the colonisers as nothing more than magic, superstition and sorcery – a certain proof that these were a primitive, inferior and harmful species. In Chapter 7, we learnt of the significant contribution which health and social care agencies made to the destruction of Aboriginal culture as a whole. It is interesting to learn, therefore, that their modern-day counterparts in Australia's nextdoor neighbour, New Zealand, have relegated western-based developmental theories in a number of practice areas (e.g. juvenile crime, child abuse) and created a family and childcare system based upon an equally complex and socially significant religion of the indigenous Maori population. This is the Family Group Conference (FGC), a source of increasing interest in childcare literature and international conferences (Churm 1999; Fulcher 1999; Hudson et al. 1996; Marsh and Crow 1997). Fulcher traces the development of this initiative, quoting from a government-sponsored report aptly entitled *Puao-te-Ata-tu (daybreak) Report of the Ministerial Advisory Committee on a Maori perspective for the Department of Social Welfare* (Rangihau 1986). This report identified 'a profound misunderstanding or ignorance of the place of the child in Maori society and its relationship with *whanau* (family), *hapu* (subtribe), and *iwi* (tribal) structures' (p.7, quoted in Fulcher 1999). In general, it exposed professionals' failure to 'understand how cultural differences shape family practices and the development of Maori children' (Fulcher 1999, p.330).

The cultural–religious origins of the contemporary FGC emphasise the importance of the relationship between Celestial and Terrestrial knowledge. Fulcher writes:

> Matters appropriately regarded as being earth bound are associated with Terrestrial Knowledge, incorporating laws that govern the physical world in which Maori live. Spiritual matters are associated with Celestial Knowledge and the two are so closely interwoven as to be nearly insepa-rable. The spiritual element is part of daily activity amongst Maori people, providing the very foundations for *Whanau Hapu Iwi* (family/subtribe/ tribe) social structures that still operate today. (Fulcher 1999, p.331)

The origin of the FGC was, according to Maori belief, a rebellious initiative by the children of Ranginui, the great Sky Father, and Papatuanuku, the matriarch Earth Mother. Cocooned in relative darkness by their parents, the children desired freedom to explore the 'outer limits of the universe'. The family conference which ensued altered the course of their lives forever.

Each Maori child's cultural identity is crucial to his or her development. Central to that identity is their genealogy or *whakapapa*, locating them through successive generations, including 'both matriarchal and patriarchal lines, and to the order of birth and its significance'. *Whakapapa* recognises the importance of all extended family relationships in the moulding of the child's identity. It would be 'unthinkable' for professionals to be deciding or planning a child's future without consideration of the contributions of extended family members. Fulcher writes: 'Great-grandparents, grandparents, parents and children from each generation were all regarded as being part of a single spiritual and economic unit. A Family Group Conference that excluded any of these members ... would ignore the important spiritual and social con-tribution they make to decision-making' (1999, p.332).

It is not possible to do justice to Fulcher's comprehensive paper in a few paragraphs. But it is helpful material for anyone providing services for religious and cultural minorities. As in all countries with displaced, oppressed and culturally and religiously different indigenous peoples, New Zealand professionals have learnt the inadequacies of efforts based upon western (religionless) theories, training, values and techniques, etc., coupled with the 'profound ignorance' (quoted in the above government-commissioned report) of important aspects of the religions and cultures of the people they are trying to serve. Such an approach is little more than a continuation and intensification of the colonial onslaught perpetrated against indigenous cultures in the first instance. The results are predictable. The high incidence of Maori clientele in the criminal justice and mental health systems are only two of the typical examples of overrepresentation found in many countries. Others include: Aboriginals in Australia (crime, alcoholism, suicide); the Irish in Britain (alcoholism, mental health); American Indians in Oklahoma and other states (alcoholism, mental health); African-Caribbean men in Britain (crime, schizophrenia). The continuing vulnerability of such groups and the failure of western-based, cultureless or culturally insensitive therapies and treatments is an inevitable consequence of their religious and/or cultural alienation in secular environments vastly different from those in which they originated. In the Family Group Conference, New Zealand's health and social care agencies have made a substantial contribution towards attempting to reverse centuries-old alienating, culturally annihilating processes. Their attempts to reach, explore, understand and respect the core of Maori culture and religion is as genuine as it is beneficial. They have much to teach us about cultural competence.

Summary and conclusion

This chapter has considered some of the challenges that religion and related concepts, such as 'spirituality' and 'faith', may pose to health and social care professionals. While western countries become more secular and irreligious, substantially populated minorities within them tenaciously adhere to their religious creeds and to the values and spirituality derived from them. In an increasingly irreligious dominant culture, it is helpful to consider available definitions of religion and the related terms as a first step in acknowledging the importance of religiosity in people's lives.

The second logical step is to listen to people saying precisely why religion is so important to them. A sizeable 'list' of perfectly good reasons – spiritual, social, emotional, psychological, communal – has accumulated in answer to that question, plus the realisation that religion is not just important as a spiritual dimension in their lives, but guides and influences virtually every aspect of daily living.

There are numerous reasons why health and social care professionals may be sceptical or cynical about religion. This becomes a matter of concern if scepticism or cynicism adversely influences their responses to devoutly religious patients or clients. Seven potential reasons for professional negativity towards religion have been explored in this chapter:

1. awareness of the role played by dominant established religions in the destruction of indigenous cultures;

2. health and social services training which ignores religion and is over-dependent upon scientific rationalism;

3. religion is perceived as too authoritative and controlling, at variance with established principles of self-determination and democracy;

4. religion is perceived as male dominated and sexist;

5. awareness of the dangers and self-destruction of some religious fundamentalists and religious cults;

6. the high prevalence of child sexual abuse among Christian clergy;

7. religion has long been an object of satire and ridicule in western societies, particularly among the professional classes.

It is useful to explore each of these potential sources of negativity. Chapter 15 will provide comprehensive self-exploration frameworks specifically for this purpose. If any of these sources reflect one's own feelings and perceptions, then it is necessary to attempt to predict their likely influence and consequences in working with those who zealously adhere to religious obligations and practices; and whose identities, personalities and responses to the world in which they live have been heavily influenced by religion and religious allegiances.

Impressive efforts are being made in contrasting locations to enhance knowledge and awareness of the influence of religion in the lives of clients. Dennis Poole, an American professor of social work, leads his students in yearly 'cultural immersion' exercises centring on a revered shrine in Chalma, Mexico. New Zealand provides a model whereby professionals have to learn to respect and utilise the ancient religion of the indigenous Maori peoples they serve. The secular sounding Family Group Conference is in effect an elaborate culture-sensitive, religion-sensitive construction. It is based upon ancient traditions of religion-inspired reverence for genealogy, the place of the child in Maori society and the rights of extended families and different generations within the same families. One of the most fundamental rights of different family members is to play a helping role in the difficulties (e.g. crime, social deviancy, childcare, child abuse, etc.) in which any individual family members may find themselves.

It can be safely assumed that the efforts in Mexico and New Zealand are mirrored in various other parts of the world, less well known, less publicised.

All such efforts represent the ultimate reversal of the negative and destructive views, feelings, perceptions, attitudes, approaches and actions towards indigenous peoples and their cultures, and the religions central to these cultures. They are truly models of cultural competence.

CHAPTER 10

Culture and Language

Introduction

Language is a significant factor in all cultures. This chapter examines some of the research findings in the context of that significance. It begins with some elementary facts about the development of language in evolution. Such development has not been without cost. Second, the centrality of language within culture will be illustrated through references to numerous historical examples. Third, a key definition of 'language' in relation to culture is provided and referred to throughout the chapter. Fourth, the importance of the paralinguistic and gestural features which accompany language will be stressed. Finally, the chapter will review the existing knowledge base in respect of health and social care services to minority language groups. Language has traditionally been a much neglected area, but has recently been given impetus by the current statutory obligation to consider the linguistic backgrounds of clients. More recent texts have included a focus upon specific language minorities and the difficulties and discriminations they face. These have contributed to a greater understanding and appreciation of the importance of language within health and social care work.

Beginnings

Language is a relatively late starter in the six-million-year evolution of the human species. Anthropologists inform us that even a million years ago the brain had not yet developed sufficiently for communication through language. Perhaps the human condition biologically recognised what was happening and resisted stubbornly. It is a well-known fact in medical anthropology in particular that our ability to speak required a substantial modification in our vocal–respiratory tract, and that this greatly increased our species' chances of both choking to death and having impacted teeth. The latter condition was invariably fatal until the nineteenth century (Haviland 1999). What a sacrifice we have made in order to be able to speak to each other.

The power of speech greatly accelerated the dawn of culture. There is much anthropological evidence indicating the importance of language in the development of cultures. Lindesmith and Strauss (1956) believe that 'language is both the vehicle by means of which culture is transmitted from generation to generation and also, an integral part of all aspects of culture' (p.6). There are numerous examples of cultural revivals pivoted on language. The Irish Gaelic revival in the late nineteenth century, and the emergence of Afrikaans as the adopted language of the South African Boers, are historically well documented (Cornell and Hartmann 1998; Moodie 1975). Perhaps less well known is how the subjugated satellites of the Soviet Union maintained and consolidated their distinct cultures and identities chiefly through the spoken word (Jones 1994). Carter and Aitchison (1986) write: 'The character and vitality of a culture is to a large extent language dependent' (p.1). So too are our social relationships (Rees 1991). The richness of human cultures is made possible primarily through languages. Dónall Ó Riagáin, Secretary General of the European Bureau for Lesser Used Languages, encapsulates the universal importance of language in relation to all cultures:

> Language is in the first instance a means of communication. But it is a lot more than that. It is a communal tool, developed and refined by its users, to express their ideas, their beliefs, their feelings. It reflects a people's development, their shared historical experience and their sense of community. It is a receptacle where a people's most intimate and finest thoughts can be recorded, stored and transmitted, not only to other contemporary members of the community, but even from one generation to the other. It is the mainspring of culture. (Ó Riagáin 1998)

Paralanguage and kinesics

Meaningful language is much more than mere words. 'Paralanguage' and 'kinesics' accompany all spoken language. Paralanguage is the system of features that often make our spoken utterances effective and unique, for example, tone, volume, voice colour, rhythm, pace, emphasis, music. Kinesics is the gestural component in language communication: for example, nodding or shaking the head, shrugging the shoulders, knitting the brow, biting the lip, crossing legs, folding arms, shaking hands (or fists), smiling, frowning, glaring, laughing, crying, mimicking, etc. Paralanguage and kinesics evolved alongside language and are of the utmost importance in communication generally. They are often as potent an expression of culture as language itself, conveying not just information, but cultural values and beliefs. Together, they convey more than 90 per cent of the emotional affect in human communication (Haviland 1999)

In Chapter 5 we witnessed enormous discrepancies in the indigenous and non-indigenous interpretations of paralanguage and kinesics. Different postures, movements, facial expressions or gestures can have the opposite meaning in different cultures. Thus we may smile to our listener(s) to indicate happiness, whereas in Japan happiness is more likely to be expressed with a straight face (Stewart and Bennett 1991, quoted in Henley and Schott 1999). Eye contact in particular varies substantially in its meaning and effect. We learn that Arab culture regards it most favourably and may perceive little of it as disrespectful. In South Asian and Eskimo cultures it is widely regarded as aggressive and rude (American influence on the training of care professionals worldwide has not been helpful in its vigorous promotion of sustained eye contact with clients, irrespective of cultures; many clients from all cultures are intimidated by such practice).

An unsuitable introduction to language

Many care workers, particularly social workers, have been introduced to the subject of 'language' through sociology, psychology, social policy, philosophy and linguistics texts. These are often characterised by abstract philosophising, medical or mechanistic jargon and analytic reductionist theorising, in which the real meaning of language and its significance within cultures can be lost. Romaine (1994), for example, believes that language has no existence apart from the social reality of its users. Denny (1998) is concerned about the link between language and discrimination, the relationship between 'quasi-technical psychiatric language and power' and also how 'social policy and practice texts are infused with a language which both subordinates and supports a personal tragedy, an individualised view of disability' (p.92). Campbell and Oliver's (1996) text is limited to the politics and social policy aspects of disability, though they make a valuable argument for regarding deaf people whose first (and only) language as a linguistic minority is sign language. The popular psychology texts of Gross (1987) and Atkinson et al. (1987) enlighten on the brain mechanisms for language and spend a great deal of time on the controversial topic of the relationship between language and thought. Hall (1976) sees great limitations in language. It is 'by nature poorly adapted to this difficult task [i.e. of enabling one to learn about another culture] ... it is too linear, not comprehensive enough, too slow, too limited, too constrained, too unnatural, too much a product of its own evolution' (p.37). Lago and Thompson (1996) believe these reductionist perceptions of language are too pessimistic for care workers grappling with the challenge of communicating with clients from diverse cultures.

Language in health and social care literature of the past

Traditionally, there has been little attention given to language in health and social care literature, perhaps because language has more often been perceived as a problem than as the pivotal expression of one's culture. Lees and McGrath's (1974) study of community work with Gujerati immigrants begins with this profile, which does not even mention language:

> The Gujerati immigrants appear to form a particularly cohesive group whose cultural identity is reinforced by the continuance of close village and kin networks, the compact area in which they now live, their strong common religious practices, and through the activities of their local Muslim Welfare Society. (Lees and McGrath 1974, p.176)

It is somewhat ironical, therefore, that the authors later tell us that 'language emerged as the greatest perceived problem' and about the limited English-speaking ability in the 43 households interviewed. 'Language problem' in this article means one thing only: the individual(s) cannot communicate with the researchers (not the other way around) and cannot be understood because they cannot speak English. Such a perception may not have changed much: Henley and Schott (1999) quote an elderly Gujarati patient who speaks no less than five languages, but tells the researchers that he is 'nothing' because he can't speak English. Yet one of the most important principles in Teaching English as a Foreign Language (TEFL) is respect for the group's own language; it is the necessary precursor for encouraging them to acquire another.

References to language in current health and social care literature and research

Current health and social care literature and practice are beginning to show some interest in language minorities. This welcome development stems mainly from two statutory obligations: (a) ensuring that all minorities are aware of the services which statutory agencies provide; (b) consideration of linguistic background in the assessment of clients and their families.

Lago and Thompson (1996) stress: 'The use of language is absolutely central to the communication process and however much good intent there is

... if misunderstandings persist, then the potential for therapy is substantially diminished' (p.55). They anticipate the possibility of the following 'language difficulties' between professionals and clients:

- One does not speak the language of the other.

- Both may be able to speak and understand English, but it's the second language of one of them.

- Both have similar language origins, but have lived all their lives in different countries (therefore have markedly different accents).

- Both have similar country and language origins, but very different styles of living (i.e. class) and speech.

Lago and Thompson believe that the professional's task is always to aspire to a quality of communication and understanding which 'evokes trust, gratitude, exploration, love and aspiration' (p.55). Then adds: 'Culturally skilled counsellors take responsibility for interacting in the language requested by the client' (p.61).

Some consequences of a language barrier

Misunderstanding

Qureshi (1989) provides numerous witty and irreverent accounts of the consequences of health professionals and patients unable to communicate with each other. Knowing no words at all will inevitably lead the health professional to a dependence upon gestures, particularly with the eyes and the arms, with some embarrassing results. Qureshi believes that most communication problems encountered can be overcome by 'patience and a positive effort'.

Misuse of interpreters

Gerrish et al. (1996) critically explore the reasons why many of their respondents – the patients of nursing and midwifery services – experienced hurt, humiliation and marginalisation as a consequence of a mutual inability to communicate between themselves and the professionals. They write about the 'absolute incomprehension of linguistic exclusion' (p.37). They comment on the inadequacies of many of the interpretative services within hospitals and highlight the risks involved in resorting to making the children and relatives of patients play that role. Henley and Schott (1999) also devote much attention to interpreters. Apart from the matter of confidentiality, this practice 'introduces a whole range of limitations into the interactions between service provider and service user' (p.38). Nursing and midwifery staff from minorities are often overused for the task of interpreting, thereby spending less precious time on their own caseloads. There is a perceptive quote which strongly implies the powerlessness experienced by patients when little effort has been made to enable them to communicate: 'When you are vulnerable by virtue of being ill and prostrate in front of someone in a uniform, it is extraordinarily difficult to have a discussion as an equal unless every effort is made to assist this to happen' (p.38).

Poorer quality of service

Papadopoulos *et al.* (1998) also predominantly address the nursing profession and acknowledge the difficulties and poor quality of service resulting from the inability of patient and nurse to communicate. They argue for the necessity of health professionals at least to acquire the knowledge of common phrases likely to be of use in many situations. They suggest that the nursing profession should 'collaborate with computer experts in order to devise appropriate phrases in different languages ... available in cheap and easily accessible pocket translators' (p.11). This is a suggestion which this author would not support in the belief that something more felt, more genuine and less mechanistic is required. Papadopoulos *et al.* (1998) draw attention to the efforts of the Greek Cypriot community in London to retain their strong sense of cultural identity and their language, chiefly through their own radio and television channels and newspapers. Many minorities now rely on such means for identical purposes.

The professionals also suffer

Henley and Schott (1999) identify numerous consequences of the language barrier, for example, poor referrals, incomplete investigations, inappropriate interventions and treatments and inaccurate files. Just as important, however, is the impact upon the professionals. It is clearly a major challenge for many professionals confronted with a client with whom they cannot communicate. They cannot provide the same diagnostic expertise; they cannot establish the necessary empathy and rapport; they cannot provide the necessary support, comfort and care. Henley and Schott are quite frank about the impact: a compromising and lowering of professional standards. They record anonymous professionals who freely admit that their ineffectiveness can lead to feelings of guilt, stress, anger, dismay and frustration. They quote from one professional who claims to have observed non-English-speaking clients being treated brutally by colleagues, of them being terrified by professionals shouting at them (presumably because they [the professionals] cannot communicate what they are attempting to do in treatment).

Blaming the clients

Blaming or misjudging the patient/client is a common deflection technique used by many professionals in these situations. For example, the professional may regard them as simply immoral, having failed in their 'moral duty' to learn the language of the country in which they have settled. Henley and Schott quote from Bowling (1990) who wrote of one official's reasoning on those who could not speak English:

> Considering the length of time the East European migrants had been living in the UK, they ought by now to be able to speak English and communicate with other English speakers. If they did not ... they had no one but themselves to blame. (Henley and Schott 1999, p.273)

Other professionals may regard the non-English-speaker as stupid or idle, believing they just couldn't be bothered to learn English. In some extreme examples, the professional may think they are inferior or odd (as some of the Irish-speaking respondents testify in Chapter 13).

Language barriers and specific minority groups

Many writers have briefly touched on language in their wider focus upon discrimination against specific minority groups. It is particularly illuminating to see how the various forms of language discrimination become manifest in health and social care practice. Here are nine such examples.

The elderly within cultural minorities in Britain

Blakemore and Boneham (1994) focus upon the impact of language difficulties experienced by elderly members of minority communities. These difficulties include: failure to get them the welfare benefits to which they are entitled; a lack of awareness about their reluctance to attend available day care and social centres; a failure to recognise the even greater significance the individual elder attaches to his or her language in moments of illness and crises (a point also stressed by Henley and Schott 1999). Those who speak some English and have picked up common phrases may be particularly susceptible to being offended by 'demeaning or condescending expressions' commonly used by professionals working with the elderly population as a whole, for example, 'luv', 'naughty boy/girl', 'little devil', etc.

Gujarati and Bangladeshi women in childbirth

Katbamna's two research groups, Gujarati Hindu and Bangladeshi Muslim women, have different experiences of health services during pregnancy and childbirth, due in the main to the differences in linguistic aptitude. The Gujarati women are better educated and speak English. Many of the Bangladeshi women are illiterate and dependent upon husbands, relatives and friends. Both groups experience cultural insensitivity and racism, but the Bangladeshi women's experiences are of a worse kind. Many of them could not read the (English) literature which health services provide for pregnancy and childbirth. They could not understand television coverage of the topic and could not attend antenatal and postnatal classes. In fact for some of them 'one of the main challenges ... was to survive in an alien environment where no one spoke their language' (Katbamna 2000, p.92).

Watson (1991) reports similar findings, concluding that poverty and ill health among the Bengali respondents might be compounded by language barriers' (p.101). A cautionary note should be struck here. Currer exposed professionals' misperceptions of her clients as helpless, when in fact they were highly confident and influential within their own domain. The difficulties described above are outside that domain, and a consequence of their interactions with culturally [i.e. language] insensitive services).

Punjabi parents

Dosanjh and Ghuman (1997) explored the attitudes of Punjabi parents 'to the core values of their community', the first of which is 'the mother tongue'. Assimilation, education, social life and many of the influences of the dominant culture make it difficult to sustain Punjabi as a living and vibrant expression of Punjabi culture. A Sikh mother articulates the dilemma:

> I want him to learn Punjabi. He talks to me in English. But I answer him in Punjabi. I tell him to speak with me in Punjabi. He tries, but after saying a few words he begins to laugh. (Dosanjh and Ghuman 1997, p.291)

Parental determination and consistency (or the lack of it) appear to be the most significant factor in maintaining the language, with one Punjabi mother admitting: 'Basically it is our fault ... We don't try to make the effort to speak

Punjabi' (p.290). She expresses a strong desire, however, that her children actually do learn the language, whatever their own efforts.

The school can play a major role in determining whether or not Punjabi children will speak their mother tongue. Dosanjh and Ghuman reveal the lack of provision in the nursery, primary and secondary education which the children of the respondents are receiving. No school had formal provision for the teaching of any community language, including Punjabi. The authors speak of the deleterious effects 'on the motivation of children to learn their mother tongue' and suggest the need for 'a degree of continuity between homes (which are bilingual and bicultural) and school, in order to achieve an all-round social and intellectual development of children' (p.291).

Pathan women in Britain

Currer's (1986, 1991) work with Pathan Muslim women in Britain (see Chapter 4) also touches on language discrimination. Her respondents are predominantly non-English-speaking. Few if any health workers can communicate with them. Those who make the effort are much appreciated (Currer 1986). Like Henley and Schott, she acknowledges the difficulties the lack of communication poses for the workers, but the most significant impact is much more profound and both professional and client are the losers:

> When difficulties of communication and differences of culture are a feature of the health care interaction, the worker's task of understanding the behaviour of patients or their parents becomes even more difficult. While actions may be credited with a rationality, this rationality is inaccessible to the worker, and often seen as based upon superstition. (Currer 1991, p.41)

West Indian children transferring to schools in Britain

Bushell's (1996) chapter on the obstacles that children from the West Indies have to surmount in British schools is informative. Language is one of the main obstacles, particularly for children who have had little or no formal education. The type of West Indian creole language they speak will depend upon the island they come from, the country of origin of the earliest colonists of that island, and the extent of the African influence. If they have had little exposure to English at home and if creole has been the only means of communication within their community, then they are likely to 'experience extreme difficulty in understanding the spoken English at school, and great anxiety in trying to cope' (p.40). Part of that difficulty stems from the perception that creole is not really a language, more of a 'broken English', a subject of ridicule. In the West Indies it is most certainly a whole language, as expressive and as core an aspect of African Caribbean culture as Irish is of Gaelic culture. Gurnah (1989) argues persuasively for the need to develop multilingual studies to support all black children in these situations. But he also sees white (working-class) children who speak various dialects of English experiencing the same ridicule. He is acutely conscious of the consequential lack of opportunity to exploit their own potential.

Bangladeshi parents' perceptions of an East London child and family consultation service

The research of Hillier and Rahman (1996) explored why there was such a low referral rate (7%) of Bangladeshi children to the only child psychiatric service available within the London borough of Tower Hamlets. Of the child population of the borough 45 per cent are Bangladeshi. In 1990, there were no Bangladeshi professionals or interpreters working in the team delivering the service. The authors mention 'language' as a possible source of difficulty for the parents and highlight the increase in referrals when the service recruited a Bangladeshi social worker, a Bangladeshi psychiatrist and an interpreter. A later study 'confirmed just how valuable such appointments were' (p.41). A Bangladeshi mother said: 'If I could have used my own language, I would have felt at ease … a Bangladeshi would have understood me … I could have expressed myself and the professional would have listened' (p.41). The authors comment: 'Few white professionals know even a basic greeting in Bengali' (p.42).

New Zealand's Maoris

Fulcher (1999) includes some interesting comments on the Maori perception of language in his paper on the cultural origins of Family Group Conferences. He refers to the Maori belief that 'language is a child's inheritance, bequeathed directly from the Celestial Sky Father and the Terrestrial Earth mother' (p.332). Fulcher's main point is that those who are organising and/or participating in the conference must realise how central the native language and the traditional manner of communication is to the child's identity. Professional jargon is difficult for any client group in any country; among Maori participants in the conference it can only reinforce confusion, undermine empowerment or generate hostility.

Child protection: Asian families in the Midlands

An emerging theme in Humphreys, Atkar and Baldwin's (1999) research was that Asian families experience discrimination in child protection work due to the inadequacy of the interpretative service. This was manifest in the lack of dependability; interpreters were quite often simply not available. Often they were male, which posed difficulties in an area of social work (i.e. child protection) in which women are perceived as central in the child's life. A male interpreter questioning an Asian mother on sexual abuse allegations is a risky prospect, for mother and interpreter alike. In home visits, fathers usually spoke English and therefore played a 'gatekeeping' role in which they marginalised the mother. In conferences and reviews, interpreters went beyond the boundaries of their role, to the extent of reinterpreting or modifying what the parent(s) was trying to say. Consequently, 'either the families' or the professional's views and questions were not being accurately relayed' (p.286). The authors reveal professionals' assumption that 'it is the family that needs the interpreter, rather than the worker needing an interpreter to assist him to understand each individual family member' (p.286).

Cultural minority parents of disabled children

Chamba and Ahmad (2000) base their article on a major survey of cultural minority parents of severely disabled children (Chamba *et al.*, 1999). As may be expected, many of the communication difficulties experienced by the groups already discussed greatly exacerbate the already formidable challenges which Chamba and Ahmad's parents face in caring for severely disabled children. They conclude that 'attainment of such basic rights as information about their disabled children and entitlements to welfare…remains impossible' (p.101).

Towards a greater focus on cultural sensitivity and insensitivity to language

All these contributions increase and enhance the knowledge base for health and social care workers. They reveal two main factors: first, that clients from linguistic minorities regard their language as significant and important in their daily lives; second, that there is enormous potential for discriminatory practice in the professionals' attitude and approach to languages other than their own. We are, however, limited in exploring these two factors, for a reason common to all the contributions: there is little information on context and there is insufficient detail about the (language) discrimination experienced. Each contribution (with the exception of Chamba and Ahmad's (2000) article) is in fact an extract from a larger discriminatory canvas which included professional responses to numerous other components of culture, and also racism and sexism. Nevertheless, the fact that so many health and social care authors are writing about discrimination revolving around minority languages is a most welcome development. The next three chapters will provide the opportunity to explore the above two factors in depth. They describe a research project carried out within a distinct cultural (and language) minority in Northern Ireland. The principal focus will be on clients' perceptions of culturally sensitive and culturally insensitive practice on the part of health and social care professionals. The respondents provide numerous examples of these opposing experiences, in such detail as to give ample opportunity for analysis and comment.

Summary and conclusion

Language has been crucial in the development of all cultures. Ó'Riagáin (1998) provides a useful definition of language conveying both its importance and its centrality. Numerous minorities in different parts of the world, living under differing systems and enduring various oppressions, have exploited the power of language to sustain their cultures and maintain their consciousness of a national and/or cultural identity. Less dramatically, cultural minorities currently experience various forms of cultural insensitivity due to their language difference.

Facial expression and gestures (referred to as paralinguistic and gestural features) which accompany language can be as important as the spoken word. They are often the principal means through which culturally sensitive or culturally insensitive practice is manifest.

Health and social care literature has traditionally given little attention to language. Languages other than English have been more generally regarded as inconveniences. The situation is changing however. Current statutory obligations to consider the linguistic heritage of clients and to ensure that they do not experience discrimination or disempowerment because of their language has compelled many writers to address the issue more realistically. There is now a substantial literature which recognises the importance of language and the discriminatory potential in professionals' response to languages. This chapter has looked at numerous examples of cultural minorities in different locations experiencing discrimination and insensitivity because of their language. Such examples enhance cultural awareness generally and contribute to cultural competence training for work with linguistic minorities in particular.

Part III

The Way Forward

CHAPTER II

Cultural Sensitivity
and Cultural Insensitivity

Introduction

This chapter describes recent research within an Irish-speaking community. The principal objective of the research is to explore the respondents' perceptions of culturally sensitive and culturally insensitive practice by health and social care professionals. The research also explores the respondents' views on culture generally. They were asked: what did culture mean to them and what were the most important components of their culture? As expected, a substantial majority regarded language as the most important. The Irish-speaking community is unique in many respects. The chapter includes a brief description of its origins and its aspirations. It highlights significant milestones in the community's development and some of the many obstacles it had to overcome. The underlying assumption in this research is that people who have to surmount formidable odds for the right to express and promote their culture are likely to be more perceptive and sensitive on various aspects of culture and on the attitude and approach of health and social care professionals towards their culture.

The chapter begins on a recent important occasion in Irish history, the signing of the 1998 Good Friday Agreement. It summarises the agreement's commitment to promoting Irish language and culture. It describes the research undertaken, explains the rationale of the questions asked and outlines the method of contact with respondents. The findings of the research will be presented in this chapter with analysis and commentary in the next.

An historic agreement

On Good Friday in April 1998 in Belfast, an agreement was made between the representatives of opposing political and paramilitary forces throughout Ireland (NI Government 1998). The agreement acknowledged the cultural diversity of Northern Ireland, and stated that all participants 'recognise the importance of respect, understanding and tolerance in relation to linguistic diversity'. It then spelt out its commitment to the support and promotion of the Irish language in particular. In the context of twentieth-century political, social and educational life in Northern Ireland, this represented a significant achievement on the part of those at the centre of a Gaelic cultural revival. In the early part of the twentieth century, for example, government ministers, including Prime Minister Craigavon, were so overtly hostile to Irish that it was banned from infant classes and all financial assistance towards its promotion ceased. As many governments discover, however, hostility and suppression of culture is usually counterproductive.

Education: the key to a cultural revival

In 1968, the parents of five families involved in the promotion of Irish purchased some land in west Belfast and built their own homes. A short time later they renovated a prefabricated building on adjoining land and organised a primary school in which their children were taught entirely through the medium of the Irish language. The parents also committed themselves to becoming fluent speakers of Irish and ensuring that their children would be reared in an Irish-speaking environment. The origins of this development lay in numerous factors. First, the group was representative of a much larger population who had long before articulated a Gaelic cultural identity to which they aspired, central to which was the Irish language. Second, they felt culturally isolated in an existing and dominant British culture (i.e. English-speaking communities, television, radio, press, English-speaking schools and employment, etc.). Third, the parents realised that full-time, Irish-speaking education was the key to a more rapid revival and development of their Gaelic culture and the moulding of a Gaelic cultural identity. Irish speaking would become the norm for both children and parents in this small Irish-speaking community; parents and children would learn from each other and parents would gain support and encouragement from other parents and from the teachers of their children.

Expansion of education through the medium of Irish

Nine children were enrolled in the first school (Bunscoil Ghaelach Bhéal Feirste) in 1971, to be taught by one teacher. In 1984, 162 children were enrolled. During that same period, the number of teachers increased from one to twelve and the original five families were joined by many more. The rate of increase in enrolment dramatically accelerated when the parents and their advisers and supporters concentrated their efforts on nursery education. The nurseries then became the principal source of enrolment for primary education. Today there are over 500 children attending that first school and more than 100 attending its satellite nursery (Bunscoil Na fuiscoige), which originally adjoined the primary school but has since had to move to larger premises. Similar enterprises occurred in other parts of the city. There are now five Irish-speaking primary schools in Belfast. With the expansion of primary education, eventually there had to be a corresponding introduction of secondary education. Meanscoile Feirste, the first secondary school, now has over 250 pupils. Irish-speaking primary and secondary schools are also operating in the city of Derry and the towns of Newry, Coalisland and Maghera. Perhaps the most significant expansion lies in the growth of nursery education. There are now more than 40 Irish-speaking nurseries throughout Northern Ireland, a guaranteed supply for the primary education to follow.

During this period, the Ministry of Education's attitude changed significantly. Having declared the proposed initiative illegal in 1967, it registered the first school An Bhunscoil Ghaelach as an independent school in 1976. In September 1978, a school inspector visited and gave a favourable report on its achievements. In April 1984, it was recognised as a grant-aided school – a major breakthrough, meaning 100 per cent financial support for running costs and staff salaries and 85 per cent grant for capital expenditure. At the time of writing, seven primary and one secondary school currently receive 100 per cent grant aid for recurrent expenditure. Four other primary schools and one secondary school have been granted independent status (DENI 1998). Additionally, there are now over 70 preschool playgroup (naíscoil) facilities throughout Northern Ireland. Clearly then, the enterprise begun by the young parents in 1968 has succeeded.

Consolidating and further expansion

Now that the foundations had been laid, the parents and their supporters would reach out to their community at large and attempt to consolidate their achievement. They would, in effect, lock into and have a significant influence on the Gaelic revival throughout the island of Ireland. There was much networking to do, establishing links with the traditional Gaeltacht (Irish-speaking) communities in Ireland. They also established links with minority language groups in Scotland, Wales and Europe, hosting visits and seminars from interested parties (Ó Riagáin 1998). Consolidation in Ireland concentrated on gaining support from influential people and institutions and actively facilitating the spread of Irish language learning. *Lá*, a weekly Irish newspaper (it means 'day') was established in 1984. A pressure group, *Meán*, was formed, with the specific aim of getting radio and television companies to provide facilities for promoting Irish. Their efforts would culminate in the Irish government's financing of the high-tech revolutionary new Irish television station, Telifis na Gaeltacht. In the spring of 2000, the Irish Language movement went online, (www.pobal.org). In September 2000, it hosted the first international conference, 'Promoting Diversity: Building our New Society'.

Reliable respondents or fanatical anti-Brits

It is reasonable to assume that the Irish-speaking community has an acute sense of the meaning of culture and when the concept is mentioned, discussed or defined it is likely to have greater resonance within that community than elsewhere. Similarly, with terms such as cultural awareness, cultural sensitivity and cultural insensitivity, a community which has surmounted so many obstacles in re-establishing and reasserting its cultural identity is likely to have a more acute sense of the meaning of these terms. Opposing assumptions, however, may be legitimately expressed about this whole development: for example (a) that such commitment and sacrifice constitutes some kind of cultural fanaticism and one of the inevitable consequences must be an insularity and intolerance towards the culture of others; (b) that the whole enterprise was nothing more than an expression of traditional Irish antipathy towards the British. Could it be, for example, merely a coincidence that the rapid development of the Irish-speaking movement took place during the significant increase in British military activity (in response to increased IRA activity) on the streets of west Belfast? The validity or otherwise of these assumptions, positive and negative, can be put to the test through research.

Principal objective and methodology

Statutory obligation

The main objective of the research was to explore the feelings and perceptions of the Irish-speaking community on the issue of cultural sensitivity and cultural insensitivity within the context of health and social care services. In effect, one is also asking: how have health and social care services and the numerous professional groups they employ responded to the rapid growth and establishment of Irish-speaking families and schools in the localities which they serve?

In an age of active, assertive consumerism, it seemed timely and appropriate that the recipients of the service should be given an opportunity to enlighten on this central question. The development of the Irish-speaking community obviously had implications for care professionals, but particularly for family and childcare professionals, constantly reminded of their statutory duty to promote the cultural identity of parents and children (The Children [Northern Ireland] Order 1995, s.6(3)(c)).

Areas of exploration

This core objective was pursued through the use of face-to-face structured interviews in which two questionnaires were completed. Both questionnaires asked some basic data questions about age, employment, whether or not one spoke Irish or was learning Irish, whether or not one had children attending Irish-speaking schools. One questionnaire explored respondents' understanding of culture and related terms. Respondents were invited to answer numerous questions grouped within the following categories:

1. culture and its most important components (e.g. religion, language, child rearing, etc.)

2. cultural identity and its most important expression

3. maintaining and consolidating one's culture

4. attitudes to other cultures (e.g. do you equally respect all cultures and if not why not?)

5. cultural sensitivity (e.g. what is the most important form of cultural sensitivity for you personally, is it respect for your religion, or your language, or your values, or your child rearing, etc?)

6. cultural insensitivity (e.g. what is the most common form of cultural insensitivity which you encounter?).

The other questionnaire explored the feelings and perceptions of respondents as they engaged with health and social care professionals; these included reception staff, GPs, psychologists, psychiatrists, social workers, paediatricians, health visitors, speech therapists, occupational therapists, teachers in special schools, opticians, community nurses, general nurses, nurses in accident and emergency (A&E), consultants, surgeons, chemists, dentists. The questionnaire initially sought to establish whether or not respondents (or their family members) spoke Irish or were learning Irish; the reasons why the Irish language was important to them, and whether or not they regarded the Irish language as the most important, or one of the most important aspects of their culture. Thereafter, it was basically divided into two parts, one concentrating upon their experiences of cultural sensitivity on the part of professionals, and another upon their experiences of cultural insensitivity. They were given the opportunity to recount experiences of both, then asked about the impact of these (good and bad) experiences and how such impacts influenced their judgements on the quality of services overall.

Pilot study

The larger questionnaire (probing perceptions and understanding of one's culture and culture generally, cultural sensitivity and insensitivity and one's attitude to other cultures) was subject to substantial pilot testing. It was in fact available on the internet long before the research took place and also attracted significant attention within the workplace. Minor modifications were made to both questionnaires on the basis of returns and they have subsequently been used for training purposes.

Making contact with respondents

The Irish-speaking community was contacted chiefly through their schools. The author approached all the principals of the schools and discussed the research with each of them. He provided circulars in English and Irish advertising the research and seeking parents' co-operation. The principals distributed these to all the children. Not all the children delivered them to their parents (nor were they expected to) which was why the author also advertised in the local English and Irish-speaking press. In initial conversations with the respondents, the point was reiterated many times: that the research would provide an opportunity for any respondent to give examples of culturally sensitive and insensitive practice. Logically of course, one assumes that if parents wish to highlight the experience of cultural sensitivity, they must at least have a clear notion of the opposite kind of experience, cultural insensitivity. Conversely, if parents wish to highlight examples of cultural insensitivity on the part of professionals, they must at least have a clear notion of cultural sensitivity. The concern about a potential exploitation of the research (i.e. a condemnation of British health and social services' treatment of the Irish-speaking community) proved to be unfounded. The majority of respondents were actually just as keen to provide examples of cultural sensitivity, which they would describe in great detail, as inclined to recall cultural insensitivity, which many of them did, but some with reluctance.

The respondents

Forty-eight adults contacted the author in response to the advertised circular and were interviewed. These respondents therefore constituted a self-selected group. Very little is said in current health, social care and social sciences research literature about respondent self-selection (e.g. Fuller and Petch 1995; May 1993; Sapsford and Abbott 1992). An obvious first question is whether or not such a group would be credibly representative of the targeted population (the sampling frame), that is the Irish-speaking population in Northern Ireland. They were representative in accordance with the principal criteria stated in the advertisements and circulars: that they or any of their partners or children could speak Irish or were learning Irish; that they or their immediate family members had contact with any health and social care personnel. Forty-four of the respondents had children. The total number of children was 104. The number of children attending Irish-speaking schools or play groups was 73. Whatever the merits or disadvantages of self-selection, the ethical principle of having no control over who was going to contact me and volunteer themselves for interview was strictly adhered to. Contrary to expectations, there was a remarkable diversity of responses, in terms of:

- geographical location: it was a most even distribution throughout Northern Ireland and included respondents from every part of every county, rather than clusters of respondents from the largest concentration of Irish speakers in West Belfast

- social class: it included unemployed people, students, managers, teachers, community workers, journalists, factory workers, civil servants, social workers (field and residential), shop assistants,

full-time family carers of elderly parents, project workers and
parents caring for their children full time

- age: the oldest respondent was 63, the youngest 18

- gender balance: the 48 respondents consisted of 32 women
  (average age 35) and 16 men (average age 41). This is a much more
  balanced gender ratio than that commonly found in health and
  social services related research, in which women constitute the
  overwhelming majority of respondents or, indeed, are often the
  only respondents (O'Hagan and Dillenburger 1995).

Duration and location of interviews

The interviews on average lasted between one and a half and two hours. They
were carried out in locations decided by the respondents. The majority of
interviews took place in their homes; the minority in a variety of locations
such as workplaces, schools, community halls, the researcher's office (some
specifically requested that they came to my office). All the interviews were
taped and transcribed in their entirety.

Confidentiality and security

All the respondents appeared to be enthusiastic about the research, but many
were also nervous. This was particularly the case when respondents lived in
isolation, in areas where no other families or individuals spoke Irish or, worse,
where there was open hostility directed against the language and those who
spoke it. Respondents therefore often answered key questions reluctantly and
hesitantly, and continually sought assurance about the confidentiality of their
replies. Their apprehensions were understandable. The harsh reality is that
there are grave risks in speaking Irish in many parts of Northern Ireland, or in
identifying oneself as an Irish speaker. One particular family crystallised this
concern more than anyone else. They wanted to know precisely how they
were going to be referred to in the research. They were conscious of the fact
that their family had numerous conspicuous features (location, community,
jobs, etc.) and that the slightest reference to any of these features could easily
identify them. The thought that I may unwittingly reveal the whereabouts and
identities of an Irish-speaking family who might then experience a sectarian
attack weighed very heavily upon me. Great care has been taken in
anonymising the respondents in this research.

Table 11.1 Respondents' understanding of culture

	The meaning of culture (What does culture mean to you?)	Most important aspect(s) of culture	Why is it (are they) the most important aspect(s) of culture
1.	A way of life. It encompasses everything.	Irish-speaking education.How we rear our children.Instilling values in our children.	It's what we believe is right (i.e. education through the medium of Irish). And it's what we're involved in.
2.	Language, sport, leisure.Something that links us within our community.	The values our culture gives us. The thought processes and beliefs within our culture.	These things make me feel part of a wider community; make me feel included, safe and supported.
3.	It's hard to define. It's something that you feel you belong with; that you identify very strongly with. You say, 'Yes that is what I am and that's what I belong to. I feel at home here.'	Language.My system of beliefs.Irish education.The environment in which our children are brought up.Family values.	They just make you aware of your culture; they're the way you express your culture; and the way you bring up your own children. They're the things that give your children an awareness of their culture.
4.	Identity, national identity; my Irish culture; which is a lot of things; day-to-day living to a great extent; the music; the language; something that the kids do; culture is something that is alive and living.	All aspects are important. There's an equality in them, and you can't separate them. It comes as one and that's what makes it.	Not applicable.
5.	Way of life. The way I live my life. It embraces my religious beliefs and my working life, my values, my past times, my married life and the way I rear my children.	My language; the way I was brought up; my relationships within my family. All our family speak Irish and that's something that unites us.	It's about the way I view my life and how I relate to people. Irish is the principal means by which I communicate with people.
6.	It's your identity and where you're from and who you are.	That you have cultured values, and that you recognise your own identity, and that you respect other cultures because you know about your own culture. When you know who you are, then you can respect others. I think values are the most important thing in culture.	You derive your respect for other people from the values your culture has given you. You also derive your respect for the environment from your culture. It's also something about the way you view and relate to the land. When you speak Irish, you get a key into your own culture that you wouldn't get otherwise. And it's almost impossible to explain.

Perceptions of culture and its most important aspects

The first three questions considered the meaning of culture, the most important component of one's culture and why that particular component(s) is regarded as the most important. Table 11.1 sets out some sample unedited replies.

Initial findings

It was predictable that many respondents, 34 (71%), would regard language (Irish) as an important or most important aspect of culture, but perhaps less predictable was the importance attributed by so many to values and child rearing. Of the respondents, 29 (60%) stated (or strongly implied) that values were an important component of culture and 21 (41.6%) included (or strongly implied) child rearing. There was a marked similarity in the ratio of male–female inclusions of values (62.5% and 59% respectively) and child rearing (43% equally). This emphasis upon values and child rearing is interesting. Few of the definitions of culture in current literature of the care professionals mention them, unlike anthropologists Ruth Benedict and Margaret Mead (see Chapter 3) who made values and child rearing the core aspects of culture. One phrase that does repeatedly appear in current and past definitions of culture is 'way of life', mentioned or strongly implied in this research by 24 (50%) respondents. Perhaps most surprising is that 10 (21%) respondents mentioned Irish sport as an aspect of their culture. One respondent regarded sport as the core component in her and her family's expression of culture.

Learning Irish, but with other things in mind

The respondents were asked how and why it was important for them or their family members to be speaking or learning to speak Irish. Their responses to this question were less politically oriented than anticipated, and much more self-interested and pragmatic: 27 (56%) said that it was an expression of their culture or identity, or cultural identity, but 15 (31%) respondents said that they wanted their children to be bilingual, as this would benefit them in various ways, such as educationally, travelling, learning a third language, etc. Although 'Irish-speaking schools' were not mentioned in this question, five parents said that the schools offered good or excellent education, which was reason enough (in addition to learning Irish) for sending their children to them. Three of these parents considered this choice very carefully, visiting and monitoring the school's results before making a final decision. One said: 'I was very impressed by those teachers, and the relationship they had with their children. I felt there was a very friendly ethos in there.' Another said: 'It wasn't just all that Irishness, it was also the community spirit that attracted me, the friendliness and the drive, and the enthusiasm.'

Only one parent gave an overtly political response to the question of how important learning Irish was: 'For me it's very much part of a resistance, a cultural resistance, to feeling marginalised, treated as second class. I mean it's very much politically motivated.' However, this is also one of the parents who carefully considered other aspects of the school's life and performance before enrolling the children. The lack of political motivation in the responses overall is similar to the findings of Maguire (1986) and refutes the suggestion that the establishment of an Irish-speaking community was motivated by anti-British sentiment (Table 11.2).

Table 11. 2 Summary of initial results	
	Respondents N = 48
Culture as a 'way of life'	24 (50%)
Language as an important or most important component of culture	34 (71%)
'Values' as important or most important component of culture	29 (60%)
Child rearing as important or most important component of culture	21 (42%)
Sport as important or most important component of culture	10 (21%)
Reasons for learning Irish include wanting children to be bilingual	15 (31%)

Frequency of contact with health and social services professionals

All respondents had contact with health and social care professionals. No attempt was made to elicit precisely how many contacts each respondent had with each professional, on the grounds that it would probably have been unacceptably intrusive and more susceptible to inaccuracies. Rather, the respondents were asked to recall merely the categories of professionals they had had contact with during the past three years, and the average frequency of contact with all the professionals as a whole. The frequency of the cumulative contacts recalled varied substantially from 2 to 200 per year (a number of families had severely disabled members, necessitating numerous contacts with a variety of professionals). The average number of contacts with health and

Table 11. 3 Recalling contacts with different health and social care professionals	
Identified professionals	Number of respondents recalling contacts with these professionals: N = 48
Reception staff	48
GPs	48
Chemists	43
Nurses	42
Dentists	36
Consultants	33
Health visitors	28
Opticians	21
Paediatricians	19
Midwives	20
Surgeons	16
Speech therapists	11
Nursery teachers	10
Social workers	7
Physiotherapists	6
Occupational therapists	6
Psychiatrists	4
Psychologists	2
Special needs teachers	4
Chiropodists	1

social care professionals was 21 per year. Contacts with certain high profile professionals were easily recalled: for example, all respondents (48 = 100%) recalled themselves or their immediate family members having contacts with their GPs and with the reception staff of GP surgeries, clinics and hospitals. A comprehensive list of professionals was recited to each respondent to facilitate recall. The results are seen in Table 11.3.

Definitions of 'cultural sensitivity' and 'cultural insensitivity'

The respondents were asked to recall professionals' culturally sensitive and culturally insensitive practice. Here are the definitions of cultural sensitivity and cultural insensitivity which were provided prior to these questions:

> *Cultural sensitivity* is action or words which are quite clearly seen and felt to be respectful to someone's culture. The culturally sensitive person is acutely aware of the fact that culture and cultural identity are highly significant and important in the lives of many people.

> *Cultural insensitivity* is action or words which are disrespectful to someone's culture, and which usually cause offence to the person. The culturally insensitive person may be aware or unaware of the offence he or she is causing.

Each respondent was invited to consider these definitions for as long as required and if they were unsatisfactory in any way, to make whatever changes he or she wished. No changes were requested. Presumably this was because each definition was general enough to be easily applied to their recall of culturally sensitive and culturally insensitive experiences. The definitions were continually referred to during subsequent interviews.

Sensitive professionals or insensitive agencies

The respondents were initially asked whether they observed any differences among agencies in the degree of cultural sensitivity or insensitivity. This question was intended to seek out generalised perceptions of health and social services agencies as a whole. Of the respondents 28 said there were noticeable differences. When asked to identify culturally sensitive and culturally insensitive agencies, many of them made a clear distinction between individual professionals working for those agencies and the agencies themselves. In other words, if a GP was culturally sensitive this did not mean that their large busy practice, including receptionists, nurses, health visitors and social workers, was equally culturally sensitive. Having described one speech therapist's cultural insensitivity, a respondent proceeded to describe the great cultural sensitivity of two other speech therapists and stressed: 'It's the individual ... not the agency or the statutory bodies.'

Extent of cultural sensitivity and cultural insensitivity

Memory recall of numbers of occurrences is always problematic in this kind of research, and asking the respondents to recall culturally sensitive and culturally insensitive practice elicited responses which were not entirely consistent.

Table 11.4 Recalling culturally sensitive and culturally insensitive experiences			
Identified professionals	Number of respondents recalling contacts with these professionals (N = 48)	Number of respondents recalling culturally sensitive practice (N = 48)	Number of respondents recalling culturally insensitive practice (N = 48)
Reception staff	48	3	14
GPs	48	21	8
Chemists	43	0	4
Nurses	42	2	6
Dentists	36	5	0
Consultants	33	4	7
Health visitors	28	3	9
Opticians	21	1	2
Paediatricians	19	1	1
Midwives	20	2	5
Surgeons	16	0	0
Speech therapists	11	2	4
Nursery teachers	10	0	2
Social workers	7	1	1
Physiotherapists	6	1	0
Occupational therapists	6	3	0
Psychiatrists	4	0	0
Psychologists	2	1	0
Special needs teachers	2	1	1
Chiropodists	1	0	0
Total		51	64

But the responses overall do say something about the respondents' perceptions and memories of contacts with professionals generally. There are clearly statistically significant differences in the recall of different professionals' culturally sensitive and insensitive practices, and for some agencies that may be a matter of concern (Table 11.4).

The relatively high number of recalls of GPs being culturally sensitive (21 = 44%) may be explained by the fact that so many of them are community based and may share the same cultural heritage as that of the respondents.

Frequency of culturally sensitive and culturally insensitive actions recalled

Many of the respondents recalled more than one occasion when a professional(s) was culturally sensitive and/or culturally insensitive. Six respondents said they could not recall any occasions of either. The total number of culturally sensitive interactions recalled in response to the questions was 51, and culturally insensitive interactions 64. Thirteen respondents (5 men, 8 women) said they could not recall any professional being culturally sensitive (perceptively redefined by one respondent as 'reaching out to me culturally'); 10 respondents (8 women, 2 men) said they could not recall any professional being culturally insensitive. This means that the 51 occasions of cultural sensitivity were recalled by 35 respondents (48–13), and that the 64 occasions of culturally insensitive interactions were recalled by 38 respondents (48–10) (Table 15.5).

Table 11.5 Recalling culturally sensitive and insensitive practice	
Respondents	**(N = 48)**
Recalling professionals being culturally *sensitive*	35
Recalling professionals being culturally *insensitive*	38
Who could not recall professionals being culturally *sensitive*	13
Who could not recall professionals being culturally *insensitive*	10
Who could not recall professionals being culturally *sensitive* or *insensitive*	6

The nature and type of cultural sensitivity and insensitivity which occurred

A substantial number of respondents (28 = 58%) experienced cultural sensitivity and cultural insensitivity principally through the professionals' responses to their language, to their Irish names in particular. But as each respondent described occurrences of cultural sensitivity and cultural insensitivity, and the impact which either had upon them, it became obvious that much more than language was involved. There was substantial variation in:

- the contexts in which either occurred
- the impact which either had
- the interpretations initially and retrospectively given to them.

Some form of prioritisation/categorisation had to be imposed upon the enormous amount of recorded material which the respondents provided. As with child abuse, bullying and domestic violence, there are different types and degrees of cultural sensitivity and cultural insensitivity. A follow-up question, 'What was the impact of the cultural sensitivity or cultural insensitivity which you have described?' helped to determine nature and degree. The following examples therefore of 'low', 'medium' and 'high' culturally sensitive and culturally insensitive actions are based primarily on the respondent's reply to that follow-up question.

Cultural sensitivity

Actions constituting 'low' cultural sensitivity

Any attempt by the professional(s) to get the Irish names of respondents right was welcomed by the respondents. On the face of it, this may not seem to require too much effort on the part of the professional, and while the impact was generally of a pleasant nature, it was seldom judged strong enough to warrant anything more than 'low' or 'mild' classification. Table 11.6 gives a random selection of descriptions of 'low' cultural sensitivity and the impact they had.

The principal theme here is unmistakably 'effort'. Respondents very much appreciate effort and no less than 29 out of the 48 described the efforts of professionals as a source of pleasure and/or gratitude, across the three levels of cultural sensitivity. The greater and more sustained the effort throughout the contact, the greater the appreciation. There is no expectation whatsoever on the part of the respondents that all professionals can or should speak Irish. But

Table 11.6 'Low' cultural sensitivity

'Low' cultural sensitivity	Impact
My GP makes a genuine effort to get our names right.	I welcome that.
The speech therapist made an effort to learn Irish words through the child.	You automatically warm to her.
The nurses tried their best to pronounce our names properly.	It gives you a good opinion of them.
A receptionist really struggled with ————-'s name. She kept trying, and eventually got it right. She was really pleased.	A very positive impact. It makes you feel good about the service.
Our dentist makes no fuss at all about our names. He just treats us like he treats everybody else. He respects you as a person. There's no cultural observation to be made.	It makes me extremely comfortable to be in that surgery, and to have my children examined.

there is a basic requirement for professionals at least to attempt to get someone's name right. Should they have any knowledge of Irish whatsoever, that's much better. A father put it like this:

> I don't want to be unrealistic about this. I mean when we invite people to address us or the children whether they be a medical person or DHSS, or a magician, or whatever, I would say to them, 'Look. We're an Irish-speaking school, what can you do for us?' And it's amazing what that triggers off ... It's really encouraging to know how many of those people tried to put in a bit of Irish, even the magician!

The last example in Table 11.6 is somewhat different from the norm. The respondent prefaced her example of cultural sensitivity by saying that the dentist was Asian and that he had no trouble with the name. There were only two other examples in which respondents similarly described culturally sensitive experience in terms of no fuss being made of the name. As we shall see, the context in one of these was very different, and the impact greater, thereby necessitating a different classification. Seven respondents described contact with doctors and dentists from countries outside the UK. Every one of them was regarded as culturally sensitive. No one recalled cultural insensitivity on the part of any of those seven professionals.

Actions constituting 'medium' cultural sensitivity

The impact of 'medium' cultural sensitivity is obviously greater than 'low' cultural sensitivity. Often it involves parents and children, and the predominantly pleasant feelings are shared by both. More importantly, the professional is observed making some favourable comment about the Irish language and lavishing praise on the children for being able to speak it. In other instances, the service being provided is enhanced through cultural sensitivity, and invariably facilitates a better working relationship and partnership (Table 11.7).

We can see from Table 11.7 that the impact is often as significant as the action, and sometimes more so. A GP merely converses in Irish with the children, asking them about their Irish-speaking school. But it is the mother who correctly interprets this more significantly than it first appears: 'It makes them feel that wee bit special. Like as if the language was their own wee thing.' The GP is in effect inducing pride, adding to their self-esteem, consolidating their sense of culture and identity, and causing many of the same pleasant feelings within the mother herself.

The midwife/antenatal case is interesting. The respondent (Mrs X) is one of the three who, when asked to recall cultural sensitivity, described situations in which professionals made no fuss about their names. The first of those three respondents is mentioned in Table 11.6 on 'low' sensitivity; but Mrs X's experience appears above under 'medium' sensitivity, because of the different contexts in which the cultural sensitivity occurred. The midwife involved may be puzzled to learn that her mere passive act of making no fuss about someone's name constituted a ('medium') culturally sensitive action (in a culturally insensitive context), bringing much relief and contentment to the respondent. It also brought the respondent back to antenatal classes, which she had abandoned because of that insensitivity from other staff.

Actions constituting 'high' cultural sensitivity

'High' cultural sensitivity actions contain some distinct and unrelated features. One of these is the greater depth of the underlying communication between the professional and child and/or parent. Another is that of the professionals openly challenging the culturally insensitive practice of colleagues (Table 11.8).

Each of the examples in Table 11.8 is interesting in its own right, but probably the third one, involving the psychologist, is the most revealing. For-

Table 11.7 'Medium' cultural sensitivity

'Medium' cultural sensitivity	Impact
Two speech therapists came to examine our child. They didn't know any Irish. But when they heard ———- speaking it, they said it was a lovely language. They asked the child to help them to learn it, to tell them what it meant in English. They kept praising him for speaking Irish and praising Irish itself.	Our perceptions were very positive. There was a much better relationship, more trust. [our child] felt great about them.
The hospital consultant spoke to my kids in Irish and conversed with them about their schools.	It's very welcome because it's good for the kids. It makes me proud of them. For them to be seeing important people like doctors learning Irish ... then it's not just a school thing. There's a real language out there.
The GP talks to the kids in Irish, and asks them how they're getting on at school.	The kids feel good. It makes them feel that wee bit special. Like it was as if the language was their own wee thing.
My child was screaming in A&E. She had had a bad fall. A nurse came over. She saw the [Irish school] badge on her blazer. She started speaking to her in Irish. She showed her these wee picture cards and asked to say them in Irish. She had her calmed down in seconds.	It was nice to think somebody could speak to her in Irish. It was reassuring ... you know somebody you know belonged to you.
I had had a tough time at the hospital with nurses and midwives making a big fuss about my name. Then in the antenatal class I went to, this midwife did the opposite; she made no comment at all about my name, and she had no bother saying it.	It was a good experience ... a relief.
I was suffering mentally and the nurse and the occupational therapist made an effort to speak to me in Irish.	We had great fun, and it was nice just feeling close to people. It really helped too. I was in hospital for the first time, I felt so isolated when I went in. The nurse and OT eased the pain. It was sensitive to my culture and identity.

midable obstacles were placed in the way of the Irish-speaking community in its early development, particularly by the Department of Education. An educational psychologist therefore, may expect some scepticism from the Irish-speaking parents generally. It appears as though this educational psy-

Table 11.8 'High' cultural sensitivity

'High' cultural sensitivity	Impact
The health visitor was carrying out developmental tests. She didn't know any Irish. My son kept answering in Irish. But the HV just kept praising him. Each time he answered, she looked over at me as if asking me to confirm he had given the right answer. She wanted me to nod or shake my head, and she'd praise him all the time.	The relationship blossomed from then. It was like a second home to me. I was so relaxed. I trusted her fully.
The GP and my son (11) got immersed in this really in-depth discussion about some obscure Irish writer they both knew about. The same GP offered to help [my son] with his Irish.	I thought this was all a bit over the top, but you could see how [my son] was loving it. It put him absolutely at ease. That was the main thing.
The educational psychologist was carrying out statementing (i.e. assessment) on our disabled child. He was very knowledgeable of Irish culture and realised immediately that 'Irish' was not the only reason we were wanted to send [our child] to an Irish school. He took account of all our views. In the end however, he advised us that the Irish school would not be the best facility for [our child].	This was not what we wanted to hear. But we trusted him and felt fully supported by him. We accepted his recommendations.
A Polish doctor objected to all the fuss and resentment the nurses and midwives were making about my Irish name. He insisted that staff should call me by that name. He did so himself, and said that it was a lovely name.	Extremely grateful, and very much at ease with this doctor.
A GP treating my daughter said: 'I will tell you what I would like you to do, and perhaps you would explain to your daughter in Irish.'	It made me feel comfortable with the service; gave me confidence in the service and treatment. The whole attitude was right. It valued my daughter, me, and our language.

chologist demonstrated skill, patience, empathy and the highest level of cultural sensitivity. The latter is, in the parent's opinion, the most significant factor in their ability to accept the validity of the recommendation he made – a recommendation which they never really wanted to hear.

The confronting and challenging of culturally insensitive behaviour by a doctor is also interesting. A more extended account of that same respondent's testimony will clarify precisely what was being done to her, and the significance of the doctor's intervention.

> I sat in outpatients and I was called into the antenatal unit for examinations, and the nurse came in ... I was sitting down in front of several parents and this nurse came in and she said '————— whatever your name is supposed to be ... you're next.' And I got a wee bit embarrassed ... And she said, 'Well, what's this name?' I said to her, 'If you just call me Barry, if it's a problem.' So then I went into a room and that was fair enough and it was left at that. And my name was written down as Barry.

> So about 10 minutes later a doctor came, and he was obviously from Eastern Europe, I think he told me Poland. He said, 'Who is the next person ...?' The door was ajar and I could hear this conversation, and the nurse who had been speaking to me said, 'Well that woman is going to be called Miss Barry ... because we can't ... that's her name in Irish, and we can't say it ....'

> And the doctor said, 'Well, why can't we call her name in Irish?' And the nurse said, 'Well, none of us can pronounce it.' And he said, 'Have we tried, I mean ... she's married and ...' He was quite determined about it.

> So I was called in, and he asked me my name, and he said that was a lovely name, and he made me feel at ease, and that was it. He examined me and everything was fine.

> Then the midwife had to come in to do the final check. She was the third woman I met and she asked me why I insisted in having my name in Gaelic, and I said my husband's name is in Gaelic and I'm married to him, and that's why my name is in Gaelic.

> I kept saying to myself: how am I going to get rid of all this hassle, I mean ... is there such a big deal?

> So now, to be honest with you, when I phone ————— hospital, I give them my medical number, I don't mention my name, I just say: my number is ...

Cultural insensitivity

That last case is typical of many which revealed instances of cultural insensitivity. Often, these too revolve around the professional's attitude to spoken Irish and Irish names in particular; but the contexts in which the insensitivity occurs can greatly magnify its seriousness and its impact. As we move from 'low' cultural insensitivity through to 'high' insensitivity, more ominous professional actions are exposed. These may well stem initially from a negative response to Irish, but they are manifest within a context that has other important components for the respondent, for example, deciding what is best for one's child, worrying over a sick child, trying to maintain one's family and child-rearing values.s

Table 11.9 'Low' cultural insensitivity	
'Low' cultural insensitivity	**Impact**
Receptionist and chemists don't make any attempt to get the children's names right. You always have to be telling them the name, and writing it down for them. But it doesn't make any difference. You go back again and again, and you go through exactly the same.	It's not good enough.
I went to casualty because I burnt my fingers. The nurse asked my name and then reacted amazingly. She was frightened, and palpitating, hyperventilating. All apparently because of my Irish name.	All I wanted was my fingers dressed. I'm not into cultural crises. I think it put the onus on me to reassure her, instead of the other way round. She should have been reassuring me about my fingers.
The receptionist at the optician told me they couldn't register ———'s name because the computer couldn't take it. They said they had to have the English of her name. I told them there wasn't any English for it.	You could feel the edge, the abruptness in their manner.
A paediatrician showed no understanding or sensitivity towards our wish to have our children assessed by health staff who could accept that our children's first language is Irish.	You become accustomed to cultural insensitivity. It doesn't lessen the service you get from all these professionals, but it makes you less comfortable in the situation.
A lot of professionals get the name wrong again and again. They don't really try. I used to say to them … but you feel a bit sort of … you know, 'you're a complainer'.	You can often sound like a complainer if you push the issue too far. If people make an effort, that's enough for me.

Actions constituting 'low' cultural insensitivity

We have seen how professionals making efforts to get one's name right were greatly appreciated by respondents, and constituted 'low' sensitivity. Conversely, there were many examples of professionals making no effort, and sometimes seemingly determined to demonstrate that they had no intention of trying to get the name right (Table 11.9).

Table 11.9 does not indicate serious instances of cultural insensitivity, but they generate a fair degree of discomfort and irritability. They clearly indicate some degree of entrenchment in a particular kind of insensitivity. The most serious impact is undoubtedly that of the final respondent: the professionals' repetitive ignoring of his child's basic right to be called her proper name induces some kind of guilt complex in him. After repeated attempts to get them to say/write the name correctly, he gives up and blames himself.

Table 11.10 'Medium' cultural insensitivity	
'Medium' cultural insensitivity	**Impact**
When our child was doing the speech test, the speech therapist insisted that she reply in English. She wouldn't move on until the child said it in English. She made such a big deal of it. (Note: there were four similar cases.)	I wondered how insensitive and hurtful she would have been if I had not been there. I think she would have demolished the child.
Hospital receptionists wanted to translate our names into English on their forms and records. I pleaded with them not to, and they assured me they wouldn't. But when I went back to the hospital, they had.	I was not a happy camper!
An optician visiting the school asked my child to read letters. The letter 'v' was there. There's no 'v' in the Irish language. My child didn't know what the letter was. He kept asking her.	That struck me as being totally insensitive and totally stupid as well.
A health visitor and her student colleague were doing an assessment of ———- in our home. They resented our child speaking Irish. One said: 'I don't know what they're saying, but they're saying it in Irish.'	I just think it's a poor service.
I was in hospital. I met a young student doctor. She spoke Irish. We both enjoyed speaking Irish to each other. When she came round with the consultant however, and I spoke to her in Irish, she didn't respond. I could see from the expression on her face that she didn't like me speaking Irish when the consultant was there.	I felt offended, slightly.

Actions constituting 'medium' cultural insensitivity

There is no overall dominant theme in the 15 recalls of incidents of 'medium' cultural insensitivity (Table 11.10). There appears to be more hurt and some indication of the respondents perceptively realising the full implications of the insensitivity.

In Table 11.10 there is a growing sense of negativity to the language in all the recalls of 'medium' cultural insensitivity. There are also some indications of the respondents perceiving the potential of professionals to offend even more. The respondent may well have been right in believing that her daughter 'would have been demolished' by the speech therapist, not literally but in the sense of being exposed and humiliated by a cultural insensitivity specifically provoked by the Irish language. The final recall of the respondent who was in hospital reveals an element of risk or fear generated by Irish language in specific contexts. We cannot know precisely why the young doctor behaved as she did, but there are numerous similar recalls across the low, medium and high classifications clearly describing an impact of offence combined with a sense of risk and/or fear. Another respondent spoke of hospital reception staff giving 'these startled, disapproving looks and gestures when I spoke to my child in Irish' and described the impact as 're-sentment, self-doubt ... it was as if I had stepped out of line'.

Actions constituting 'high' cultural insensitivity

Although there was a substantial number of 'high' culturally insensitive actions, they are less diverse than in the other classifications (Table 11.11). 'Risk' and 'fear' are more manifest and in one case a couple endure a terrible ordeal. As one would expect, the impact is greater, both in terms of the degree of emotional and psychological pain inflicted, and in the duration of that pain. It also has a profound impact upon respondents' perceptions of the individual professionals involved. (As already observed, the respondents are not inclined to condemn or criticise whole agencies because an individual employee was culturally insensitive.)

The greater the help needed, the more insensitive the service

The examples of 'high' cultural insensitivity in Table 11.11 heighten one's sense of irony pervading all the examples. That is, that the parents are in need of help of some kind; they are in receipt of a service supposed to respond to

Table 11.11 'High' cultural insensitivity

'High' cultural insensitivity	Impact
A speech therapist said learning Irish would make ——-'s situation worse (she has learning difficulties). She told the nursery teacher (without me knowing) that she should discourage my daughter speaking Irish. 'You should only communicate with her in English.'	I was furious. The nursery teacher was distraught.
The speech therapist said that ———'s speech delay was not a developmental problem, but due to her being brought up bilingually.	We distrusted her.
Our child was in hospital for a long time. A teacher gives kids lessons there. When he heard she went to an Irish school, he just turned on her. He said: 'I can't do anything with you.' He belittled her deliberately. Our child said: 'He made me feel stupid.'	Anger, distrust. We felt it was an attack upon our culture.
My child is autistic. The speech therapist said I was putting an extra burden on him, sending him to an Irish school, At the time I was questioning what I was doing. I wanted to do the best. I had decided the Irish school was the best, not just because of the Irish.	I thought it was very insensitive. It made me feel I had made an important choice for my children without giving it full consideration.
A professional who didn't know that male and female Irish surnames in the same family are different, told me that I shouldn't use these different surnames, as people would think my children had different fathers.	I burst out laughing.
A doctor in A&E asked: 'What kind of name is that … I've never heard anything like that before?' He was looking at me as if I was some kind of freak.	I was very upset. My wee boy's registered disabled. He was very ill at the time, and he couldn't breathe properly, and this doctor was being actually insulting and very hurtful about our name.
The health visitor asked: was the Irish school and the bilingualism not another pressure for my child? My child wet the bed recently, and the HV asked: could it have to do with the school? She just continued to go on about the pressure we were putting on her.	I really felt that she was putting me down. That really hurt me more than anything. I'm the mother and it was me who was being hurt. She was criticising my way of parenting.
A speech therapist dismissed my wanting to send ————- to an Irish school. She thought it would be detrimental. She didn't realise how important it was to me.	I wanted an informed opinion, not an off-the-cuff decision. She dismissed the intention too quickly. I just thought it wasn't a good service, certainly not for Irish-speaking families.

Our child was very ill one night. We phoned the emergency GP office. The receptionist asked loads of questions about ———'s name. You could tell she was hostile to the name by her tone. She was making it out to be a real weird name. We were worried sick about our child, and she went on and on about his name. Then she told us to take the child to a clinic in ———. It was 15 miles away. We didn't know this at the time, but it was right in the middle of this notorious loyalist area. It was covered in Union Jacks and red, white and blue bunting, and anti-Catholic graffiti. There were a lot of drunks about. coming out of bars and clubs. We eventually found the place.	We were petrified. And angry. We found out later that we could have taken ——— to the hospital in ———.

that need; and delivery of the service is characterised to varying degrees by a cultural insensitivity which can cause great offence.

INSENSITIVITY THROUGH ASSOCIATION

Cultural insensitivity is 'actions or words which are disrespectful to someone's culture'. But there is something else at play here, something more serious. Four speech therapists and a health visitor discourage children from speaking Irish on the basis of some ill-defined reasoning that it will do them harm. Four of the children have special needs, for example, autism, physical disablement, an apparent speech delay and unspecified behavioural problems and bedwetting. None of the five respondents recalls any of the professionals involved explaining why precisely they believed learning and speaking Irish or becoming bilingual would do the child harm. The remark: 'I wanted an informed opinion not an off-the-cuff decision' is illuminating, and probably typical of the remaining four respondents' wishes. Like the vast majority of all of the respondents, this parent (in the full response given) finds it difficult to point the finger and criticise one particular professional. One senses his/her turmoil. The Irish language is 'very very important' to him/her. But it is precisely this language which is being identified as a potential source of difficulty for their child. One can easily imagine the impact of the speech therapist's 'advice' on the moment-by-moment interactions between parent and child.

PROFESSIONAL OPINION OR PERSONAL PREJUDICE

Another parent had an identical difficulty, trying to discover the reasoning behind a speech therapist's recommendation that her child should not learn Irish. She could not find any reason, and imagined that the general attitude within the agency seemed to be: 'Do you think, given ———'s problems, that she should be there [in an Irish school] learning Irish.' This parent also valued the language, saying, 'It's something I felt I wanted my children to learn, and to nurture, and to use in everyday speech.'

Wherever one looks in the extensive transcripts, there is no indication of the respondents knowing or understanding what precisely is going on in the professional's mind that leads the professional to discourage or oppose the parents' wishes to have their children educated in Irish schools. The lack of evidence and/or reasoning for this apparent concern only exacerbates the parents' predicament. The professionals are influential people, trained, articulate, professionally qualified, well-established in the community and operating under statute. Frustration and anger frequently well up from parents' testimonies and some seek reassurance about being 'a good enough' parent to their child:

> Whenever the health visitor left, and I started thinking about it, there was no way that she was being culturally sensitive. She was supposed to be here to see ———— (our other child), but she just concentrated on ————- and her behavioural problems. Are ————'s behavioural problems something that happened at school? She just continued to go on about the pressure that we were putting on her. I spoke to the nursery teacher the day after it, because I was very concerned about it. The more I thought about it, I really felt that she was putting me down. And I spoke to the teacher, and the teacher said to me, she thought it was totally out of order. She said that she [the HV] should have been telling me how good I was in pushing ————- further, instead of knocking me back for pushing her on. And she said the fact that ————- is bilingual at such an early age is a real credit to her.

The mother's answer to the question about the impact of the insensitivity included:

> Well ... I'm the mother of the child, and it was me who was being hurt. It really did hit me. I was very annoyed. I really felt that she was putting me down. That really hurt me, more than anything ... she was criticising my way of parenting her. And then she invited me to a parenting course the next week, and I thought ... no way. I said: 'Well ... I'll keep her at arm's length the next time she comes.'

Perception is vital. Like four other parents who had similar experiences, the most serious aspect is the parents' sense of being undermined. The professionals are in effect (though undoubtedly without realising it) attacking something even more profound than language: the respondents' systems of beliefs and values underpinning their parenting and their self-worth.

AN UNFRIENDLY CURIOSITY

A number of interpretations can be made about the behaviour of the doctor in A&E who repeatedly enquired about the patient's name, and responded to hearing the name with some kind of incredulity ('looking at me as if I was some kind of freak'). The repetition and the incredulity may simply have been a mask to conceal a more serious perception of the language and those who used it – contemptuous, discriminatory or sectarian. This could apply anywhere in the world, where professionals duty-bound to offer the best possible service their profession can give nevertheless cannot control a curiousity at best, a negativity or hostility at worst, about some aspect of the client's/patient's life and culture which they encounter. Let us hear the respondent recall her experiences in more detail:

> One particular incident, a doctor in the A&E ... he was the doctor in charge. My wee boy was very ill at the time, and he was brought in and he couldn't breathe properly, and this doctor proceeded saying to me: 'What kind of name is that?' And I said, 'His name is ————-. It's an Irish name.' And he said: 'I've never heard anything like that before ... ———————— what a strange name.' He kept repeating it, and saying how strange it was. And I was very upset, and I was very upset mostly over the child ... He was actually insulting and very hurtful the way he went about the whole thing, because he could see that he was talking to me at a time when I was very upset ... my wee boy could hardly breathe. He was put on a nebulizer, and it wasn't the time for him to bring up his educational background in Irish history or whatever. It wasn't the appropriate time. But the difference there, I noticed thinking back, of that particular doctor was: he was crossing that barrier not just dealing with the name ... he wanted to get into a discussion ... he was actually making a comment on the culture. Sometimes this happens ... a professional wants to talk about your culture, but wants to talk about it more positively ... they're genuinely interested in your culture ... You know: 'that's a very interesting name' ... and they mean it ... But this doctor wasn't doing that. He was actually being dismissive of the name and the culture.

We may better understand this response by looking at the respondent's opposing experiences of cultural *sensitivity* on the part of nurses in another hospital. She then said of that sensitivity:

It does give me a good opinion of them. More so for my children. Because I would find that ... I don't want my children affected by someone's negative attitude towards their name. They might be saying it to me, but it is my child who will feel that there is something that is wrong with their name. And that really bothers me. Because I don't want them to feel that there is anything wrong or different.

In answer to the question whether this cultural sensitivity made a difference to the quality of the service provided, the respondent replied:

Oh yes ... as I say, it makes me feel more relaxed; it puts me at my ease. I also think it makes me think they're more professional; that's one aspect of it ... that someone actually does take the time, and cares enough to try to say the name ... It also makes a difference to the children; they appreciate it too when professionals make an effort to get their name right. Otherwise the children would have very negative feelings. *I mean if someone is sensitive to them, in something so fundamental and important as their name, it does make a difference to how the child is going to feel.* (author emphasis)

CULTURAL INSENSITIVITY ENDANGERING LIFE

The final example of 'high' cultural insensitivity emphasises the importance of timing and context. It is another case in which parents are in great need of reassurances about a sick child, and speedy and effective medical treatment. A persistent, hostile enquiry about their child's name has to be overcome first.

The time is 1am. A three-month-old baby appears to be very ill. The parents contact the GP emergency duty service. The receptionist is preoccupied with the child's name: 'What kind of name is that ... I've never heard that name before ... where did you get that name from ...?' The parents' only concern is their sick child, but the receptionist goes on and on about their child's name. There is no friendliness in the tone of enquiry.

Eventually, the receptionist instructs the parents to take their child to a surgery in a certain location, in the centre of a notorious Protestant paramilitary estate. The parents may or may not be Irish Catholics, but they have certainly given their baby a name undeniably associated with Irishness and Catholicism. As the couple get near this particular location, they endure anxieties that arise from different sources. The most obvious one arises out of their thoughts and fears about the baby's illness; they both know that three-month-old babies are very vulnerable. Another source of anxiety arises from the growing realisation that they are in dangerous territory. The

Protestant emblems and anti-Catholic graffiti on every gable wall intensify this realisation. But it is the third source of anxiety that is more significant and actually fuels the other two; it is the repetitive questioning (and their constant memory of it as they journey towards danger) which they had to endure from the receptionist because of their child's Irish name.

There are many examples of professionals' preoccupation with respondents' names, but when it prefaces an instruction to Irish Catholic parents in the middle of the night to take their sick three-month-old baby to a surgery in a Protestant paramilitary location, then it is a little more than mere cultural insensitivity. The receptionist was in effect ensuring that the parents would be far more conscious of (and consequently far more nervous about) their differentness as they neared a location where such differentness could so easily have cost them their lives. The sight of drunk men coming out of the pubs and the clubs in this location did indeed 'petrify' them (many sectarian murders in Northern Ireland have a pub-club-alcohol component). If the family had had the misfortune to be stopped and questioned at one of the illegal guarded roadblocks which periodically litter Northern Ireland, their fear (fuelled by memories of the receptionist's exaggerated reactions to their child's name) would surely have exposed them. It is inconceivable that this duty receptionist deliberately dispatched these parents and their baby into a highly dangerous situation. Yet there were six respondents who experienced some sense of fear and/or danger as a consequence of the cultural insensitivity they were describing, and the contexts in which it occurred.

All the main findings of the research will be discussed with reference to relevant literature, in the next chapter. To conclude this chapter, however, the responses to one of the more general questions is worthy of note. The respondents were asked whether there was any culture, apart from their own, which they respected more highly than other cultures they were aware of. Thirty-two respondents (75%: 13 men, 19 women) gave a total of 55 cultures which they respected highly. The culture of the American Indians was by far the most admired (22 respondents: 15 women and 7 men), the reason being their struggle to survive and their relationship with the land. Other minority cultures whose adherents were similarly perceived by the respondents as having endured oppression and struggle predominated in the total list and included the cultures of Palestinians, Australian Aborigines, New Zealand Maoris, Tibetans, South Africans, Israelis, Nicaraguans, Iraqis, Muslims, Chinese minorities in Northern Ireland and Mexicans.

Summary and conclusion

This chapter described research carried out within a small community of Irish speakers in Northern Ireland. It has provided an outline profile of the community and the historical and political contexts in which the community originated and developed. The underlying assumption has been that this particular community, having overcome many obstacles in pursuit of the right to promote its culture, would be particularly sensitive to culture generally, would have an acute sense of the meaning of culture, and could provide interesting insights on the issue of the cultural sensitivity or otherwise of the various care agencies which serve its members. There were considerable differences in the recall of culturally sensitive and culturally insensitive experiences. Much of the cultural sensitivity and insensitivity recalled by respondents revolved around their Irish language, and Irish names in particular. But there was much variation in context and timing, thereby leading to differing impacts and interpretations, and impinging upon many other important aspects of culture. There were varying degrees and types of sensitivity and insensitivity, so much so that a grading framework was devised, identifying instances of 'low', 'medium' and 'high' cultural sensitivity and similarly with cultural insensitivity.

Instances of 'high' cultural sensitivity were characterised by an awareness on the part of the professional of the profound importance of the Irish language in the lives of respondents, and a corresponding empathy and sensitivity in the delivery of whichever service the parent(s) was receiving. They also included some impressive examples of professionals combating blatantly insensitive attitudes of colleagues towards culture. Instances of 'high' cultural insensitivity included professionals suggesting or inferring that Irish education was detrimental to some children's development. The most serious impact of cultural insensitivity occurred when parents felt that (a) their values and child rearing were being questioned and found wanting; (b) that they were made to feel they were not serving the best interests of their children; (c) that they sensed fear and danger both to themselves and their children in speaking Irish.

CHAPTER 12

Commentary on Research Findings

Introduction

This chapter will comment on the research findings and attempt to elicit their contributions to an increased knowledge base underpinning professional practice. The parents' sometimes very detailed responses make original contributions in at least eight areas of interest. First, the fact that their first language is English heightens their perception of how professionals respond to hearing them speak Irish. Second, they can convey to English-speaking professionals (and readers) precisely what speaking Irish means to them. Third, they demonstrate a balanced and reasoned perspective on how professionals have treated them, often providing detailed observations of culturally competent as well as culturally incompetent practice. Fourth, their testimony suggests that key professionals are not adequately meeting the challenge of bilingual education. Fifth, that same testimony demonstrates the need for constant reminders of the standards set by the governing bodies of the relevant professions. Sixth, the findings raise questions about the level of critical self-awareness in some professionals, in respect of their actions and the impact of those actions. Seventh, considerable insight is gained through the parents' detailed accounts of how professionals react to 'foreign' language names. Finally, they provide the opportunity to learn about the Irish naming systems, enabling professionals to avoid embarrassing pitfalls.

With regard to the last two contributions, a framework of analysis applicable to all languages will be provided. This will grade culturally insensitive responses to 'foreign' names in terms of their impact upon the client. It will demonstrate that location and context can greatly exacerbate the pain and hurt that culturally insensitive practice can cause. There is convincing evidence of cultural insensitivity towards language worldwide, and the chapter concludes by considering political influences underpinning language intolerance.

Enhancing the knowledge base on the importance of language

1. Describing professional responses to Irish in English

In health and social care work, language minorities do not usually speak English as a first language as do the Irish. Some may think that this particular characteristic limits any contribution their responses can make to the existing knowledge base, because their experiences are vastly different from (and less difficult than) those of many non-English speaking minority groups. But it is precisely because the Irish-speaking community are fluent in English that their contribution is a valuable one. They do not, as do some non-English speaking minorities, experience a crippling sense of inferiority or lack of confidence due to an inability to speak English; nor do they live day to day (as those non-speaking minorities may do) constantly fearing being exposed and humiliated by some insensitive (and linguistically racist) English-speaking people. Being able to speak English enables them to be conscious of how people react to them (or their children) speaking Irish. They have the presence of mind which enables them to concentrate on such things. Their first major contribution to the knowledge base, therefore, is to describe cultural sensitivity and cultural insensitivity in such detail, using English language concepts, vocabulary and images, that English-speaking researchers and readers like myself cannot fail to understand.

2. Conveying the status and meaning of language in their own terms

Many of the respondents gave detailed and expansive replies to questions about the importance of their language. More informatively, that importance arises not just from the qualities and attractions of the language itself (i.e. its poetry, music, etc.), but more so from its cultural and historical context. In their own words: 'The thing that expresses my culture most ... language is the key to culture and cultural exploration ... the most distinctive factor ... it symbolises a lot of other things ... you experience your culture through language ... the most proactive way I can communicate my Irishness ... etc.'.

There are many incidents recorded by the respondents that convey the hurt and anger which can be generated by an insensitivity to one's language. One parent spoke of her fear about not being present during the developmental testing of her child since she said she thought the professional 'would have demolished the child'. Her child is being asked to respond to different shapes and colours which the professional holds up to her. She says *ciorcal* and *cearnóg* in response to the 'circle' and the 'square'. She says *dearg* in response to the colour 'red'. The professional does not accept these Irish words and insists on the child speaking in English. The mother cries out to the researcher: 'Of course it's *dearg* [for red]. A child needs all the praise you can give her … in saying "no" to *dearg* you're also saying no to my culture. It's more than just the language. You're saying no to everything I believe in.'

3. A balanced contribution

The third contribution the parents make lies in the balance of their opposing experiences, that is, cultural sensitivity and cultural insensitivity. We have seen in the literature that many minority respondents in health and social care research have been given the opportunity to highlight the shortcomings of the services provided. But few have spent as much time as this particular minority group in describing both culturally sensitive and culturally insensitive experiences. They recalled and described a whole array of culturally sensitive practice which can only be a source of satisfaction for the agencies and individuals involved. Additionally, many of the respondents tolerated cultural insensitivity, six of them proclaiming that professionals had a difficult enough job without having to reach out to their clients culturally. Empathy and tolerance was also demonstrated. One respondent, repeatedly hurt by a health visitor who insisted that her child answer in English during a series of developmental tests, actually downgraded the offence and said: 'It's not being outright rude or anything … it's just a sort of indifference to what information I'm giving her [i.e. that my child's first language is Irish].' She later added: 'I'm not expecting her to go out and learn Irish … but just to be aware a second or a third time after it's been pointed out.'

Another example was a respondent's reaction to a professional's suggestion that people might think her children had different fathers because they had 'different surnames'. This was a mistaken assumption on the professional's part, not knowing anything about Irish naming systems (see below). In many locations in Britain, such a suggestion would most likely have led to a complaint, followed by some publicity and then a reprimand, if not disciplinary proceedings. In this case, the respondent merely burst out laughing and explained the 'misunderstanding' to the bewildered professional, whereupon they both then had a good laugh. One of many examples of balance and tolerance is provided in its entirety in the previous chapter, and highlights the hugely positive impact of culturally competent practice upon the thinking of a young mother who also experienced a cultural insensitivity bordering on the horrendous. No justice is done to these respondents without careful study of their opposing experiences and the impacts of those experiences. It is invaluable material for training purposes.

4. The challenge of assessing bilingual children

Their fourth contribution to the knowledge base reflects a deeper (and more painful) level of experience arising from professionals' assessment of their children. Like many other minority parents from different countries, speaking different languages, the Irish-speaking parents raise a legitimate concern about non-Irish speaking childcare professionals assessing their children in crucial areas of development, in particular, speech. If the professionals are not knowledgeable of and/or do not share the culture of the parents, and if they have no ability at all in speaking the first language of the children they are assessing, can they provide an accurate assessment of their linguistic and intellectual capacities? Eleven respondents were unhappy, resentful, puzzled or angry because periodic developmental tests were being administered in English to their Irish-speaking children by professionals who could speak no Irish. These professionals gave the parents no indication of awareness of the potential shortcomings in such practice. The parents felt unable at the time to articulate a deep unease and suspicion that there were shortcomings, and were apprehensive about the long-term implications of results. Here is a parent expressing the initial dilemma this posed for her (she has already provided a simple, yet powerful example of 'high' cultural sensitivity from her GP):

> I've wondered for example whether or not my child developed a stutter. She didn't have a stutter as such. But sometimes she'd be very hesitant in speaking … this is a child who would talk the legs off a stool by the way … I have noticed tendencies in her towards repetition and hesitation and things like that, which may be quite natural. But I would like to know whether or not that's a thing of her having to translate and having to move backwards and forwards and I want to know what impact this is having on her conceptual awareness. I would like to know that if my child needed speech therapy, for instance, that the health professionals would be able to spot that in a bilingual child, and I don't have confidence that they necessarily would. I don't have confidence that if a child stuttered or had a hesitation or an impediment, that in Irish they would pick it up, if it wasn't also there in English. And I know without a shadow of a doubt that someone who's listening for a speech problem [i.e. in a child speaking Irish] … unless I've spotted problems, they're not going to spot it. I know that, because they don't know the language that she's talking.

In response to the question about the impact of cultural insensitivity, the parent replied:

> It makes me more anxious, about the service and the child's development; I suppose it makes me more … yes 'anxious' is the word, because it makes me wary, if there are problems, then I'm the one who has to spot them, but then I don't necessarily know what to do about them. You know I don't feel that there's somebody I can contact; I don't feel there's a support system there outside of the Irish speaking community.

This mother probably didn't realise that her concerns lie at the heart of current debate and research in speech and language therapy. She articulates those concerns accurately: the inability to speak Irish is not the problem, it is the fact that important judgements are being made about children on the basis of that professional inability. Such practice has been the subject of critical debate in other countries (Barnes 1995; Keats 1997) and has featured prominently in UK conferences and publications (Holm *et al.* 1998). There is a substantial Bilingualism database (available on the internet), listing hundreds of publications and research on the subject. Key individuals within the association have made significant advances. Stow and Pert (1998), for example, two speech therapists in Rochdale (where school children speak 35 languages in addition to English), have created The Rochdale Assessment of Mirpuri Phonology (RAMP). This is a bilingual phonology assessment they designed specifically for children speaking Mirpuri (a dialect of Punjabi), Punjabi and Urdu. But the principle underlying it applies to all bilingual situations: children develop separate phonological systems for each language they speak and professionals should assess these phonological systems for all languages spoken by the child. This is precisely the purpose of their assessment tool (RAMP).

5. Deviations from professional standards

The experiences above should remind one of the standards set by one's own governing bodies. The Royal College of Speech and Language Therapists lists many principles and procedures underpinning an effective speech and language therapy service. Here are some of them, taken from the Royal College's handbook: *Communicating, Quality 2*:

- The profession recognises that bilingualism in a child is an advantage.

- The speech and language therapist will make every effort to assess in both (all) languages to facilitate differential diagnosis.

- Clients and carers should never be advised to give up speaking in their home language as a means of supporting language progress in English.

- Information in referral and assessment will be available in the language of choice.

- Appropriate language assessment material should be available in the required languages. This will encompass phonology, vocabulary, syntax and fluency.

- As language assessments do not readily translate from one language to another due to cultural bias, they should be used as part of a qualitative assessment.

- The team needs to be aware of the implications for assessment and intervention in situations where there is no bilingual worker available in the client's home language.

- It is essential that a bilingual professional, para-professional, co-worker or translator in the client's home language is involved.

BILINGUAL CO-WORKERS

- A bilingual co-working service acknowledges the rights of all individuals who are referred to the speech and language therapy service to receive the service in a language of their choice.

- Bilingual co-workers … take the case history in the client's/carer's home language, including, with children, to advise on play observation as appropriate to the culture.

- Bilingual co-workers contribute to the process of diagnosis between primary language difficulties and English as a second language.

- As bilingual co-workers are more accessible to the carers of bilingual clients, they play a vital role in empowering carers to participate in management of the client's speech and language difficulties. (Royal College of Speech and Language Therapists 1996, p.294)

Although a number of health and social care trusts in Northern Ireland do provide an interpretative service available to all the professions, there are no bilingual co-workers trained by the speech and language therapy services for the specific responsibilities listed above. The consequences of this are clearly visible in the experiences described by many parents.

6. Knowing oneself culturally and one's own cultural bias

There is an enormous challenge in the sixth contribution which the parents make concerning the vital necessity for all professionals to know themselves culturally and to know precisely what culturally motivates them; to utter advice and guidance within any powerfully felt cultural context (such as that of the Irish-speaking community) only after the most careful, objective consideration of available evidence and research. There is something particularly disturbing about many of the experiences described by some of the Irish-speaking parents, and there are some questions that need to be asked. Did those professionals who were culturally insensitive in different ways realise precisely what was motivating them when they were, for example (a) refusing to recognise and accept Irish; (b) insisting that children spoke English; (c) suggesting or actually claiming that learning Irish would be detrimental to the children's development? Was there the slightest element of cultural bias in their attitudes and approach? The recorded experiences from which such questions arise remind one of the attitudes of health, social care and educational professionals to the languages of the Australian Aboriginals and American Indians. There is nothing unique about such cultural insensitivity. It simply reinforces the argument that professionals and their agencies delude themselves in thinking that they are incapable of repeating the mistakes of their predecessors – a harsh reality that child protection workers in particular, in virtually all the health and social care professions, have been compelled to accept.

7. Irish names

The Irish respondents remind us, first, of how important are their names to human beings and, second, how easy it is culturally to offend in response to names. Names are vitally important as the most potent symbol of identity, cultural identity in particular. Names are the principal means by which we register our existence in this world and by which we establish our social relationships. It is difficult to imagine living without a name.

There were many examples of insensitivity in response to Irish names, but this was only the tip of an iceberg. Respondents collectively could have provided literally hundreds of such occurrences (it was not the researcher's objective to extract every single recall of a culturally insensitive incident). This particular type of insensitivity was so frequently perpetrated by health and social care professionals that it reinforces an earlier point demonstrated repeatedly in the *Bringing Them Home* report (Commonwealth of Australia 1997): that language and hearing a particular language spoken (the first word in that language is likely to be a name) can just as easily trigger off discriminatory (racist) responses as the sight of someone of a different colour. Qureshi (1989) writes: 'As with colour shock, name shock is a real entity, adversely influencing rapport' (p.83). It was not uncommon for a respondent to be culturally offended numerous times within a few hours by professionals' reactions to his or her name, for example, first by reception staff, then by medical staff, third by the reception staff again as they left the surgery. There was the possibility too of the chemist then being culturally insensitive in response to the name on the prescription (four such recalls). Most of the examples given in the previous chapter are classified under 'low' cultural insensitivity, but some did graduate to 'medium' and 'high' in accordance with their particular contexts and impacts.

Irish forenames have become increasingly popular in the English-speaking world. They are often steeped in legends and myths, deriving from particular families or clans, famous saints, kings or queens. Their meanings are often fantastic and/or poetic and their sounds euphonious. Names such as Niamh ('brightness, radiance, lustre'), Aoife ('beautiful, radiant, pleasant, like a goddess') and Fearghus or Fergus ('man-strength') are not likely to pose any difficulty; they are quite commonly used by the famous and the public alike. Many other popular 'Irish' names among the respondents are not actually of Irish origin, but are derivatives from biblical names or from Irish versions of Norman and other European imports. But the spelling of these names may have been problematic for the professionals: Pádraig (Patrick), Mícheál (Michael), Máire (Mary), Proinnsias ([St.]) Francis), Eibhlín (from the Norman Avelina) and Siobhán (from the French feminine form of John).

Then there are the original Irish names, which one may assume definitely did pose problems, in both pronunciation and spelling: Meadhbh or Méabh (pronounced 'mev' and meaning 'intoxicating, she who made men drunk'; the Anglicised version of this name, Maeve, is very popular too); Íte or Íde (pronounced 'id-e', who according to legend fostered the child Jesus and was once called 'the bright sun of the women of Munster' (O Corráin and Maguire 1990); Eógan (or Eoan, pronounced o-n, and meaning 'born of the yew').

Irish family names (surnames) are likely to be even more problematic. They are often lengthy, three or four syllables at least, with spellings and pronunciations not easily guessed. Here are some of them, with the approximate pronunciation in brackets: Ó Searcaigh (O'Sharkey), Ó Flatharta (O'Flaharta), Ní Dhomhnaill (Nee Ghone-nall), Chóil Mhaidhc (Call Whack), Ó Neachtain (O'Neachtin), Ní Churraigní (Nee Chureen), Macgiolla Shuligh (Magillah Who-al-lee). Such names figure prominently in Irish-speaking families in both Northern Ireland and the Republic of Ireland.

The experiences of the Irish-speaking community are not dissimilar from those of other minorities. Mares (1982), for example, quotes from a Vietnamese man: 'Why is it so difficult to get a Vietnamese person's name right? What if I always called you by the wrong name. How would you feel? … People are always getting the wrong bit of your name, or pronouncing it so you can't recognise it' (p.103).

There can be much more serious consequences: one of the Irish-speaking respondents who was expecting her first child spoke of her hospital experiences. Both her forename and surname are distinctly Irish. When she arrived at hospital the responses to her name were, on the basis of previous antenatal visits, predictable: incredulity, unfriendly curiosity and puzzlement, constant questioning about the name and spelling (this mother had described previous incidents of cultural insensitivity, some of which are categorised under 'high' in the previous chapter; she had also described 'high' culturally sensitive experiences). Six months previously, she had undergone ECG tests in another larger hospital because of a suspected heart murmur. The doctor seeing her could not find the results of the test. These were imperative, as they could have dictated pre-delivery, precautionary measures. A search was initiated. The suggestion was made that the patient's name may have been the cause of the difficulty. This was incomprehensible to the doctor, a German, who, according to the mother, complained. The results were eventually found. The mother spent seven days in hospital. She recalls mealtimes thereafter and hearing staff refer to her as 'the woman with the funny name'. She described the overall experience as 'the worst seven days of her life' and has since lodged an official complaint.

Probably the most tragic case involving cultural insensitivity towards a non-English name is that of Aliyah Ismail, a 13-year-old Muslim girl who drifted into drugs and prostitution and died alone in a North London bedsit, after taking a lethal overdose of methadone (Brindle 1999; Hassan 1999). This tragedy has been interpreted in many ways, but there can be little dispute about one of the findings of the official inquiry report, that more than 230 professionals had been involved in trying to help Aliyah and she had been subjected to 68 movements among different carers during her brief life. Often professionals did not know what was happening to Aliyah Ismail, or what other professionals were doing to help. One of the reasons for this was that some professionals were careless and culturally insensitive enough not to learn precisely what her name was. Consequently, a number of agencies had a number of different files for the same child; she was given three different surnames and both forename and surname were spelt in different ways.

8. Naming systems

Numerous writers have drawn attention to the challenges posed by names and naming systems within minority groups (e.g. Henley and Schott 1999; Mares 1982; Qureshi 1989). Nationalities and particular languages and religions which are referred to on this matter include Vietnamese, Nigerian (Yorobo and Ibo), South Asian Muslim, Middle Eastern Arab/Muslim, Eritrean (Tigrinya and Tigre), Chinese, Greek, Turkish, Somali, Muslim, Sikh and Hindu. Health and social care professionals therefore may well have been alerted to the numerous pitfalls revolving around names and naming systems. You do not, for example, ask a Muslim 'What is your Christian name?' In the traditional Chinese naming system, the family name comes first. Sikhs are often guided by a religious ruling that actually precludes them from using their family name (they adopt a male title, e.g. Singh, or female title, e.g. Kaur. Turkish people are traditionally addressed first by their forename followed by Bey (for a man) or Hanim (for a woman). Henley and Schott (1999) demonstrate the laughable consequences of imposing the English naming system upon any of these groups, a common practice in health and social care practice.

Health and social care professionals unfamiliar with Irish are not likely to know of the main pitfall awaiting them regarding Irish family names. Most surnames in Ireland, irrespective of whether people speak Irish or not, are actually of Irish origin. The family names of men and boys usually begin with Mac (son) or Ó (grandson). Thus, MacAnnaidh, Mac Coy, Mac Guigin, MacGill and Ó Muilleoir, O'Hagan, O'Flaherty and O'Neill. If a family surname begins with Mac, then the girls and unmarried women in that family have Nic (daughter of) at the beginning of the surname. Some married women may choose the traditional Bean Mhic (wife of) before their surname, but this is increasingly being discarded. If the family name begins with Ó, the Nic becomes Ní and the Bean Mhic becomes Bean Uí. The important point to remember, however, is that the boys and girls in the same families will have different family names (Ó Dónaill and Ní Churraighin 1995).

The experiences of the Irish-speaking community add considerably to the testimonies of individuals from other minority groups. But their detailed accounts provide something more: a means to identify and categorise the nature of this particular cultural insensitivity and its impact. Here we learn of the location and context of the insensitivity to names, the attitude, tone, facial expression, action, etc., all of which influence the extent of the offence caused. This is useful training material and can be applied to learning about the experiences of all minorities whose names are not familiar to English-speaking health and social care professionals (Table 12.1).

Table 12.1 Gradations of cultural insensitivity in respect of Irish names

Professional's culturally insensitive response to client's name	Professional's culturally insensitive response to client's name within a social group context (more serious)
Not attempting to pronounce the name correctly.	Exposing a name to some form of social ridicule with the remark: 'I wouldn't even attempt to say that name!' (location: e.g. social services, hospital reception).
Conveying to the patient or client that their name is 'awkward' for their files and records.	Loudly complaining about a name and asking someone repeatedly to repeat their name, with an expression of incredulity or contempt each time the name is repeated (location: e.g. chemist's shop, reception area).
Writing the name down incorrectly (e.g. just as it sounds) in the presence of the client.	Two or more professionals making fun of, and/or sharing their incredulity about client's name in the near presence of client and others (location: e.g. behind a reception screen).
Writing the name down incorrectly, even though previously having been repeatedly told the correct way to write the name.	Two or more professionals sharing incredulity about client's name within hearing distance of client and others. Facial expressions and tone compatible with what they are saying (location: e.g. reception area).

Not attempting to pronounce the name correctly, having been told on numerous occasions the correct pronunciation. Repeatedly spelling the name wrongly on the appointment card sent to the client.	Two or more professionals sharing negative or culturally biased views about client's name within hearing distance of client and others. Facial expressions and tone compatible with what is being said. (location: e.g. reception area, chemist's shop).
Actually deleting or scoring out the correctly spelt Irish name on official records and substituting an English translation, or what one thinks is an accurate English translation	Two or more professionals resisting client's wishes (in the presence of other clients) for name to be spelt right; professionals jointly conveying their prejudice, resentment, hostility or mockery towards the client and name (location: e.g. queue in social services office, casualty department).
Repeatedly resenting having to make the effort to pronounce or write the name correctly, and increasingly expressing that resentment more strongly; conveying this resentment through facial expression (frowning, exasperation, anger, etc.) and tone of voice.	Two or more professionals develop a mocking attitude over client's name, in the client's presence, both seeking to outdo the other in the nature and degree of ridicule directed against the name (location: e.g. behind a reception screen, hospital or social services waiting area).
Conveying incredulity (through facial expression and/or exclamation) on hearing an Irish name and expressing that incredulity with the question: 'What sort of name is that!'	Two or more professionals develop a mocking attitude over client's name and, without realising it, increasing the mockery to the point of humiliating client (location: as above).
Rejecting the name, by saying something like: 'I can't write that name down ... I can't put that name into the computer ... That's not her real name.' Conveying this rejection through irritable tone of voice and/or an expression of annoyance, limited or no eye contact.	Professional(s) try to engage other patients, clients or members of the public (i.e. getting them to join in the 'fun') and, without realising it, mocking and humiliating someone because of their Irish name (location: hospital ward, and/or similar to above).
Repeatedly translating name into English or guessing and writing down what seems to be the English spelling of the name: both of these actions against the express wishes of the client/patient.	Professionals (e.g. receptionists, nurses, doctors, etc.) are negatively curious and questioning about a child's name, while the parents' only preoccupation is their sick child (location: casualty dept, health clinic).

Political influences on language intolerance

What is the cause of the prevalence of insensitivity and intolerance to language? Probably there are many causes and one of the most conspicuous is political exploitation of the potency of language. In Canada, Belgium, Turkey, India, Pakistan or Bangladesh, to name just a few, politicians and community leaders have sought to exacerbate language divisions and exclusivity in pursuit of broader political objectives. 'Language riots' have often resulted, sometimes ensuring a legacy of hatred and bitterness, but also accelerating break-up and the creation of additional states and boundaries. In India alone, the politics of language and the periodical disturbances revolving around language led directly to the emergence of no less than six new states long after the country had achieved its independence (Das Gupta 1975).

The struggles of the Irish-speaking community to legitimise their educational activities and promote their language have produced a much smaller scale 'language politics', but no less fractious and no more lacking in political opportunism. Their efforts have been punctuated by repeated attempts by hostile, opportunistic politicians, attempting to condemn, denigrate, ridicule, humiliate and mock both the Irish language and its adherents, and to block any financial or other support that might have come their way. A brief scan of any Northern Ireland newspapers will reveal the paranoia and prejudices of its politicians during the past 30 years. These politicians have warned of the threat of an 'unstoppable Gaelic onslaught'; have dismissed this 'foreign Irish Gaelic culture'; and have threatened to throw street names in Irish 'into the river'. The Chairman of the Northern Ireland Assembly Education committee was reported as saying: 'Irish ... has no relevance, no bearing and no long-term usage in the modern world' (*Irish News*, 7 December 1999).

The appointment of Martin McGuinness, a former IRA leader, to the post of Minister of Education predictably provoked an outcry among such politicians. Few could predict, however, the extent to which they would go in mobilising opposition to McGuinness. School children 'went on strike', walked out of classrooms and gathered petitions which were then handed to such politicians. Senior political figures 'sympathised' with the children. The same chairman of the education committee quoted above felt compelled to issue a press release in which he 'strongly rejected claims that the Minister of Education will force feed the Irish language to Protestant school children'. In radio and television interviews the children made it clear that they would physically prevent the education minister from visiting their schools. They waved their placards to the cameras, denouncing the minister and the Irish language. They verbally mocked the language, insisting that it would never be taught in their schools. Of all the images captured in more than 30 years of conflict, none were so depressing as those of school children conditioned and indoctrinated in the most extreme forms of cultural insensitivity, capable of being provoked into a fury at the mere sound of Irish and the sight of anyone who dared to speak it.

The precise reasons why numerous health and social care professionals in Northern Ireland have demonstrated insensitivity towards Irish are unknown at this point. But there can be little doubt that 'language politics' have influenced some of them. The fundamental requirement remains: that such influence must be exposed and eradicated in training and that trainers, managers and practitioners should be vigilant in preventing its return.

Summary and conclusion

This chapter has focused upon some of the findings of the previous two chapters, which revealed the extent of cultural insensitivity towards language in particular. The findings contribute to the knowledge base of health and social care training in numerous ways: they provide detailed descriptive accounts in English of how health and social care professionals respond to a language other than English. They record health and social care clients (a) defining culture in their own terms; (b) conveying the magnitude of meaning which language has for them. They enhance professionals' awareness of both cultural sensitivity and cultural insensitivity in respect of language and contribute to the current debate on professionals' assessment of bilingual children. They highlight deviations from professional standards in the assessment of bilingual children and facilitate enquiry into the possibility of cultural bias in professional responses to particular languages. Crucially, they demonstrate the significance of cultural self-awareness in professional practice.

The findings also re-emphasise the importance of clients' names in their own language and culture and provide basic information about Irish forenames in particular. They add to the considerable knowledge of naming systems in different languages and alert professionals to one of the most common pitfalls in the Irish naming system. The latter two contributions have facilitated the construction of a framework in which the location and context of cultural insensitivity towards any language can be identified and its differing manifestations and impacts can be graded.

Insensitivity towards language should be seen in a global and historical context. 'Language politics', in which the potency of language has been exploited for political gain in many parts of the world, has been well documented. Northern Ireland is no different in that sense from other locations. There are major structural and political hurdles to be overcome to facilitate its health and social care trainers pursuing the objective of cultural competence in working with all language minorities.

CHAPTER 13

Agency Perspectives

Introduction

Culturally competent services ultimately rely on front-line professionals, on the quality of their training, on their culturally oriented knowledge, values and skills, their experiences, interests and personal attributes. There is greater likelihood of culturally competent practice, however, if their managers and agencies have specified cultural awareness and cultural competence as objectives of policy. This chapter looks at some of the relevant agency perspectives on the development of an Irish-speaking community in Northern Ireland, and the legislative frameworks under which they operate. There are numerous contributions.

Every health and social care trust received a letter informing them about the research and asking whether or not specific policies and guidelines relating to the Irish-speaking community had been formulated. All but two of the fifteen trusts responded. A meeting with a senior manager of one of these trusts took place. The author had two lengthy meetings with speech therapists. A number of respondents were critical of comments made by speech therapists (and health visitors) regarding their children's speech difficulties and attempts to become bilingual. Discussions also took place with

- a senior partner in a GP practice serving Irish-speaking families
- the Department of Education for Northern Ireland
- the 'Policy and Legislation' section of the Northern Ireland Office.

Finally, relevant literature pertaining to the Irish language, produced by staff in the various agencies, was made available to the author.

Responses from the agencies

Cultural diversity and cultural competence are not normally matters of concern for senior managers in large health care institutions. This fact is apparent even in the titles of publications for management (Department of Health 1992a; Ferris and Graddy 1989; Forder and Knapp 1993; Kelly 1992), many of which indicate the more pressing 'macro' issues and convulsive reorganisations thrust upon them by successive governments during the last two decades. Yet we have seen in previous chapters that governments have also recently awakened to the cultural diversity of their electorate, and are legislating demands for an appropriate response from all public bodies. It was encouraging therefore that so many senior managers took the trouble to respond to my enquiry, which told them about the research and asked about relevant policies and guidelines. Here are extracts from the replies:

> 1. Currently our policy [towards Irish speakers] is … if the patient wishes us to record his/her name and/or address in Irish, we are happy to do that, and to address any correspondence to the patient accordingly. In addition … the Health and Personal Social Services has been supportive of officers wishing to take the Diploma in Irish Studies at Galway University designed to equip staff in the public sector with the ability to work effectively with the Irish-speaking community.

> 2. We have been researching our catchment area in order to identify minority groups whose first language is not English.

> 3. We have literature available in the Irish language in the A&E dept. and there is a current project to make a similar provision within the outpatients' department. [We are] attempting to ensure similar communication services to others including visually impaired … We are currently reviewing the availability of hospital literature and services for those who are not fluent in English and for those who require extra large print, Braille or audio cassettes.

> 4. The Trust has not produced any policies or guidelines in Irish.

> 5. I am not aware of any new policies or guidelines that have emerged … concerning the development of the Irish language.

> 6. We have on the few occasions where there seemed to be a demand for it produced leaflets in Irish … We have one leaflet on Speech and Language Therapy, and one on the Disability Network Scheme.

> 7. There are no such policies within —————-.

8. From 1996 ... we enlisted the help of a local teacher who kindly volunteered to help in this regard [i.e. as interpreter].

9. Currently in ——————— there are 7 Irish language playgroups inspected by the Early Years Team ... we are at the early stages of discussing with an Irish language umbrella group about the possibility of leaflets concerning Early Years provision in Irish.

10. Where a user expresses a preference for communication in the Irish language they are referred to one of our Irish-speaking members of staff. However the field of psychiatry and psychotherapy is particularly specialised, and if treatments are to be conducted through the medium of Irish, it is necessary for both the therapist and the patient to have a thorough knowledge of idiomatic and specialist terms. This does present some difficulties.

11. The Trust does not have a formal policy ... but it does have access to translation services outside the Trust, to enable it to deal with correspondence which is written in Irish or other languages.

12. A data base has been developed ... which records members of staff fluent in a 2nd language which is not English. There is a total of 20 people currently on the data base ... 3 of whom are Irish speakers ... Although currently none of the Trust's information leaflets are made available in Irish, where a request is made, every effort is made to meet this request.

13. The Trust is currently preparing its Draft Equality Scheme for consultation ... It is therefore very opportune that you have made contact at this time – I would be most happy to meet with you on this matter.

The legislative context underpinning agency responses to Irish

The Draft Equality Scheme referred to in the last quote was mentioned by 11 of the 13 trusts that replied. This is a legislative requirement stemming from s.75 and Schedule 9 of the Northern Ireland Act 1998, and all Trusts were engaged in the process of submitting their draft proposals for inspection by the government; hence the comment that my enquiry was timely.

The legislative context underpinning agency response to the Irish language and Irish speakers has undergone radical change. Reference has already been made to the 'illegality' of teaching through the medium of Irish a mere 30 years ago, and the near impregnable resistance to any change in the status quo from leading civil servants, particularly in the Ministry of

Education. By 1995, these conditions had by and large been eradicated and the Local Government (Miscellaneous Provisions) (Northern Ireland) Order of that year removed the legal prohibition on the erection of non-English street names and gave district councils the right to erect street names in another language (meaning in effect Irish) alongside the English name. The government also issued a Central Secretariat Circular (1/95), the first paragraph of which states: 'Correspondence with the members of the public who wish to use the Irish language should be treated with due courtesy.' It clarified the legal entitlement of anyone assuming 'any name he or she wishes – in English or any other language, and if she is generally known by that name, it is valid for purposes of legal identification' (para.3). The government obliged all health and social care departments to 'respect the wishes of any individual who has indicated a desire to be known by a personal name in the Irish language', and later specifies: 'Unless it appears that he or she is not generally known by that name, a personal name in Irish should be accepted for all official purposes, including correspondence and official documents.' (para.4). As always in legislation and guidelines like this, however, there are loopholes which enable professionals and their agencies to avoid the essential responsibilities decreed. One obvious loophole above is the phrase 'unless it appears that he or she is not generally known by that name', giving anyone the opportunity to argue that 'I certainly don't know the person by that name'. Nevertheless, the 1995 Order represented real progress and was a precursor of subsequent more liberal approaches, climaxing in the commitments to the promotion of Irish in the Good Friday Agreement and the Northern Ireland Act 1998.

S.75 of the Northern Ireland Act requires each trust 'to have due regard to the need to promote equal opportunity ... between persons of different religious belief, racial group, age, marital status or sexual orientation, between men and women generally, between persons with a disability and persons without, between persons with dependants and persons without ... Each Trust shall in carrying out its functions, have regard to the desirability of promoting good relations between persons of different religious belief, political opinion or racial group.' There is no mention of culture or cultural diversity here, nor is there any mention of linguistic diversity or linguistically distinct groups. Consequentially, no agency may feel obliged to make reference to the Irish-speaking community. This again emphasises the importance of wording in legislation, to avoid creating loopholes on the one hand and to prevent exploitation on the other. One trust, in explaining its equal opportunities in communication, intentionally or unintentionally excludes consideration of the Irish-speaking community in its phrase 'members of ethnic groups whose first language is not English'. This is not the fault of the trust, but of the legislation directing their policies. The two consultations made with the Policy and Legislation office of the Northern Ireland government explained the omission of reference to 'culture' in s.75. They said it followed to the letter the wording of the relevant section on equal opportunities in the historic Good Friday Agreement. There are actually two Rights, Safeguards and Equality of Opportunity sections in the agreement. The first is the one where there is no mention of 'culture' (pp.16–17). But the second (pp.19–20) actually has the words 'cultural issues' in its subheading, and most of that section is a commitment to respecting the linguistic diversity of the country generally, and to promoting the Irish language in particular. Thus the explanation given by the government office does not make sense and trusts that seek to avoid having to respond to any requests in respect of the Irish language by arguing either (a) that Irish is no different from any other minority language spoken, or (b) that for those who speak Irish, it is their second not their first language, are acting contrary to both the spirit and the letter of the agreement.

Comment on agency management responses

There is much that is positive in the responses from the agencies, and many of them rightly emphasised their responsibilities to all groups irrespective of the differences between them. As expected, there was considerable diversity in their replies. Such diversity is easily explained in the vast differences in numbers of Irish-speaking people in each trust area. Not surprising either is the fact that the Draft Equality submissions are couched in general terms and lack the specific detailed guidelines required in alerting staff to different expressions of cultural sensitivity and cultural insensitivity. The consultation with a senior manager focused on the nub of the problem from the agency perspective: the fact that Irish-speaking people all speak fluent English. English for most of them is their first language, so it would be unrealistic to expect professionals to learn Irish. As the research demonstrates, however, the respondents do not expect professionals to learn Irish, but to respect the language and those who speak it.

Some of the seemingly less than interested responses above, notably (4) and (7), are strange and inaccurate. I discovered that numerous initiatives were taking place in those two particular locations. These included meaningful consultations with the Irish-speaking community, the allocation of Irish-speaking workers, the publishing of trust literature in Irish, both specific (e.g. family and childcare services) and general (e.g. Irish/English information packs about services as a whole). There is nothing unusual about chief executives being unaware of the excellent work being done in their name. As Thorpe (1994) also discovered in his child protection research in Australia, front-line staff are more often needs-led by the realities around them than by policy directed from above.

A senior GP's perspective

Discussion took place with the senior partner of a large GP practice in west Belfast. This practice featured very favourably in the recall of respondents. Words such as 'empathy', 'sensitivity', 'culturally sensitive', 'like home from home', 'knowing me', 'I feel so confident/comfortable/trusting going in there' were frequently used. The GP told me of an early realisation of the development of the Irish-speaking community. He and his partners set about attempting to provide an additional 'consultation service in Irish'. He researched in numerous academic quarters and within the professional bodies to which his staff and practice were affiliated, particularly the Irish Association of Medical Practitioners. He sought technical advice on graphics for signs, brochures and leaflets. He also needed to seek approval from the health and social services trust covering his area (the major concern there was ensuring that bilingual notices said the same things). Finally, and probably most importantly, he and his colleagues decided that they should employ at least one Irish-speaking GP.

These innovations were made not without apprehensions. They believed they were doing the right thing and that it would benefit both patients and practice, but they also wondered whether it might be perceived as a publicity stunt. Subsequent developments reassured them, with many professionals, including doctors and dentists and the business community (supermarkets, banks, shops, sports centres) now all providing information bilingually. The more important measure of the success of that particular GP's practice, however, is the gratitude of their Irish-speaking patients.

Speech therapists' perspectives

Speech therapy services were significant for many parents. In the context of national figures, Irish-speaking children were overrepresented in referrals to speech therapy. Reflecting their openness and interest in the research, they invited me to speak to speech therapists and submit questions for their consideration. The opening questions explored their developing awareness of the Irish-speaking community, the first referrals of children attending the Irish-speaking schools, and whether or not they recalled their agencies becoming similarly aware, and if so, whether it led to any policy or guidelines. They had gradually over a ten-year period become increasingly aware of the community. One therapist said it made her conscious of the fact that she had given up Irish, and the experience rekindled her enthusiasm for the language (many professionals had similar experiences). They all believed their agencies and managers were becoming aware of the increasing diversity of the population as a whole (reaffirmed in the written response by management). When management did begin thinking in terms of policy and guidelines, it was in response to this overall demography.

The most striking reflection of the speech therapists in my view was their acute consciousness (again mirrored in the response of the senior manager to whom I spoke) of the fact that all the Irish-speaking parents and children spoke fluent English; indeed English was for nearly all of them their first language. The significance of this point is evident in its frequent emergence in response to different questions. For example, towards the end, they were asked about contacts with speech therapists on the mainland of Britain, who have substantial working experience with minority cultures. Had advice or help been sought from these sources? The Northern Ireland therapists did have regular contacts but, they rightly stressed, the situation in Britain regarding minority cultures and the languages within those cultures was very different. Their professional counterpoints there were dealing with minority groups whose second language is English.

Three questions addressed the possible contexts of speech difficulties and related problems emerging:

1. What was the consensus among speech therapists about the origins/causes of these problems?

2. What were the major challenges for speech therapists revolving around these problems?

3. Did they think socio-economic factors such as poverty, deprivation, family fragmentation, etc., played any part?

On the first and second of these questions, there was no consensus; nor was there a perception that speech difficulties in Irish/English-speaking children constituted a 'major problem'. On the third question about possible socio-economic influences, the response included:

> No, these factors [e.g. poverty and deprivation] don't affect the situation. I would say that even though there are fragmented families, and poverty and all the rest, these people remain very committed to learning Irish; in fact I would say that, generally, the parents are very articulate, very motivated, and there are very good networks established within the community. There's actually more community cohesion here, despite things like poverty and/or broken families, more cohesion than you're likely to get in the general population, which is much more disparate.

Another question explored agency and managerial response to the increasing awareness of the Irish-speaking community, and in particular to the growing realisation that children from the Irish-speaking schools were being referred. Speech therapists did not receive or expect expert help and guidance from within their agencies about approaching/working with the parents of these children. It was not unique in that sense; it was common with all situations where a speech therapist has to convey to any parent that their child has speech difficulty, and that rectifying it was likely to be a long-term project over maybe three or four years:

> General training for speech therapy and our professional body prepares for this eventuality. This is about relationships with parents in general; about helping the parents through that process, discussing with them different and difficult issues.

I shared with the speech therapists the fact that some parents recalled speech therapists and health visitors making a connection between learning Irish and speech difficulties developing. I shared with them my own perception that these parents would have been particularly vulnerable to such a suggestion. The following is an edited version of the (very lengthy) response to that question:

> I take the point that there could be even more sensitivity required in respect of the point you're making ... but you've got to remember that we have this challenge with all parents irrespective of what group they belong to. The parents may say what do you mean? ... are you telling me that my child has a speech and language problem? And we've got to be very careful with all parents in the way that we respond to that situation.

A second response to the same question produced this answer:

> We've found it very useful to go out to the Naíscoil [Irish playgroup/ nursery]. There is an informal group that meets with the playgroup leaders and some of the parents, the mums in particular. It was very useful to illustrate where speech and language therapy fits in. And certainly they were very receptive, and we are very keen for further contact. It's something that we would hope to keep up and develop.

I made the point that there were other professionals mentioned who provoked the same feelings in the parents: that they were somehow doing their children harm by sending them to Irish-speaking schools; that there was a link being made between the difficulty experienced (speech impairment, autism, etc.) and the fact that the child was learning Irish. I asked a supplementary question as to whether or not any of the therapists sensed this was how parents were actually perceiving and interpreting what they were attempting to do. Could they recall ever seeing a parent's expression that would have conveyed that this was what they were thinking?

> We want to work with whoever is looking at how we develop. We can always improve. I think it's best done in the local patches, where people feel that they can relate to the professionals.

A second reply stated:

> Yes, I think you do be sensitive, and you try to be guided by parents and carers and the input [verbal and expressive] they're showing. You may then want to revisit the matter another time, to repeat and reinforce the right message over and over again, and not just in one visit, but the next time and the next time.

The speech therapists believed that there was a dearth of literature and research on the speech therapy aspects of what the Irish-speaking community was attempting to do, and that such literature and research would be very much appreciated. One therapist said:

> We're still at the information-gathering stage, it has to be said. But our professional body is helpful, and we have lots of contacts with colleagues in other trusts, and it could be that they are dealing with similar groups ... children or adults ... similar speech disorders. We have specific interest groups, groups of therapists coming together who are interested in the same area of work. And there's a lot of literature on bilingualism. That's probably where we're at as a professional group. It's the sharing, recognising that perhaps we could improve. We're doing that all the time.

This discussion with speech therapists was enlightening in numerous respects. No attempt was made to reinterpret or reframe some of the parents' unpleasant experiences with professionals who somehow found a causal link between learning Irish and speech malfunctioning. But the most lasting impression was of the inherent contradiction in the therapists' responses (mirroring precisely the same in management). On the one hand, they rightly stressed their obligations to all minority groups and also emphasised that the Irish parents were no different from parents from other minorities in the challenge they presented to speech therapists on learning of their children's speech problems. Yet, on the other hand, they also stressed the fact that these Irish families, both children and parents, spoke English as their first language and Irish as their second. The therapists (and managers) agreed that this made it a very different (and unique) situation. There is not the slightest hint in these responses of the kind of negativity and/or hostility to Irish recalled by parents. Yet it must be said that within that apparent contradiction there lies the potential for stresses and strains between individual front-line workers and their clients.

A framework for looking at professionals' responses to minority cultures

There are numerous indicators in this chapter and the previous two chapters that some agencies and their front-line professional staff perceived and approached the Irish-speaking community and their language with an attitude not conducive to cultural competence. If agency management is actively pursuing the goal of cultural competence in respect of all minorities, through quality supervision, support and monitoring, the problem will be exposed and effectively dealt with. If not, it will get worse. The agency context is crucial and with the help of a simple imaginary framework of (agency) self-exploration we can consider the potential fusion of positive and/or negative attitudes and approaches towards minority cultural/linguistic groups on the part of both agency and worker (Table 13.1).

Possible origins of worker–manager cultural insensitivity

There are many locations in the world where communities are divided, ideologies and cultures conflict, and internecine strife abounds. It is vitally important for health and social care managers in such situations to self-explore. One obvious area of exploration is 'how endemic and narrow one's socialization has been' (McPhatter 1997) in relation to conflicting sides.

Table 13.1 Worker plus agency factors leading to cultural sensitivity and cultural insensitivity		
Attitude/ approach of professional	Pertinent factors in agency context	Possible impact of attitude and approach and of agency context, on worker's thinking and actions
Positive	Agency is aware of the emergence of a new, culturally and linguistically distinct group. It consults with group; produces bilingual literature, draws up or amends existing guidelines on work with minority cultures. It monitors the development of the group, and the challenges it poses to its workforce.	Curiosity, interest, wanting/needing to learn about this group. Admiration for a group certain about its identity. Rekindling aspects of one's own identity and culture. Being motivated to learn the basics of the language of this group. Conveying interest, enthusiasm and empathy in interaction with group members.
Indifferent	Agency knows nothing about this group; has no intentions of learning about it; says all groups are treated the same	Uninterested in hearing anything about the culture of this group, makes no attempt to reach out culturally.
Negative	Predicts and resents new group placing additional burdens on hard-pressed staff. Is determined not to appear to be offering special favours to this group. Suspects that group is critical about agency in any case.	Resents even having to think about this groups needs. Sees it as just another 'exclusive' minority group trying to impose its differentness on everybody else. Begins to think of it in negative terms, seeking out perceived negatives in the way it lives, rears its children etc.
Hostile	Agency regards the group as alien and hostile, another extension of rampant anti-state activity. Shares the opinions of local politicians hostile to the group. Key managerial personnel are determined to pay lip service only to statutory obligations towards this particular minority group.	Worker regards individual group as potential enemies. Associates them with terrorism and/or sponging off the state. Makes the same association about their language. Impulsively reacts against any request by group member to respect their names, their language in particular and their culture generally. Takes advantage of any opportunity to undermine client's cultural convictions, for example, linking child's developmental problems with key aspects of culture, e.g. language, religion or diet.

There are many managers in these locations of division who have grown up in environments inhabited only by people like themselves with the same culture and the same language, religion, values and child rearing within that culture; 'monocultural early socialization' McPhatter calls it. I recall a conversation in Belfast with a former care manager who was a Catholic. The same age as myself, she told me she had never set foot on the Protestant Shankhill Road (a relatively safe place in those days) at any time in her childhood or teens . This does not necessarily make a manager biased and prejudiced, but it increases the possibility of him or her becoming so. If the divisions in the country are such that the distinct and different cultural groups feel threatened by each other, and if managers share that sense of threat and have had nothing other than that monocultural socialization and upbringing within one of those cultural groups, then there is the greater likelihood of a bias and prejudice, manifesting itself in cultural insensitivity and cultural incompetence. The manifestation may lie within their own attitude and behaviour towards the 'other' culture, or worse in how they influence and direct their front line staff responsible for delivering a service to those who share that culture.

This may be difficult for managers to accept. They invest much time and effort in projecting the best possible image of themselves and of their agencies, an important function in any manager's job. They daily polish their own veneer of professionalism, objectivity, discipline and neutrality. There is no incentive for them to engage in the painful 'peeling away and restructuring' in a 'process of enlightened consciousness' (McPhatter 1997). They are unlikely to admit to themselves or to others how current turbulent events impact upon them, or how such events influence the quality of their work. Yet in Northern Ireland events have not just been turbulent, for the Protestant community in particular they have been catastrophic (McKay 2000). Here is a female member of the Protestant Orange Order articulating her sense of cultural loss (she has nothing to do with health and social care, but I have little doubt that her words echo in the minds and hearts of some health and social care staff and their managers throughout Northern Ireland):

> A quiet stillness descends over the crowd, prompted by the Commons' Silver Band's decision to play a hauntingly beautiful piece of music, and which I hope will remain locked deep within my heart forever. The over-powering feeling that you do not belong is a strong and memorable one. And like the Ulster-born author Alexander Irvine 'I am a stranger in the [town] of my birth.'

I have lived all my life in an area, Newry town, which accepts me as a ratepayer, but continually rejects me as an individual with an unique – and, more importantly, a genuine and legitimate – cultural identity. I have a ready affinity with the poet T.S. Eliot, who in his poem 'The Wasteland' cried out: 'I can connect nothing with nothing.' I live through my own cultural 'wasteland', and like the lady who adorns the banner I also cling to my rock as do 761 other souls like me, for they too are strangers. (McClure 1999, p.13)

Again managers and their staff may protest that whatever cultural anguish they are experiencing, they remain professional and detached at all times, serving everyone equally. Doctors in particular will rightly claim that they respond to life-threatening crises anywhere in the world, instinctively, professionally and effectively, saving life irrespective of who or what their patient represents. But this is not an appropriate analogy. Most health and social care work is not about life-threatening events. It is often carried out in a much more complex social, environmental and political context, in which one has time to think and reflect and form opinion and judgement about aspects of the client's life far beyond the problem they present. There has obviously been both positive and negative thought and reflection by professionals serving the Irish community, and more than a little discriminatory opinion and judgement accompanying the services they provided.

Summary and conclusion

Contact and discussion with many representatives of agencies provided the foundation for this chapter. Those representatives included chief executives, managers, equality project leaders, team leaders, speech therapists, civil servants, social workers and general practitioners. There was considerable diversity in response, which is a reflection on the areas in which the Irish-speaking community is concentrated. The present legislative context underpinning agency responsibilities to Irish-speaking people was reviewed. While this indicates radical reform, there are still loopholes which are conducive to acts of cultural insensitivity, intentional or otherwise. There is little mention of culture in the present submissions being made by trusts in accordance with the Northern Ireland Act 1998, a fact which would seem to be at variance with both the spirit and letter of the historic Good Friday Agreement.

Speech therapists are key personnel in respect of a considerable number of Irish-speaking families. The contents of a lengthy discussion with four speech therapists were recorded and extracts provided in this chapter. They reveal a considerable degree of professionalism and sensitivity towards the families of these children, though they stress their obligations to all minority linguistic groups. No attempt was made to explain some of the disturbing experiences recalled by respondents in their contacts with a small number of speech therapists and health visitors.

It is obvious from this and previous chapters that the Irish-speaking community and its language pose difficulties for some agencies and their front-line professionals. An attempt was made to explore the origins of such difficulties, within both the Northern Ireland and international contexts of working in seriously divided communities. It seems evident that workers and managers who have emerged from one side only of any community divide, and who may experience some sense of threat from aspects of life on the other side, are unlikely to be able to perceive and respond to both sides with equanimity. The workplace, including its management, supervision, support and monitoring, and its overall commitment (or lack of) to culturally competent practice, will greatly influence the approach and attitude of front-line professional staff towards minority cultural and/or linguistic groups. The detailed descriptive account of experiences provided by the respondents indicates that some professionals were not adhering to the legal, professional and ethical principles governing their work.

CHAPTER 14

Defining Culture
Completing the Task

Introduction

Inadequacy of definition can lead to misunderstanding. We have looked at many critical comments about culture in health and social care literature. The striking feature about such comment is that it is invariably based upon definitions that are incomplete, ambiguous, confusing or very similar to definitions of different concepts (such as 'ethnicity'). We have also seen 'culture' being harshly questioned and criticised without any definition being provided at all. Culture is a complex, multifaceted concept and not easy to define; but sufficient ground has now been covered to enable us to complete the task begun in Chapter 3. This brief chapter will now list the principal components of culture and attempt to summarise their meaning and function. Cumulatively, this is a reasonable basis upon which to provide a comprehensive definition of 'culture', 'cultural identity' and 'cultural competence'. Such definitions should be generally useful. They should not be mere abstract substitutes for ordinary people's everyday understanding of culture. The primary objective is to provide definitions which are particularly meaningful and applicable for health and social care practitioners. They should be helpful reference points in relation to fulfilling statutory obligations, for example, to consider religious persuasion, racial origin and cultural and linguistic background of clients (Children Act 1989). They should also enhance professionals' self-awareness about the approach, attitude and actions which best constitute cultural competence.

Culture: a way of life

The most common term used in definitions of culture generally, and in anthropological definitions in particular, is 'way of life'. This was also the most frequently heard term in response to the question 'What does culture mean to you?' (Chapter 11) This term should therefore occupy a prominent place in any definition. It is manifestly obvious that previous definers and theoreticians and current respondents do not mean any sort of way of life. On the contrary, culture means a very special way of life, in accordance with a system of values, underpinned by certain ideas, perceptions and meanings.

Values and the ideas, perceptions and meanings underpinning them

Ruth Benedict's preoccupation with the values of ancient cultures is well founded. Many today regard values as a core cultural attribute and the associated ideas, perceptions and meanings as integral to such values. All these combine to provide the individual's life map: values, ideas, perceptions and meanings by which they know and understand and relate to the world around them; a precious and priceless guide which enables them to integrate within their own culture and to negotiate successfully the often alien terrain of other cultures (possibly submerged in very different values, ideas, perceptions and meanings).

It is misleading to apply the term culture to some movement, cult or ideology whose ideas, perceptions and meanings have proven destructive to humanity, for example, fascist culture or apartheid culture. These are contradictions in terms. Concepts like fascism, communism and apartheid have no value base (in the true meaning of the term value within health and social care), and their associated ideas, perceptions and meanings consistently demonstrate the illogicality and destructive and self-destructive essence at their core. They are doomed from initial conception, though they may initially give the impression that they are developing and expanding irreversibly. They wreak havoc upon humanity long before their self-destructive core begins to manifest itself. In making the theoretical proposition that the whole way of life is central to the meaning of a culture, one is also asserting that that way of life has proven to be and still proves to be productive and effective for the greater good of those who share that culture.

The essence of culture (stemming from its original meaning and reaffirmed by virtually every one of the respondents) is its benefit and worth to those who share in it, and to humanity as a whole. Culture's life blood is its value base, governing and serving all aspects of function. The ideas, perceptions and meanings which have evolved historically within cultures have created and also underpin their value base. The two sets of components – values and ideas, perceptions and meanings – are mutually serving.

Relationship with the physical environment

A definition of culture must include acknowledgement of the relationship between peoples and their physical environment and the cultural significance of that relationship. The environment includes home and homeland, mountains, deserts, seas, lakes, the stars and skies, the sun, wind, moon and rains and, crucially, the climate. These all determine and shape the lives and ways of life of individuals, their living habitats and the manufacture of tools with which they exercise some control over that environment. Literature, art, anthropology and archaeology all provide evidence that the physical environment is immensely influential in the evolution of values, ideas, perceptions and meanings of a culture, and in the emotional and psychological lives of individuals within it.

Clothes and diet

The physical environment influences both clothes and diet. Clothes and diet have also assumed religious and spiritual significance within cultures and remain the most visible expression of cultural identity. In a culturally insensitive setting, clothes and diet are often the first target of ridicule, with no conception whatsoever of the meaning of clothes and diet to the individual. Gerrish et al. (1996) refer to food as the 'vehicle for a rich variety of ritual and meaning across the range of cultural mores' (p.43). Doctors in particular are only likely to see food in terms of whether healthy it is or not, and are quick to associate specific minority diets with numerous ailments (Katbamna 2000; Qureshi 1989). Gerrish et al. discovered that health professionals' ignorance of the cultural significance of food was 'one of the most frequent signs of ethnocentric thoughtlessness' (p.43).

Similarly, Henley (1982), Henley and Schott (1999) and Qureshi (1989) reflect on the cultural and religious significance of clothing and appearance (highly significant in the experiences of Arooj and her sisters in Chapter 2). The Sikh turban and kirpan, the Scottish kilt, the Muslim woman's yashmak or hijab, her burqa or chador, the Jewish prayer shawl and phylacteries, the black suits and tall hats worn by orthodox Jews, the Muslim taviz, these all have cultural and/or religious meaning for the wearers (as well as the potential for cultural insensitivity on the part of the observer).

The arts

The values, ideas, perceptions and meanings underpinning culture may be expressed through particular art forms such as music, literature, poetry, drama and dance. When people state that music is the most important aspect of their culture and the most frequent expression of their cultural identity, they may be referring to numerous factors; for example, the music may embody differing and important cultural characteristics (e.g. strong rhythm, energy and dynamism, or conformity, passivity and hierarchy, etc.). The music may also capture the history of a people and convey, as no other medium can, their struggle, sacrifice and eventual freedom. The emotional and 'cultural' power of music is immense, generating strong emotions and a sense of sameness and belonging to a particular cultural group. The 'multicultural experience' on the streets of London, New York and Paris is as much audible as it is visible, the distinction between cultures more emphatically drawn through music than through any other cultural component. Similarly with other arts, they can trigger cultural recognition, identity, loyalty and pride. Conversely, however, the arts can be a vehicle for attacking, mocking or belittling someone else's culture or some particular aspect of that culture. The impact can be devastating, as the Salman Rushdie affair demonstrated.

Family, child rearing, relationships and care of the elderly

A number of the respondents declared that 'family values' was the most important aspect of their culture. They spoke about the 'way they brought up their children', 'the values they instilled in them', 'the way they taught them the difference between right and wrong', 'the way they were brought up themselves', the 'obligations and responsibilities between differing generations'. All these behaviours, they believed, were attributes of their culture (which echoes the work of Ruth Benedict, for whom culture 'is an expression of core values which most people learn and absorb'; Moore 1997, p.83). Such values do not extend merely through childhood; they are equally manifest in attitudes and behaviour towards adolescence, marriage, the elderly and death. Differing cultures perceive these stages of life and our responsibilities within them differently, but the fact that so many cultures regard at least some of them reverentially, is reason enough to refer to them in any definition of culture. This is taken for granted in the caring professions. Whatever neglect of culture in the past, front-line professionals collectively witness the cultural significance of family life, child rearing, family and social relationships and attitudes towards the elderly every working day (Blakemore and Boneham 1994; Currer 1991; Dosanjh and Ghuman 1997).

Religion

In Chapter 9, we saw that religion was a core component of culture for many people. Archaeology and anthropology inform us that religion evolved from the earliest dawn of human existence and always played a central and crucial role in the development of culture (Haviland 1999). Organised religion and culture are often fused (Haynes 1993), as with the billion Muslims many of whom might consider the separation of culture and religion as incomprehensible.

Language and education

Language and education have been crucial in the attempts of indigenous peoples to rediscover and re-establish particular cultures. Much has been written about the success of American Indians in this regard, and of the Irish-speaking community in creating their own education system in Northern Ireland. The latter is an endeavour closely followed in Scotland, where similar efforts are being made to revive Scottish Gaelic culture. The current campaign by Muslims for a separate Islamic education system is as much to do with maintaining Islamic culture as it is with criticism of the moral and academic standards in mainstream western education. Any definition of culture must refer to language, religion and education.

Myth and legend

We are slowly beginning to realise the significance of myth and legend within distinct cultures. Irish-Gaelic culture is a prime example, having sustained and cultivated various myths and legends established in its pagan-Celtic past. More relevant, however, is the utilisation of Maori myth and legend by New Zealand's present day health and social care personnel in enhancing their services to Maori people. Cotterell (1999) says that the influence of myths 'can still be felt in our languages, religions and customs' and that they 'remain an essential element of everyday life and culture'.

Sport

A substantial minority of respondents said Irish team sports were an important aspect of their culture. One respondent used sport to illustrate cultural insensitivity, while another explained how all-consuming sport was within her family. Team sports are often equated to religion in the degree of pride and passion they can arouse and the depth of loyalty they can command. Sport as 'culture' or 'religion' should surprise no one, as often the competition in many sports is prefaced by religious prayer and/or tribal ritual, the most famous example of which is the Maori hakka before each New Zealand rugby match. Team sports as an aspect of culture are manifest precisely as they were described by one of the respondents: they necessitate socially constructive relationships, selflessness, pride, seeking inspiration through reflection and perception beyond oneself; contributing to the construction and maintenance of sporting social and welfare institutions and, most important of all, respect for competition and one's opponents. Sport as culture embraces the concept of individual striving for physical and psychological perfection, but such perfection in national team sports is in the service of and fully integrated within a greater whole. Sport is often manifest alongside other aspects of culture such as religion, music, language and literature.

Sporting events are often the occasions when certain individuals and groups indulge in the most grossly insensitive, racist, criminal and destructive behaviours, provoking judgements such as the 'culture of thuggery' associated with sport. Sport itself is often riddled with bribery and corruption and great sporting heroes are often exposed as cheats. Various other verbal compounds that include 'culture' are then invented, further degrading the concept and preventing people from understanding and appreciating the powerfully cohesive and beneficial influence which a sports-dominated culture may exercise. It also makes it more difficult to respect and easier to ignore those who say sport is the core aspect of their culture.

Definitions of 'culture' and 'cultural identity'

Brevity and succinctness are laudable goals in literature. But it is obvious now that 'culture' and 'cultural identity' cannot be defined in one-liners. They are concepts which are too complex and all-embracing, needing explanation and exposition. Definitions must reflect the knowledge and literature of disciplines which have enhanced our understanding of the concept and have given it a much higher profile than traditionally afforded to it within health and social care literature (for example, in anthropology and culture studies). Definitions should in effect help counter the ignoring or downgrading of culture already noted in some literature. For health and social care professionals in particular, definitions of culture and cultural identity should additionally give a very clear indication of the meaning of 'cultural sensitivity' and 'cultural insensitivity' and should convey the extent of potential for culturally sensitive and culturally insensitive practice. Most important of all, they should enhance professional awareness and understanding of the meaning of 'cultural heritage' and the statutory obligations pertaining to culture. Finally, a definition of culture should function as the principal foundation upon which culturally competent practice is based. Here then are the definitions of culture, cultural identity and cultural competence.

Culture

Culture is the distinctive way of life of the group, race, class, community or nation to which the individual belongs. It is the first and most important frame of reference from which one's sense of identity evolves.

The 'way of life' within particular cultures has been determined in part by space, physical environment and geographical location, all of which in turn influence physical characteristics and the development of perception, emotion, cognition, communication, mobility and gesture. Our space and physical environment provide much of the dynamic context for the processes and practices which give shape and form to culture.

The 'way of life' within cultures has also been determined and shaped by the values, ideas, perceptions and meanings which have evolved over time. These values, ideas, perceptions and meanings constitute the individual's knowledge and understanding of the world in which he or she lives. They have contributed to and are strengthened by the creation and establishment of significant components of culture, such as myth, legend, language, religion, morality, systems of belief, mores and customs, dress and diet, art and sports, education and the manufacture and use of functional tools and material objects. Culture embraces all of these, and the individual may regard each of them, or any number of them, as culturally significant.

Our attitudes and behaviour towards and within social relationships, family life, birth, child rearing, adolescence, marriage, growing old, disability and death are all strongly influenced by our cultures; they are influenced differently in different cultures (Figure 14.1).

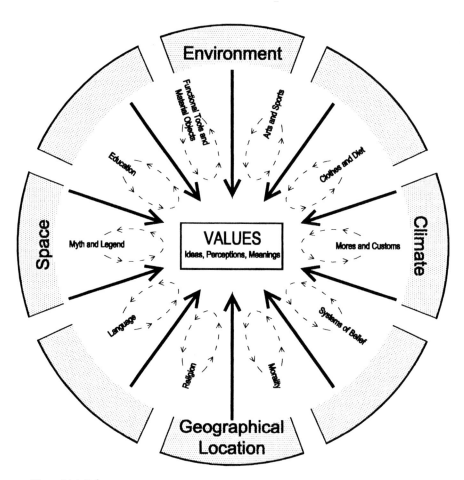

Figure 14.1 Culture

Cultural identity

Cultural identity is the sense of sameness and belonging which the individual experiences in living, sharing and in expressing a particular culture. That sense of sameness and belonging may vary according to the many differing expressions of culture. For example, sharing the same language may generate the greatest sense of cultural sameness and belonging for one individual, whilst sharing the same attitudes to the elderly may generate the greatest sense of cultural sameness and belonging for another. Individuals may regard some or all of these expressions of culture as significant in the formation and articulation of their cultural identity.

'Culture' and 'identity' are crucially important in the development of the individual and the group, race, community or nation to which he or she belongs. But they are both dynamic concepts, subject to influence and change. Progressive development of cultures and identities depends upon pervasive interaction, accumulated knowledge, and mutual respect.

Cultural competence

Cultural competence is the ability to maximise sensitivity and minimise insensitivity in the service of culturally diverse communities. This requires knowledge, values and skills, but most of these are the basic knowledge, values and skills which underpin any competency training in numerous care professions. Their successful application in work with culturally diverse peoples and communities will depend a great deal upon cultural awareness, attitude and approach. The workers need not be (as is often claimed) highly knowledgeable about the cultures of the people they serve, but they must approach culturally different people with openness and respect – a willingness to learn. Self-awareness is the most important component in the knowledge base of culturally competent practice.

Conclusion

These definitions of culture, cultural identity and cultural competence may not be universally acceptable within health and social care, but they do at least convey the importance and the multifaceted nature of the concepts. They lend support to the convictions of those policy and law makers who have formulated the professional's statutory and ethical duty to consider and respect culture. The definitions are the results of the cumulative learning of previous chapters. Much ground has been covered, many references made and the experiences of very many culturally diverse peoples around the world have all been considered before the final formulations. They are probably much more expansive than previous definitions in health and social care literature, but I make no apology for that. There may well be a connection between the brief and inadequate definitions of the past and the proven negativity to culture in health and social care literature of the present. Hearing ordinary people define their own culture in their own very positive terms, and expressing concern and respect for the culture of others, has been particularly influential in my arriving at the above definitions. Since the ultimate goal in all of these endeavours is the promotion of cultural competence, that too has been defined. It is hoped that all these definitions will serve as useful reference points for health and social care workers statutorily obliged to provide culturally competent services in a multicultural society.

CHAPTER 15

Training for Cultural Competence

Introduction

Progress is being made in health and social care training in preparing workers for the multicultural world in which they will operate. Agencies and trainers in specific locations have embarked upon innovative projects and commitments to provide services to specific minorities, and the representatives of minorities are increasingly impacting upon the thinking and actions of trainers and management. Much of the structure of training is soundly based, beginning with the legislative frameworks underpinning multicultural work and often stressing the importance of self-awareness of one's own biases and prejudices. There is also the opportunity to learn about the principal differences in cultures, about the importance of religion and language in many cultures, and about cultural characteristics that need to be known in order to avoid embarrassing pitfalls. These efforts are producing results and should be acknowledged.

Conversely, however, many deficiencies in working with cultural minorities have been revealed. They fall into two main categories:

- lack of cultural knowledge and awareness
- negative and hostile attitudes and approaches towards culture in general.

Within these categories, cultural incompetence has taken various forms:

- frustration and anger when unable to communicate
- an inability to listen 'culturally'
- overt criticisms of or indifference to some central cultural and religious tenets

- a tendency to blame aspects of culture (e.g. language, child rearing, diet) for impaired development, illnesses and unacceptable behaviours.

These issues represent a major challenge for trainers.

This chapter begins by exploring the issue of 'relevant' and 'non-relevant' subject areas for health and social care work. Second, it will promote the use and application of concepts such as 'culture', 'cultural sensitivity' and 'cultural competence' in place of outdated, restrictive concepts, increasingly limiting in a multicultural world. Third, it will critically review the knowledge base underlying training for cultural competence. It will identify and list the knowledge components usually required for cultural competence, but will additionally advise some caution about the knowledge base generally. Fourth, the chapter will provide frameworks for self-exploration, based upon many of the lessons of previous chapters. Finally, it will contest the assumption that people from minority cultures expect too much from hard-pressed, front-line professionals and place intolerable burdens upon them.

Relevant and non-relevant subjects: the case for anthropology

One of the obstacles to cultural competence in medicine is the exclusivity of the knowledge and qualification requirements for entry to training; invariably biology, chemistry, maths and physics are the only subjects regarded as significant. Other care professions strongly favour the social sciences as a firm foundation. In fact, many training departments, particularly social work, specify social sciences as the relevant and preferred subject area. Surprisingly however, anthropology is not normally included in the given examples of relevant social sciences degrees (i.e. sociology, politics, psychology, social administration). Yet we know that cultural anthropology teaches more about cultures than any other subject area.

There are however indications of change, at least in the literature. There is a growing recognition of the significance of cultural anthropology and medical anthropology in medical and psychiatric literature (e.g. Fernando 1991; Guéllar and Paniagua 2000; Helman 1994; Herrera, Lawson and Sramek 1999; Kleinman 1980). In nursing, midwifery and health visitor training, Gerrish *et al.* (1996) 'draws very heavily on anthropological insights into specific cultures' (p.26). In family therapy, Maitra and Millar (1996), a psychiatrist and psychologist and both experienced crosscultural family therapists, speak of the 'much needed sense of relativism to the Western clinical sciences' brought about by anthropological studies (p.113). In occupational therapy, Creek's (2000) standard text now contains a lengthy chapter on the 'cultural context', in which numerous references are made to texts heavily influenced by anthropology. In child care, Jill Korbin (1997), a professor of anthropology, continues to enlighten many different professionals in child protection work with her prolific outpouring of research and publications on differing aspects of the cultural contexts of child maltreatment around the world (Korbin 1997, 1987, 1981).

Outdated, narrow and restrictive concepts

During the 1990s, anti-oppressive and anti-discriminatory practice gradually replaced anti-racist practice. This was obviously an improvement, but change based upon discomfort and ridicule (Phillips 1993) or on serious criticism (Macy and Moxon 1996) is not likely to provide more reliable and more permanent foundations. The fact is that the seemingly all-embracing anti-oppressive and anti-discriminatory practice departed little from the concentration upon racism and anti-racism. There are some notable exceptions, including Dalrymple and Burke (1995) and Boushel (1991).

Also during the 1990s one began to see health and social care (and related) texts and articles carrying titles, chapters and sections containing the words 'culture', 'cultural' and 'cultural competence'. These include Ahmad (1996), Chamberlayne *et al.* (1999), Channer and Parton (1991), Fernando (1991), Fulcher (1999), Gerrish *et al.* (1996), Hall and du Gay (1996), Henley and Schott (1999), Kavanagh and Kennedy (1992), Keats (1997), Kelleher and Hillier (1996), Lago and Thompson (1996), Leigh (1998), Lorenz (1999), McPhatter (1997), McRoy, Oglesby and Grape (1997) Ahn (1993), O'Hagan (1999), Papadopoulos *et al.* (1998), Poole (1998), Rogers and Potocky (1996), Reschly and Graham-Clay (1989), Sewpaul (1999), and Sinha (1998). A few of these publications, notably Ahmad, Fernando and Lorenz, find the concept of culture problematic and, like Ahmed (1987) and Thompson (1993), believe it conceals racism. Nevertheless, the fact that serious critics of culture now feel the need to challenge a concept which they and their professions have ignored over decades may indicate a realisation that this concept is fast gaining ground. A few quotes from some of the texts which actually promote culture and cultural competence will demonstrate the increasing use of the concept:

The time has come for the nursing profession to embrace competence in managing cross-cultural interaction as being as much a part of their professional competencies as aseptic techniques or the administration of drugs. (Gerrish *et al.* 1996, p.26)

Culturally competent professionals recognise similarities and differences in the values, norms, customs, history, and institutions of groups of people that vary by ethnicity, gender, religion, and sexual orientation. They recognise sources of comfort and discomfort between themselves and clients of similar or different cultural backgrounds. They understand the impact of discrimination, oppression, and stereotyping on practice. They recognise their own biases towards or against certain cultural groups. And they rely on scientific evidence and moral reasoning to work effectively in cross-cultural situations. (Poole 1998, pp.163–166)

The development of cultural sensitivity, cultural competence and respect for cultural diversity is enhanced by increasing our knowledge of service users' frames of reference. Through the use of a qualitative, interpretative feminist research methodology, the study upon which this paper is based is aimed at understanding the cultural and religious aspects of infertility. (Sewpaul 1999, p.742)

Principles of importance to those aspiring towards culturally competent social work practice: (1) I accept that I have much to learn; (2) I appreciate regional and geographical factors related to people of contrasting cultures; (3) I follow the standard that knowledge is obtained from the person in the situation and add to learning about the situation from that person before generalising to others; (4) I demonstrate the capacity to form and sustain relationships with people from contrasting cultures … (Leigh 1998, pp.173–4, paraphrased in Fulcher 1999, p.336)

The current level of cultural incompetence can persist only at vast detriment to children, families, communities, the child welfare system, and society as a whole. (McPhatter 1997, p.274)

Cultural awareness should be a part of every health professional's training at either basic, undergraduate or post qualification level. (Bailey 1996, p.91)

These texts are written by health and social care academics, researchers, trainers and practitioners on four different continents. Collectively, the quotations convey a concept of culture that assimilates the principles and convictions of those trainers who have so vigorously promoted anti-racist, anti-oppressive and anti-discriminatory practice. It is clear now, from the content of many of the chapters in this book, why Bailey's advice to trainers should not go unheeded. The traditional negativity in health and social care literature (and practice) towards the concept of 'culture' is not dissimilar from the hostility (from that same literature) towards the concept of 'competence' in the early 1990s (Timms 1991). The latter resistance to the challenge of 'competence' has long since evaporated and it should not be too difficult now to acknowledge that the professions' traditional negativity towards 'culture' is likely to endure a similar fate.

The knowledge base for culturally competent practice

Papadopoulos et al. (1998, p.13) speak of 'a dearth of culturally sensitive knowledge to inform professional carers', two of the reasons being:

- a reluctance on the part of trainers to concentrate on specific groups, in case of stereotyping
- the entrenched view that 'individualised client care deals with all client needs'.

In addition to general knowledge about cultural differences, the trainers of the care professionals must concentrate upon how culture may impinge upon their specific area of work; for example, surgeons should be made aware of the importance of where they position a stoma on Muslim patients who use only their left hand for toilet function, and nurses, physiotherapists and occupational therapists should consider the implications of this cultural factor for post-operative periods generally. Medical students may learn about 'the cultural meaning of high blood pressure' (Morgan 1996), or African-Caribbean lay beliefs about diabetes (Pierce and Armstrong 1996). Trainee social workers may be required to explore the cultural significance of a Bangladeshi mother's reluctance to use available childcare facilities (Hillier and Rahman 1996). More generally, the knowledge base will also necessitate exploration of:

- statutory, agency and professional underpinning of obligations to serve equally all cultural groups
- the nuances and conventions of particular cultures, including one's own culture, awareness of the impact these may have on other cultures and the reasons underlying such impact

- information on the demography of cultural minorities and their origins preceding immigration and settlement

- how parents, families, extended families and communities within many minority cultures may influence the lives and decision making of individual members, and how any or all of these may traditionally have played the roles of professionals, i.e. helpers in pregnancy, bereavement, child minding, fostering, adoption, etc.

- religion and religious practices, commitments and requirements; the prominent role of religious elders in family and community life

- communication, including differing interpretations of expression and gesture, elementary language teaching, focusing upon words and phrases most likely to arise within the service being provided and the necessity of interpreter/translation resources

- family structures, child rearing, gender roles; differing perceptions of birth, development, gender, illness, care of the elderly, death; moral issues such as contraception, abortion, euthanasia, child protection (what constitutes child abuse/neglect in different cultures)

- how particular cultural groups may be more subject than other groups to (a) structure-based discrimination; (b) socio-economic disadvantage (e.g. inadequate housing and unemployment); (c) racism and racist-driven violence; (d) greater risk of ill-health (physical and mental); (e) higher rates of morbidity and mortality

- coping and survival strategies in a culturally hostile world

- the differing naming systems within cultural groups and how to address different family members

- avoiding common pitfalls of misinterpretation, which lead to acute embarrassment on the part of both professional and client (see in particular Hall 1959, 1966, 1976a)

- learning the dominant forms of acculturation processes which minority groups may undergo, which will include language, education, diet and religion.

Whatever the subject area, it is vitally important to incorporate clients' perceptions in the learning process, and much of the research referred to in numerous chapters will contribute. The works of Blakemore and Boneham (1994), Henley and Schott (1999), Hillier and Rahman (1996), Katbamna (2000), Lago and Thompson (1996), Sewpaul, (1999) and Tanno and González (1998) are especially recommended.

A contrasting perspective on knowledge

There are some notes of caution about acquiring knowledge in cultural competence training which revolve around the following areas.

Acquiring knowledge and expertise about a particular culture

McPhatter (1997) writes: 'Practitioners and educators alike consistently perceive themselves to be considerably more effective in their cross-cultural work than they, in fact, are' (p.275). That misperception may stem from a preoccupation with one culture to the exclusion of all others. Both the definition of culture in the last chapter and the quotations by writers in different continents given above convey the inclusivity of culture and the common experiences of humanity throughout cultures. Some writers and researchers restrict their learning efforts to one particular culture. They may know the culture thoroughly, belong to it, speak the language and be able to function as an interpreter. They are truly experts and will have no difficulty in working effectively within that culture. This does not necessarily mean that they will be culturally competent working within and providing a service for all cultures. If they are uninterested in other cultures which they encounter in their work, they cannot be culturally competent. Cultural competence, as Leigh (1998) states, is about demonstrating the capacity to form and sustain relationships with people from contrasting cultures. It is about sincerity, effort and openness in response to all cultures encountered in one's professional practice.

Diversity within a culture

Cultures are seldom uniform. Those who share a particular culture may differ in fundamental ways. Their social and economic lives may be vastly different, as will be their standard of education and their status. Ahmad (1996) provides accounts of three different experiences of childbirth by three Muslim Pakistani women. His point is that although all three women 'are part of the Pakistani culture and tradition on pregnancy and childbirth' their entirely different perceptions and experiences arise from the substantial differences in their social class, their living environments (rural–urban) and their access to health care. (It seems to me, though, that Ahmad's rich Muslim woman is consciously making choices about her pregnancy that have nothing to do with culture; they are more indicative of an advanced acculturation into the conveniences and luxuries of upper middle class western lifestyles). Health and social care workers should be aware of these inequalities within a culture. They should not interpret the adverse health consequences which result for some as the fault of culture, or poverty-stricken individuals' inability to adhere to cultural obligations as a diminution of cultural allegiance.

The dynamic and changing character of culture

The definition in the previous chapter concluded with an emphasis upon the dynamic and changing character of culture. This dynamism and change has numerous sources, not the least of which is interaction with other cultures. The status of the components of culture may alter as a result of acculturation processes. An individual who once perceived diet, dress, music, religion, language or values as the most important component within his or her culture may think that any of these are even more important, or less, as a consequence of the influences of other cultures around him. The caution therefore is never to assume that one can empathise and achieve cultural competence without assessment that accurately locates clients culturally.

Knowledge not in the pursuit of cultural competence

Henley and Schott (1999) impress with their knowledge and understanding of countless countries, nationalities, cultures, religions and languages (though the indigenous cultures of the Americas and Australia are conspicuously absent). Potentially valuable as this resource is, one may get the sense of the authors deviating from the goal of teaching professionals how to enhance services to the minorities within those cultures; that the work is more a demonstration of just how knowledgeable the authors are about the various cultures. There is, for example, a whole chapter about the Jain community in Britain, which has some 30,000 members. We learn about the central tenets and rituals of their creed, including daily Jain prayers, which are the essence of humility, forgiveness and love. This is pleasant reading, but it does not challenge. Elsewhere in health and social care literature, we may learn countless statistical facts about minorities, their numbers, ages, family sizes and languages; for example, we may read that half of the 80,000 Eritrean refugees in Britain speak Tigrinya and one-third Tigre. But we do not learn anything of the cultural and historical significance of these two branches of the same language, nor of any struggle in maintaining either of them during, for example, the tyrannical Menguista years (details probably far more relevant in cultural competence training).

Burnham and Harris (1996) caution against the creation of 'a "grand narrative" about cultures' which may actually promote a 'static view of culture', a concern also voiced by Ahmad (1996). They add: 'One needs to guard against the development of a myth that more knowledge means less racism, or that more knowledge necessarily means more understanding' (p.133).

CultureGrams

CultureGrams are one of the latest of many US cultural competence teaching tools. Such tools of convenience are not likely to make a significant contribution to cultural competence training. They are merely a more sophisticated version of the basic information texts in which authors list unusual or startling facts about particular cultures, and advise the readers about the dos and don'ts of interaction with cultures different from their own. They make little or no allowance for the diversity within cultures, nor for the diversity of cultures within countries. They invite rote learning, which is not conducive to the in-depth reflection and preparation required for cultural competence.

The knowledge base is crucial in cultural competence training, but as all these cautionary notes indicate, so too is critical discernment.

Tackling negativity and hostility to culture

Training should help facilitate exploring the expression and the origins of professional negativity and hostility to culture. The Irish-speaking community saw and heard the expression take various forms:

- choice of words ('what kind of a name is that?', 'foreign language', 'we can't accept that', etc.)

- facial expressions (e.g. 'looking at you as if you were mad', 'as if you had horns in your head')

- tone of voice (e.g. 'not friendly like', 'curious but not in a friendly sort of way').

These professionals' responses are similar to those described in Henley and Schott (1999) in relation to many minority groups and are alluded to in Lago and Thompson (1996). The professionals appear to be feeling awkward, annoyed, frustrated, or angry because they are lacking knowledge. They cannot speak the language and they do not understand the culture. Their lack of knowledge and understanding is exposed, and they are not used to this. They are normally very competent people, satisfying both their patients and themselves. Henley and Schott's professionals actually turn in on themselves in their frustration at not being able to communicate with clients.

Loss of power and control

This sense of inadequacy may be exacerbated in other scenarios: first, if the client engages in cultural practices or is determined to fulfil cultural religious obligations which the professional perceives as obstructive (e.g. Currer's 1986, 1991 pregnant Muslim women respondents adhering to the Ramadan fasting against the advice of their GPs); second (relating specifically to the Irish-speaking community) if clients are actually far more familiar with the culture of the professional and fluent in the language of that culture (i.e. English) than the professional is with the client's culture and language; third, if the latter clients, in the presence of the English-speaking professional, actually choose to speak in another language to their accompanying children, family or friends.

Cornell and Hartmann (1998) speak of feeling 'a sudden distance' in hearing one speak a language other than one's own. McPhatter (1997) believes that professionals in such situations 'experience a great deal of personal and professional discomfort' and that this may manifest itself in 'nervousness and insecurity' (p.263). My interpretation of the findings is not dissimilar. I believe that some professionals experience a loss of power and control when they encounter the differentness of cultures. The problem is made worse if there is a residual racist or sectarian inclination within the professional. The loss of power, the consequential discomfort, nervousness or insecurity are then more likely to manifest themselves in an overt negativity and hostility.

Some aspects of existing training

Training should adequately tackle these issues. McPhatter (1997) is one of the few health and social care writers to attempt to construct a comprehensive training programme, which she refers to as the Cultural Competence Attainment Model. Her paper is structured around three central pillars: enlightened consciousness, grounded knowledge base and cumulative skill proficiency.

Enlightened consciousness 'requires a radical restructuring of a well-entrenched belief system, that perceives oneself and one's culture, including values and ways of behaving, as not only preferred but clearly superior to another's ... The ultimate goal is ... to create a belief in, and acceptance of others' (p.262). McPhatter believes that the grounded knowledge base 'begins with the premise that everything must be exposed to a process of critical analysis' (p.265). She lists and elaborates upon ten components of the knowledge base, encompassing many of the subject areas mentioned above. McPhatter emphasises the 'process' nature of skills development. She believes that one of the most crucial skills in cultural competence is 'the ability to engage a culturally different client's reality in an accepting, genuine, non-offensive manner' (p.272). Much of what she writes about skills may be more appropriately termed general goals of cultural competence training. She herself acknowledges that they are 'assessment and intervention skills in a broad sense' (a point also stressed by Burnham and Harris 1996). These include: the ability to 'intervene skilfully at every level – organisational, community, social, political and economic; to think and act at the 'macro level'; to be able to communicate cross-culturally (those who don't will 'function in a vacuum and will not achieve even minimal levels of effectiveness in their work with culturally different clients').

Other texts approach the training issue differently. For example, Kavanagh and Kennedy (1992), Lago and Thompson (1996) and Papadopoulos *et al.* (1998) invariably concentrate on set piece scenarios, involving professionals and culturally diverse clients. The professional is 'culturally' challenged by numerous aspects of the client's responses and behaviours, not the least of which is the client's scepticism about getting a fair deal in the first instance. The student playing the professional has the opportunity to explore perceptions and feelings about cultural differentness along the way.

Another method is extended case history, in which cultural issues are explored alongside social and economic conditions and family relationship dynamics (Kavanagh and Kennedy 1992). The structure presented by Papadopoulos *et al.* (1998) for training in 'transcultural care' has four main pillars: cultural awareness, cultural knowledge, cultural sensitivity and cultural competence. Within each of these pillars, there is heavy dependence upon knowledge and skills generally, without too much depth in the self-awareness requirements. Henley and Schott (1999) adopt a more narrative form of training, with frequent pauses and pointed questions throughout all their chapters.

There is a wealth of training material in many of these texts, but I suggest that cultural competence training begins at a much more basic level. Nearly all health and social care trainers rightly stress the importance of self-awareness and self-exploration. This needs to be rigorous and challenging. It needs to be facilitated within frameworks that confront the pervasive theme of negativity towards culture observable in health and social care literature and practice over many decades. The small group exercises and subsequent sharing and discussion (Table 15.1), will clearly reveal the students' understanding, perception of and feeling towards culture.

Table 15.1 Exploring culture			
Exercise 1	**Exercise 2**	**Exercise 3**	**Exercise 4**
Ask students to define culture.	Ask students to describe their own culture.	Ask students to list the most important (i.e. positive) aspects of their culture.	Ask students to say why they are the most important aspect of their culture.

The exercises in Table 15.1 may look simple and condescending, but they are guaranteed to stimulate, challenge and amuse. It is a necessary beginning exercise (beginning to think positively about culture). The objective of cultural competence cannot be achieved if negative and hostile perceptions of the central concept are never acknowledged, explored and effectively challenged within small group environments.

Exploring the potential for repeating history: effective self-exploratory exercises

Having critically discussed definitions of culture and the various components of culture, students should be invited to say what components of other people's cultures are problematic for them. These should be listed in terms of priority and can be divided into two categories: audible and visible components of culture (language, race, physical characteristics, dress, diet, etc.); the sometimes inaudible and invisible components (values, religion, child rearing, etc.). Students should then be asked to explain to the group:

1. the nature of the difficulty which each of the components poses;

2. the impact it has (on the student);

3. how they may overcome whatever difficulty (or impact) they have referred to;

4. to what extent the particular components identified as problematic can be tolerated by the student, by the placement agency and by society;

5. what action they might consider in curbing or controlling:

   - the particular cultural practices of individuals (perhaps perceived by the student as cruel, oppressive, dangerous or harmful)
   - certain expressions of particular cultural beliefs
   - the expanding and consolidating of particular cultures.

Table 15.2 sets out a framework which has been completed with purely imaginary responses to some of these questions.

Table 15.2 'Problematic' components of culture		
Components of culture regarded as problematic		**Exploring why these components of culture are problematic** (all questions in this column can be asked of each entry in first two columns)
Audible, visible components	Inaudible invisible components	
Language	Religion	What is the nature of the difficulty which each of the components you've identified pose for you?
Race, physical features	Values	What impact do each of these 'problematic' components have upon you emotionally or professionally?
Rituals	Child rearing	How do you think you may overcome the difficulty which each of these components poses for you?
Strict adherence to diet	Morality: e.g. stricture on contraception or abortion	To what extent do you think these particular components you've identified can be tolerated by you, by your agency, your society?
Educational system	Law (e.g. Islamic law)	What action might you consider in curbing or controlling components of culture you believe are cruel, oppressive, dangerous or harmful?

The exercise shown in Table 15.2 is obviously a more complex and challenging one. It is in effect an indirect self-exploration of one's own cultural base and the values (and biases) stemming from it. Trainers often advocate that workers reflect upon such matters before engaging with families and clients, in order to 'deconstruct' whatever subjective hypotheses and prejudices they may carry (Burnham and Harris 1996). But the extent and nature of anti-culture tendencies is such that a more robust approach is necessary. Everybody knows, for example, that aspects of Islamic culture will pose problems for some non-Islamic students; or that the dominant western perception of India's 'arranged' marriages may create difficulties for feminist

Table 15.3 Perceived associations between cultures and undesirable forces		
Culture	**Perceived to be associated with**	**Impact (if any) of these perceptions when meeting, interacting with, and providing service for client**
Islamic culture	International terrorism The abuse of women The ritual slaughter of animals Extremism in general	?
Irish Gaelic culture	IRA terrorism Irish nationalism Alcoholism	?
West Indian culture	Abuse of women Mental illness Gangsterism Obesity	?
Culture of travelling people	Child neglect Welfare dependency Lawlessness	?
American culture	World domination Capitalist exploitation Commercialism Materialism	?
African tribal cultures	Female circumcision Promiscuity and AIDS Dependency on international charity Lawlessness Slavery	?
British culture	Intitutional racism Colonialism	?

workers in particular. We may all find something incomprehensible and unacceptable within different cultures. Trainers must facilitate students to discover (if they don't already know) what that something is and, more importantly, how its impact may adversely impinge upon all aspects of practice.

Perceived associations between culture and destructive forces

The exercise in Table 15.3 extends the challenge further. Students should explore how they may associate particular cultures with movements, politics, ideas, ideology or characteristics that they consider harmful or destructive. The students' task is to list all possible associations, in priority, and then to ask themselves how they think these perceived associations impact upon their provision of services to the individuals involved. Table 15.3 shows an imaginary response within such a framework.

Acknowledged associations and exploration of their potential impact upon the quality of services represents a major step forward in self-exploration. The exercise in Table 15.4 focuses on components of culture regarded by the majority of students as problematic. Let us imagine that most regard religion as such. They should then return to and explore in depth one of the questions asked in Table 15.2, i.e. the nature of the difficulty which this particular component poses. It may well be any of the convictions discussed at length in Chapter 9. These and other possible convictions can be put directly to students with the question: 'Do you feel that …?

Table 15.4 Exploring possible reasons for negativity/hostility to culture arising from conviction about the religion within that culture	
Organised religions have played a significant role in colonisation and oppression of indigenous people?	Yes/No
Health and social care training courses should not be teaching about particular religions?	Yes/No
Organised religion is too authoritative and controlling?	Yes/No
Some religions have an intolerant, oppressive 'morality', e.g. anti-contraception, anti-abortion, etc?	Yes/No
Established religions are intolerant of alternative life styles?	Yes/No
Religion is male dominated and sexist?	Yes/No

Religious fundamentalism and religious cults have caused untold suffering to innocent peoples?	Yes/No
Religious clerics have exploited their control and authority, particularly over children, by sexually and physically abusing them?	Yes/No
Religion is worthy only of satire and ridicule?	Yes/No

Answering yes to each of the questions in Table 15.4 need pose no problem whatsoever in health and social care work. In fact, probably most health and social care professionals (including the author) are more likely to answer 'yes' than 'no' to most questions. But these questions only preface the far more important self-exploration. When one does answer yes, does this impede in any way the quality of service to clients for whom religion is very important. Does a yes answer tend to invoke any of the following reactions:

1. an indifference to religions?

2. disinclination to learn about various aspects of the religion(s) practised by a substantial number of your clients?

3. lack of interest in how adherence to religious practice and customs influences your clients' responses to the help and advice you're trying to provide?

4. make you critical and resentful of a particular religion when you learn that it is heavily influencing the thoughts and actions of clients?

5. provoke you into explicit criticism of what you believe is the harmful influence of religion?

6. ignore or downgrade the express wishes of clients for:
   - facilities to maintain religious worship
   - dietary, clothing and other requirements necessary in religious adherence
   - appropriate attention to religious ritual and formalities in illness and death
   - due respect to the body and organs of loved ones, as emphasised by certain religions
   - placement in residential care which will encourage and promote the continuance of the child's education and religion as parents have chosen

- choosing same religion foster parents when children are taken into care
- considering same religion adoptive parents?

All the cultural components regarded as problematic can be dealt in this way. From the training, professionally qualifying point of view, they are only problematic if they lead to any of the above behaviours and attitudes in the worker. But it is essential that such behaviours and attitudes, and the underlying causes, are revealed during basic training.

Cultural competence

What is it that clients are asking for?

Trainers should help dispel a myth which may sustain hostility and negativity towards culture. This myth convinces some that cultural minority groups expect preferential treatment; that they expect workers to be knowledgeable of and deferential to all components of their cultures; that they place intolerable burdens on hard-pressed, front-line staff. The origins of this myth may lie in a misinterpretation of available literature on culture. For example, in Gerrish et al. (1996), Henley and Schott (1999) and Katbamna (2000) there are pertinent examples of culturally insensitive practice. Often in response to the pain and offence this causes, the respondents will make comments to the effect that the workers would not be so culturally insensitive if they came from the same country, spoke the same language, shared the same values, or knew about the way the presenting problem or issue (e.g. childbirth) was dealt with within the client's culture and country of origin. This is entirely different, however, from the interpretation which may be placed upon it, that the client expects all those things.

My research demonstrated that the respondents were realistic and generous in their expectations of workers (and often exceedingly tolerant of culturally incompetent practice). As has already been stated, not one respondent expected individual health and social services staff to be able to speak Irish (they did expect teams of health workers visiting their schools to have at least one member fluent in the language). Nor did any respondent expect staff to be knowledgeable of all the different components of their culture such as family values, Irish music, literature, art, sport, etc. 'If only you professionals could realise … it's the small things that really count,' said one respondent, meaning small gestures, small words, with the right attitude and approach. First and foremost, the respondents wanted respect on initial contact. Second, they wanted workers to appreciate why the client's culture was so important, which would necessitate them being at least aware of those components the client may regard as crucial (e.g. religion, language, family values). Third, the client welcomed genuine and friendly curiosity about his or her culture. Fourth, should a worker reveal some ignorance about some aspect of the culture, they should respond appropriately. Such responses may include a simple admission of ignorance (not an apology); a commitment to take the learning on board and not make the same mistake again; and perhaps the most appropriate response of all, particularly when shared with the client, laughing at oneself. Inappropriate responses on the part of professionals are a refusal to admit anything, annoyance at being caught out, a resentment towards the client who has (most probably unintentionally) exposed the worker's ignorance, a lack of interest in the client and in his or her presenting problem. Burnham and Harris (1996) make a similar point in writing about family therapy with cultural minorities: 'We learnt that it was better to be 'clumsy' than not to do anything, to be prepared to learn from our clients and from our mistakes' (p.131). There is a delicate balance to be struck here by trainers preparing students for professional practice: to be thinking, speaking and acting confidently, yet fostering that precious capacity for humility.

The primacy of effort over knowledge

The 'respect on initial impact' mentioned above is commonly manifest in the professional's response to the client's name. Trainers must ensure qualified staff leave their courses with an acute sense of the importance of names, and an awareness of the potential for sensitive and insensitive practice in respect of names. The Irish respondents did not expect professionals to be able to pronounce or spell their names correctly; but they wanted professionals at least to respect their names and to cease reacting to Irish names as if there was something terribly odd or even threatening about them. When they enlightened professionals about spelling and pronunciation, they expected the professionals to make the effort to get it right next time or, having been enlightened second time round, to get it right on the third occasion. The respondents themselves identified 'effort' as constituting cultural sensitivity in respect of names: 'the speech therapists were making a real effort to learn Irish through the child'; 'the GP makes an effort to get spelling and pronunciation of our names right'; 'the optician takes the trouble to learn how to spell the name and how to pronounce it'; 'the receptionist really struggled with ————'s name; she kept trying and eventually got it right.'

Conversely, those professionals who still made no effort to get the spelling and pronunciation right, after being told on numerous occasions, were often regarded as culturally insensitive: 'receptionists in clinic and hospital not making an effort to get our names right'; 'even when I spell it out they write it down wrong'; 'receptionists and chemists not making any effort to get our children's names right'; 'a lot of professionals get the name wrong again and again; they don't really try; I used to say to them ... but you feel ... you're a bit of a complainer.' These testimonies add considerably to a growing literature exposing cultural insensitivity revolving around attitude and approach to personal and family names within minority cultures. Newly qualified health and social care staff can make a significant contribution to eradicating such practice.

Attitude and approach

The all-pervasive challenge in cultural competence training and practice is adopting the right attitude and approach. This is achieved when 'awareness, sensitivity and genuine acceptance towards culturally different others are internalised' and 'our whole affective demeanour' becomes one of 'openness to engagement' (McPhatter 1997, p.264). Clients do not have unrealistic expectations that busy front-line health and social care workers will additionally: (a) learn another language; (b) acquire knowledge and expertise in interpreting the Holy Qu'ran's stipulations on parental obligations; (c) have explored differing interpretations of the laws of karma within the Hindu faith; (d) have studied the cultural meaning and experiences of childbirth in some remote Himalayan settlement; (e) know the meaning of Celtic names and their origins in the legends and myths of ancient Ireland; or (f) be familiar with any of the countless culturally significant terms and phrases with which writers often regale their texts. Even less do clients expect professionals to 'be one of us'. The notion that minorities are generally making unrealistic demands upon already overburdened professionals is manifestly absurd.

Summary and conclusion

Much of the lack of understanding of culture and the failure to recognise its significance in the lives of cultural minorities can be traced back to the requirements of professional training courses. Anthropology, and cultural anthropology in particular, are subject areas immensely valuable for cultural competence training. These subjects should be incorporated within all health and social care training, both pre-qualifying and in-service training. Literature, research and training are increasingly including concepts such as cultural awareness, cultural sensitivity (and insensitivity) and cultural competence. They are replacing the narrower, more restrictive concepts such as anti-racist, anti-oppressive and anti-discriminatory practice. The knowledge base for culturally competent practice was reviewed. Some important additions were listed and some reservations about certain components of knowledge were expressed. In the light of substantial evidence of negativity and hostility to culture, much of this chapter was devoted to the construction of frameworks for self-exploration. Trainers, individual students and small groups can use these frameworks to explore potential sources of difficulties which culture or the differing components of culture may pose. The final section of the chapter challenged the assumptions that people from minority cultures expect too much from hard-pressed, front-line professionals or that they place intolerable burdens upon them. The research findings in this text demonstrate the opposite.

Epilogue

Life is unpredictable. If during the final year of the last millennium someone had said that I would leave my job, move to another country and be homeless, all in the first six months of the new millennium, I would not have believed it. I have not been set upon by some catastrophe, I should add; my wife and I merely retired early (I hope to write more), sold up and left Ireland, and returned to mainland Britain. That's where our three adult children are. We don't yet have a home of our own. After much consultation, decision making and preparation, we are living temporarily with our son, daughter-in-law and grandchild.

What has this got to do with culture and cultural competence, you may ask. Moving in with one's adult children and grandchildren is not the 'culturally appropriate' thing to do in mainland Britain, certainly not for white, middle-aged, professional people. The whole thrust of modern living in the west goes in the opposite direction. It begins when young professionals depart their family nest as quickly as they can, move as far away as their circumstances allow, partner and have children (and later maybe partner again and have more children), and return to let their parents see the grandchildren on set occasions such as birthdays, anniversaries and Christmas. The prospect of parents/grandparents moving in at some point along the way is inconceivable.

Consequently you may see many an enthusiastic grandparent at railway stations and airports patiently awaiting sight of their one- or two-year-old grandchild, recognisable only because he or she is in the arms of their own adult son or daughter. You will see many a child stiffen with apprehension as the eager, unaware grandparent (often a complete stranger to the child) quickly relieves mother of that child and smothers her with love and kisses and oohs and aahs, telling all and sundry that she really is the most beautiful child this earth has ever produced (unfortunately the child sees nothing to smile about at that particular moment in time). A few days later, when grandparents and children have adapted to each other, the process of separation begins. I reckon there are millions of permanently pining grandparents in the western world.

I've often thought about scenarios like these, in reading and writing about different cultures. There were three main stimulants: my own situation, an article by Kedar Nath Dwivedi (1996) and my reflections on living with a Bengali family in Calcutta, some 20 years ago.

When I told friends and professional colleagues of our plans, some looked at me with undisguised sympathy and not a little incredulity. One asked bluntly: 'Are you sure you know what you're doing?' Another cited examples of mere holidays ending in disaster because people who thought they knew each other simply couldn't survive more than a couple of days living together. Another suggested that it was precisely because our relationships were good (as I often maintained), that I shouldn't be contemplating doing something which may jeopardise them.

Dwivedi's article sheds some light upon these concerns, which are in effect cultural concerns about independence, individuality, boundaries, separateness and privacy. He traces their origin back to the American War of Independence and the subsequently increasing (and ultimately enveloping) influence of a western (American) culture which regarded independence as the cherished ideal, and dependence as most undesirable. He quotes from Tamura and Lau (1992): 'In western cultures, individuality is the prime value, and relatedness is secondary' (p.332). The pursuit of all these objectives takes place within an 'egocentric perspective', and Dwivedi appears to suggest some linkage with the 'rising tide of narcissistic disorders' in the west.

In contrast, many eastern cultures and their religions do not regard a person as individual or independent. They are more likely to be perceived as 'dividual' or 'divisible', part of an 'embedded interconnectedness of relation-ships' and the concept of dependency, pejoratively perceived in the west, is framed very differently as 'long term intergenerational reciprocity' and incul-cated in children from the earliest age.

This contrasts sharply with many westerners' scant knowledge and limited understanding of large Asian extended families (e.g. overcrowding, living in each other's pockets, no privacy, no independence, etc.). Dwivedi clarifies this with a fascinating theoretical exposition of the cultural and ideological under-pinning of such families. He believes that growing up in the extended family is for most Asians the 'cultural ideal of mastering narcissism'.

> The cultural ideal of filial loyalty and fraternal solidarity stipulates common economic and social life, common residence, ritual activities and cooking arrangements. The joint celebration of religious festivals, family rituals and traditional ceremonies within the extended family helps further to consolidate family ties. (Dwivedi 1996, p.29)

The western nuclear family units (husband, wife and 1.72 children) threaten the whole edifice and bonding within extended family, because 'the natural tendency of love is to be concentrated within that particular unit' and potentially excludes all the other extended family members and their interests. This danger not only necessitates vigilance, but also 'proactive training'.

As for parents moving in with their adult children, and the alarm and the concern such a prospect may generate in any western heart and mind, Dwivedi quotes Vatuk's indignant response: 'To make one's home with adult children is not associated with emotions like shame or guilt' (Vatuk 1990, p.66, quoted in Dwivedi 1996, p.32).

There is the temptation here to romanticise one culture and demonise the other; also to ignore the fact that millions of Asian families, having settled and acculturated in the west, may neither recognise nor desire any of these features of Asian family life which Dwivedi is describing. I am not going to succumb to those temptations. The main intention in this epilogue is to illustrate in a different form just how challenging the goal of cultural competence can be (but ultimately how rewarding); to demonstrate the often unbridgeable divides between cultures, and between the beliefs and ways of life within cultures. I think all health and social care professionals should acknowledge that cultural diversity generates a major challenge, and that even with the best intentions in the world they may not always surmount it.

I lived with a Bengali family in Calcutta 20 years ago. I kept a very detailed diary of my experiences. There were countless cultural learning opportunities, including all the predictable ones, like family naming systems, gestures, touch and non-touch, words and expressions, the meaning of and proper pronunciation of forenames, family values, arranged marriages, child rearing, education, diet, clothes, religion and prayers (my limited understanding and narrow prejudicial perceptions on many of these underwent fundamental change). The day I joined the family, I really did become part of the family. I was 'uncle' to the two teenage boys in the family, Armitav and Sujat. I was also the subject of enormous curiosity on the part of the extended family. Arriving in Calcutta, exhausted and disoriented, I quickly fell asleep in my room. When I awoke many hours later, some eight or nine beautiful friendly faces encircled my bed.

They had obviously been there some time. Armitav and Sujat were among them. They introduced me. The abiding memory of that moment is of my astonishment at this wholesale invasion of my privacy and the corresponding facial expressions of warmth and welcome which had not the slightest hint of awareness that they were invading anything of the kind.

During my extended stay, I went to Darjeeling at the foot of the Himalayas, and then into Nepal, for a short break. Before going, I purchased presents for my wife, children, relatives and friends – I was due to leave India for home a day after I got back. I wrapped the presents carefully and asked Armitav whether he would kindly look after them for me. Of course he would. When I returned, all the presents were opened. I enquired of Armitav. He could not understand my enquiry. I tried to convey to him as gently and as diplomatically as I could that I expected the presents to be as I had left them. But they were exactly as I had left them. He had merely looked at them. He could sense my irritation, but he apparently couldn't fathom its cause.

These are only two minor incidents in an overall learning experience which I regard as the most intense and the most fruitful of my professional life, to say nothing of the generosity and hospitality, which on occasions overwhelmed me. So my purpose, again, is not to criticise another's culture, but merely to highlight one professional's difficulty in coping with certain aspects of that culture. The experiences illustrate some of the cultural themes and principles which Dwivedi so perceptively writes about. I was not capable then of recognising the 'embedded interconnectedness of relationships' underpinning behaviours, only preoccupied with the personal discomforts it was causing me.

All these memories came flooding back when I was doing the research. As a front-line professional in family and childcare work over a 20-year period, I often thought of the discomfort and challenge felt by many health and social care professionals in contact with the Irish-speaking community. Each time I interviewed a respondent, I tried to imagine myself in the situation of the professionals whose cultural sensitivity and cultural insensitivity were being described to me. I imagined myself back in Britain, arriving on the doorstep of some client whom I knew, knowing that their first language was English. They then told me that they had decided to recreate their lost cultural heritage and to learn the language of their culture; that they had adopted the equivalent of their own names and addresses in that language and henceforth would like me to call them by these 'new' names, and to record their names and addresses in this new language. I imagined myself listening to this and looking at my clients with some incredulity. Having had the typical stressful week of the professional care worker – frequented by mental health crises, assailed by the relatives of elderly at risk, invoking emergency legislation for abused children, or seeing a fostering placement break down for the third time – I have to confess to a powerful impulse to yell out to my new language aspiring client: 'You must be joking!' I always concluded, however, that such a predictable, understandable response might just be unhelpful and grossly culturally insensitive, but understandable nonetheless.

I exaggerate of course. The Irish-speaking community neither demanded nor confronted. All they wanted was a little bit of respect and effort, the right attitude and approach and (as they were so keen to inform me) many workers to their credit gave a lot more, but regrettably many gave a lot less.

My racism-obsessed training and its negativity to culture could not have prepared me for either of these situations. It did nothing to enable me to approach my Bengali family with complete openness and respect; nor would it have equipped me with the knowledge sufficient to understand the sacrifices people may make to retrieve their cultural heritage. Training is improving gradually on these matters, but there are still formidable obstacles. I mentioned one of these obstacles in Chapter 2, how the words 'culture' and 'cultural' are so frequently misused to describe every conceivable kind of undesirable behaviour by human beings that the words themselves take on a wholly pejorative meaning. I provided numerous examples: cultural apartheid, cultural racism, cultural oppression, cultural violence, etc. During the writing of this book I have read of many more, particularly in health and social care texts and in the loftier editorials of Britain's broadsheets: 'culture of cruelty', 'culture of delays', 'yob culture', 'culture of cronyism', 'dustbin culture', 'a culture rotten beyond repair' (Ashworth Hospital, The Guardian, 13 January 1999). As I have said, there are literally hundreds of these terms. My award for the worst, most offensive, most contradictory and most extraordinary goes to Libby Purves (2000) whose otherwise intelligent article on sex education concludes that Britain is now a 'shag culture'.

Is it any wonder that for so many the term 'culture' assumes a negativity and destructiveness all of its own? Can we really be serious about improving services for minorities who regard their culture as the most important thing in their lives if we do not attempt to rein back from this deeply offensive, linguistic nonsense, in which we have all most likely indulged?

Cultural competence is 'the ability to maximise sensitivity and minimise insensitivity in the service of culturally diverse communities'. The more we

respect both the word 'culture' and 'culture' as a concept of profound importance in the daily lives of millions of people, the nearer we move towards the
goal of achieving cultural competence.

Cultural competence is not however fundamentally about 'avoiding'
hurting people culturally; it is more proactive than that – encouraging
workers to explore, as much as they should respect, different cultures. It
further enhances clients' pride in their culture and in their sense of (cultural)
identity stemming from that culture. For those clients inhibited by fear or
ridicule from expressing their culture (such as some of the Irish-speaking
respondents), it confronts the source of that fear and ridicule head-on.
Cultural competence emerges from rigorous self-exploration; it expands the
professional's empathic repertoire, ensuring there is no culturally biased
instant response, on learning of actions or behaviour which might otherwise
be incomprehensible or alarming: Ramadan fasting during pregnancy, for
example, or temporarily moving in with one's adult children. It also makes
professionals aware of the enormous dimensions of culture; that it may well
embrace such diverse or related components as values and the relationship
with the physical environment, family life and child rearing, care of the
elderly, religion, language, education, myth and legend, the arts and sports.
Cultural competence makes it that little bit easier to understand that each or all
of these components may be profoundly significant to the client.

To know just how significant, we may return to Arooj and her sisters. The
yashmak she wore, for example, represents infinitely more to Moslem women
than a headscarf worn by millions of other women. From the fiction and the
fact (her interview on Channel 4 news) one got the sense that Arooj's Islamic
faith and culture were woven into the fabric of her everyday existence. A little
more explicitness may be called for. Here is another young Muslim woman
just recently expressing her gratitude on returning to her Islamic roots:

> Within these four walls I am at peace. Once I was weak; once I was lost.
> Now there is no question without answer. There's so much I need to ask,
> and so much only He could answer. He, to whom I submit. Where I
> thought I was going to lose, there's so much now to gain. The purpose of
> life is worshipping the creator, all of God's creations. The sun and the
> moon and the earth and the stars also worship him. This is what drives me,
> saves me, frees me. (BBC2 'Arena' 2000)

Cultural competence makes no demand on workers to accept or to believe
what others may accept and believe within their own cultures; the major challenges are to be open and aware, to understand and to respect.

References

Abas, M.A., Phillips, C., Carter, J., Walter, J., Banerjee, S. and Levy, R. (1998) 'Culturally sensitive validation of screening questionaires for depression in older African-Caribbean people living in south London.' British Journal of Psychiatry 173, 249–254.

Agathonos-Georgopoulou, H. and Browne, K. (1997) 'The prediction of child maltreatment in Greek families.' Child Abuse and Neglect 21, 8, 721–735.

Agency Network Programme (1999) The Long Walk. (Website: www.navajo.org/lwalk.html)

Ahmad, W. I. U. (1996) 'The trouble with culture.' In D. Kelleher and S. Hillier (eds) Researching Cultural Differences in Health. London: Routledge.

Ahmad, W.I.U., Baker, M.R. and Kernohan, E.E.M. (1991) 'General practitioners' perceptions of Asian patients.' Family Practice 8, 1, 52–56.

Ahmed, L. (1992) Women and Gender in Islam: Historical Roots of a Modern Debate. New Haven CT: Yale University Press.

Ahmed, S. (1986) 'Cultural racism in work with Asian women and girls.' In S. Ahmed, J. Cheetham and J. Small (eds) Social Work with Black Children and their Families. London: Batsford.

Ahmed, S. (1987) 'Racism in social work assessment.' In BASW Social Work and Racism Group. Birmingham: BASW.

Ahmed, S. (1994) 'Anti-racist social work: a black perspective.' In C. Hanvey and T. Philpot (eds) Practising Social Work. London: Routledge.

Ahn, H.N. (1993) 'Cultural diversity and the definition of child abuse.' In R. Barth, J. Duerr Berrick and N. Gilbert (eds) Child Welfare Review, vol. 1. New York: Columbia University Press, pp.28–55.

Aldridge, D. (2000) Spirituality, Healing and Medicine: Return to the Silence. London: Jessica Kingsley Publishers.

Amiel, B. (1993) 'Lady Bountiful's lethal little society list.' The Times, 11 October.

Amin, K. (1998) 'Ethnic minorities and religious affiliations: their size and impact on Britain and social work.' In N. Patel, D. Naik and B. Humphries Visions of Reality, Religion and Ethnicity in Social Work. London: CCETSW.

Andrew, A. and Sarsfield, P. (1984) Innu Health: The Role of Self-determination. In R. Fortuine (ed) Circulpolar Health '84: Proceedings of the Sixth International Symposium on Circumpolar Health, Seattle: University of Washington Press.

Anonymous (1998) 'The AWWAS group.' In N. Patel, D. Naik and B. Humphries (eds) Visions of Reality: Religion and Ethnicity in Social Work. London: CCETSW.

Appelbaum, S.A. (1973) Psychological mindedness: word, concept and essence. *International Journal of Psychoanalysis 54*, 35–36.

Asad, M. (1980) *The Principles of State and Government in Islam*. Gibraltar: Dar al-Andalus.

Aspinall, P.J. (1997) 'The conceptual basis of ethnic group terminology and classifications.' *Social Science and Medicine 45*, 5, 689–698.

Atkinson, R.L., Atkinson, R.C., Smith, E.E. and Hilgard, E. R. (1987) *Introduction to Psychology*. Florida: Harcourt Brace Jovanovich.

Aziz, E. (1989) *Enhancing Child Welfare in Aboriginal Communities (Child Protection Issues)*. Perth: Department for Community Services.

Azzam, A. (1979) *The Eternal Message of Muhammad*. London: Quartet.

Bailey, C. (1996) 'The health needs of children from ethnic minorities.' In K. Dwivedi and V. Varma (eds) *Meeting the Needs of Ethnic Minority Children*. London: Jessica Kingsley Publishers.

Bakken, B. (1993) 'Prejudice and danger: the only-child in China.' *Childhood, A Global Journal of Child Research 1*, 1, 46–61.

Barnes, P. (1995) *Personal, Social and Emotional Development of Children*. Oxford: Blackwell.

Barstow, D.G. (1999) 'Female genital mutilation: the penultimate gender abuse.' *Child Abuse and Neglect 23*, 5, 501–510.

Bateson, G. and Mead, M. (1942) *Balinese Character: A Photographic Analysis*. New York: New York Academy of Sciences.

BBC1 (1998) *Inside Story* 3 February.

BBC2 (2000) *Arena* 25 May.

Bean, P. and Melville, J. (1989) *Lost Children of the Empire*, London, Unwin Hyman.

Beevers, D.G. (1981) Ethnic differences in common diseases. *Postgraduate Medical Journal*, 57(674), 744.

Benedict, R. (1959) *Patterns of Culture*. New York: Houghton Mifflin Co.

Bennett, T. (1997) 'Towards a pragmatic for cultural studies.' In J. McGuigan (ed) *Cultural Methodologies*. London: Sage.

Berndt, R.M. (1974) *Australian Aboriginal Religion*. Leiden: Institute of Religious Iconography/Groningen: State University.

Bhate, S. and Bhate, S. (1996) 'Psychiatric needs of ethnic minority children.' In K. Dwivedi and V. Varma (eds) *Meeting the Needs of Ethnic Minority Children*. London: Jessica Kingsley Publishers.

Bhui, K., Brown, P., Hardie, T., Watson, J.P. and Parrott, J. (1998) 'African-Caribbean men remanded to Brixton Prison: psychiatric and forensic characteristics and outcomes of final court appearances.' *British Journal of Psychiatry 172*, 327–344.

Biestik, F. (1961) *The Casework Relationship*. London: Unwin.

Blakemore, K. and Boneham, M. (1994) *Age Race and Ethnicity: A Comparative Approach*. Buckingham: Open University Publications.

Blom-Cooper, L. (1985) *A Child In Trust: Jasmine Beckford*. London: Brent.

Boushel, M. (1991) 'Anti-discriminatory work on placement: helping students prepare.' *Social Work Education 10*, 3, 51–69.

Bowling, S. (1990) *Elderly People from Ethnic Minorities: A report on four projects*. London: Age Concern Institute of Gerontology/Kings College, London.

Brah, A. (1992) 'Women of South Asian origin in Britain: issues and concerns.' In P. Braham, A. Rattansi and R. Skellington (eds) *Racism and Anti-Racism: Inequalities, Opportunities and Policies*. London: Sage.

Bray, W. and Trump, D. (1982) *Dictionary of Archaeology.* London: Penguin.

Braye, S. and Preston-Shoot, M. (1995) *Empowering Practice in Social Care.* Buckingham: Open University Press.

Brindle, D. (1999) 'Drug death girl shuttled among carers.' *The Guardian,* 5 October.

Brissett-Chapman, S. (1997) 'Child protection risk assessment and African American children: cultural ramifications for families and communities.' *Child Welfare 86,* 1, 43–63.

Bryson, J. (1967) *Matthew Arnold, Poetry and Prose.* London: Rupert Hart Davis.

Burchfield, R.W. (1972) *A Supplement to the Oxford English Dictionary.* Oxford: Oxford University Press.

Burnham, J. and Harris, Q. (1996) Emerging Ethnicities. A Tale of Three Cultures. In K.N. Dwivedi and V.P. Varma (eds) *Meeting the Needs of Ethnic Minority Children,* London: Jessica Kingsley Publications.

Bushell, W. (1996) 'The immigrant (West Indian) child in school.' In K. N. Dwivedi and V. P. Varma (eds) *Meeting the Needs of Ethnic Minority Children: A Handbook for Professionals.* London: Jessica Kingsley Publishers.

Campbell, J. and Oliver, M. (1996) *Disability Politics: Understanding Our Past: Changing Our Future.* London: Routledge.

Canda, E. R. (1998) 'Edward R. Canda's response.' In N. Patel, D. Naik and B. Humphries *Visions of Reality, Religion and Ethnicity in Social Work.* London: CCETSW.

Canino, I.A. and Spurlock, J. (1994) *Culturally Diverse Children and Adolescents: Assessments, Diagnosis and Treatments.* New York: Guilford Press.

Carpenter, I. and Brocklington, I. (1980) 'A study of mental illness in Asians, West Indians, and Africans living in Manchester.' *British Journal of Psychiatry 137,* 201–205.

Carter, H. and Aitchison, J. (1986) 'Language areas and language change in Wales: 1961–1981.' In I. Hume and W.T.R. Pryce (eds) *The Welsh and Their Country.* Llandysul, Dyfed: Gomer.

Central Council for the Education and Training of Social Workers (CCETSW) (1991) *Towards Racial Justice: The Teaching of Anti Racism in Diploma in Social Work Programmes.* London: CCETSW.

Central Council for the Education and Training of Social Workers (CCETSW) (1995) *Assuring Quality in the Diploma in Social Work – 1.* London: CCETSW.

Chamba, R. and Ahmad, W.I.U. (2000) Language, communication and information: the needs of parents caring for a severely disabled child. In W.I.U Ahmad (ed.) *Ethnicity, Disability and Chronic Illness.* Buckingham: Open University Publications.

Chamba, R., Ahmad, W.I.U., Hirst, M., Lawton, D. and Beresford, B. (1999) *On the Edge: Minority Ethnic Families Caring for a Severely Disabled Child.* Bristol: Policy Press.

Chamberlayne, P., Cooper, A., Freeman, R. and Rustin, M. (1999) *Welfare and Culture in Europe: Towards a New Paradigm in Social Policy.* London, Jessica Kingsley Publications.

Chandler, M.J. and Lalonde, C. (1998) Cultural Continuity as a Hedge Against Suicide in Canada's First Nations. *Transcultural Psychiatry 35,* 2, 199–221.

Channel 4 (2000) *Dispatches: The Fight For a Child,* 10th February

Channer, Y. and Parton, N. (1991) 'Racism, cultural relativism, and child protection.' In: Violence Against Children Study Group *Taking Child Abuse Seriously.* London: Unwin Hyman.

Chatwin, B. (1988) *The Songlines.* London: Picador.

Choo, C. (1990) *Aboriginal Child Poverty.* Child Poverty Review 2. Melbourne: Brotherhood of St. Lawrence.

Churm, C. (1999) 'Cultural lessons.' *Community Care*, 13–19 May.

Collier, A.F., McClure, F.H., Collier, J., Otto, C. and Polloi, A. (1999) 'Culture-specific views of child maltreatment in a Pacific-Island community.' *Child Abuse and Neglect 23*, 3, 229–234.

Collier, M.J. (1998) 'Researching cultural identity: reconciling interpretive and postcolonial perspectives.' In V. Tanno and A. Gonzalez (eds) *Communication and Identity Across Cultures*. London: Sage.

Colton, M. and Roberts, S. (1997) *Unequal Access to Health Care: The Experiences of Black and Ethnic Minorities in Swansea Neath and Port Talbot*. Swansea: University of Wales Swansea and Swansea Bay Racial Equality Council.

Colton, M., Drury, C. and Williams, M. (1995a) *Staying Together: Supporting Families under the Children Act*. Aldershot: Arena, Ashgate.

Colton, M., Drury, C. and Williams, M. (1995b) *Children in Need*. Aldershot: Arena, Ashgate.

Commonwealth of Australia (1997) *Report of the National Inquiry into the Separation of Aboriginals and Torres Strait Islander Children from Their Families. [Bringing Them Home* report.] Sydney: Human Rights and Equal Opportunities Commission.

Corby, B. (1993) *Child Abuse, Towards a Knowledge Base*. Buckingham: Open University Press.

Cornell, S. and Hartmann, D. (1998) *Ethnicity and Race: Making Identities in a Changing World*. California: Pine Forge Press.

Corral-Verdugo, V., Frías-Armenta, M., Romea, M. and Muñoz, A. (1995) 'Validity of a scale measuring beliefs regarding the "positive" effects of punishing children: a study of Mexican mothers.' *Child Abuse and Neglect 19*, 6, 669–679.

Cotterell, A. (1999) *Encyclopedia of World Mythology*. Bath: Paragon Press.

Creek, J. (2000) *Occupational Therapy and Mental Health*. Edinburgh: Churchill Livingstone.

Crossman, V. and McLoughlin, D. (1994) 'A peculiar eclipse: E. Estyn Evans and Irish studies.' *The Irish Review 15*, 79–96.

Currer, C. (1986) 'Health concepts and illness behaviour: the case of some Pathan mothers in Britain.' PhD thesis, Department of Sociology, University of Warwick.

Currer, C. (1991) 'Understanding the mother's viewpoint: the case of Pathan women in Britain.' In S. Wyke and J. Hewison (eds) *Child Health Matters: Caring for Children in the Community*. Buckingham, Open University Press.

Curtis, E. (1907) *The North American Indian: The Complete Portfolios*. London: Taschen (1997).

Dalrymple, J. and Burke, B. (1995) *Anti Oppressive Practice: Social Care and the Law*. Buckingham: Open University Press.

Dalrymple, J. and Hough, J. (1995) *Having a Voice: An Exploration of Children's Rights and Advocacy*. Birmingham: Venture Press.

Dartington Social Research Unit (1995) *Child Protection: Messages From Research*. London: HMSO.

Das Gupta, J. (1975) 'Ethnicity, language demands and national development in India.' In N. Glazer and D. P. Moynihan *Ethnicity: Theory and Experience*. Cambridge, MA: Harvard University Press.

Day, P.R. (1987) *Sociology in Social Work Practice*. Basingstoke: Macmillan.

Debo, A. (1995) *A History of the Indians of the United States*. London: Pimlico.

Denny, D. (1998) *Social Policy and Social Work*. Oxford: Oxford University Press.

Department of Education, Northern Ireland (DENI) (1998) *Enrolment in Irish speaking schools in Northern Ireland, 1996.* Bangor: Department of Education.

Department of Health (1991) *The Patient's Charter, Raising the Standard.* London: HMSO.

Department of Health (1992a) *Review of Adoption Law. Report to Ministers of an Interdepartmental Working Group. A Consultation Document.* London: HMSO.

Department of Health (1992b) 'Implementation of caring for people: corporate contracts.' Letter from A. Foster, Deputy Chief Executive to Regional General Managers, 7 February.

Department of Health (1992c) *The Health of the Nation: A Strategy for Health in England.* London: HMSO.

Department of Health (1993) *Ethnicity and Health: A Guide for the NHS.* London: Department of Health.

Department of Health and Social Security (1974) *Report of the Committee of Enquiry into the Care and Supervision Provided in Relation to Maria Colwell.* London: HMSO.

Devore, W. and Schlesinger, E.G. (1981) *Ethnic Social Work Practice.* London: Mosby.

Dingwell, R., Eekelaar, J. and Murray, T. (1993) *The Protection of Children: State Intervention and Family Life.* Oxford: Blackwell.

Dominelli, L. (1988) *Anti-Racist Social Work.* London: Macmillan.

Dosanjh, J.S. and Ghuman, P.A.S. (1997) 'Punjabi child rearing in Britain: development of identity, religion and bilingualism.' *Childhood: A Global Journal of Child Research 4, 3,* 285–303.

Dwivedi, K. N. (1996) 'Culture and personality.' In K. N. Dwivedi and V. P. Varma (eds) *Meeting the Needs of Ethnic Minority Children: A Handbook for Professionals.* London: Jessica Kingsley Publishers.

Dwivedi, K.N. and Varma, V.P. (eds) (1996) *Meeting the Needs of Ethnic Minority Children.* London: Jessica Kingsley Publications.

Dwivedi, R. (1996) 'Community and youth work with Asian women and girls.' In K. N. Dwivedi and V. P. Varma (eds) *Meeting the Needs of Ethnic Minority Children: A Handbook for Professionals.* London: Jessica Kingsley Publishers.

Editorial (1988) 'Race, anti-racism and the editorial collective.' *Critical Social Policy 21,* 4–7.

Editorial (1999) 'Reluctant brides.' *The Times,* 29 May.

Elkin, A.P. (1933) *Studies in Australian Totemism,* Oceania Monographs no. 2. Sydney: Australian National Research Council.

European Commission Director General V (1994) *The Demographic Situation of the European Union.* Brussels: EC. DGV-COM (94) 595.

Evans, E.E. (1984) Ulster: The Common Ground. Mullingar.

Fabb, W.E. and Marshall, J.R. (1996) *The Nature of General Family Practice.* Lancaster: MTP Press.

Fernando, S. (1988) *Race and Culture in Psychiatry.* London, Croom Helm.

Fernando, S. (1991) *Mental Health, Race and Culture.* Basingstoke: Macmillan.

Fernando, S. (1995) *Mental Health in a Multi Ethnic Society, A Multi Disciplinary Handbook.* London: Routledge.

Ferrara, N. (1999) *Emotional Expression Among Cree Indians: The Role of Pictorial Representations in the Assessment of Psychological Mindedness.* London: Jessica Kingsley Publishers.

Ferris, J. M. and Graddy, E. (1989) 'Production costs, transaction costs, and local government contractor choice.' Mimeograph. School of Public Administration, University of Southern California, Los Angeles.

Fitzgerald, T.K. (1993) *Metaphors of Identity*. Albany NY: State University of NY Press.

Flekkøy, M.G. and Kaufman, N.H. (1997) *The Participation Rights of the Child: Rights and Responsibilities in Family and Society*. London: Jessica Kingsley Publishers.

Forder, J. and Knapp, M.R.J. (1993) 'Social care markets: the voluntary care sector and residential care for elderly people in England.' In S. Saxon-Harrold and J. Kendall (eds) *Researching the Voluntary Sector: A National, Local and International Perspective*. Tonbridge: Charities Aids Foundation.

Forsythe, B. (1995) 'Discrimination in social work – an historical note.' *British Journal of Social Work 25*, 1–16.

Foster, E. (1992) Women and the inverted pyramid of the black churches in Britain. In: G. Sahgal and N. Yuval-Davis (eds) *Refusing Holy Orders: Women and Fundamentalism in Britain*. London, Virago.

Fox Harding, L. M. (1996) 'Recent developments in "children's rights": liberation for whom?' *Child and Family Social Work 1, 3*, 141–150.

Franklin, B. (1995) (ed) *The Handbook of Children's Rights: Comparative Policy and Practice*. Routledge: London.

Freeman, R. and Rustin, M. (1999) 'Introduction: welfare culture and Europe.' In P. Chamberlayne, A. Cooper, R. Freeman and M. Rustin (eds) *Welfare and Culture in Europe: Towards a New Paradigm in Social Policy*. London: Jessica Kingsley Publishers.

Fromm, E. (1967) *Psychoanalysis and Religion*. New York: Yale University and Bantam Press.

Fulcher, L. C. (1999) 'Cultural origins of the contemporary group conference.' *Child Care in Practice 6*, 328–339.

Fuller, R. and Petch, A. (1995) *Practitioner Research: The Reflexive Social Worker*. Buckingham: Open University Press.

Gaasholt, Ø. and Togeby, L. (1995) *Danskernes holdingner til flygtninge of invandrere*. Århus: Politics.

Geertz, C. (1973) The Interpretation of Cultures, Selected Essays. New York: Basic Books.

Gerrish, K., Husband, C. and MacKenzie, J. (1996) *Nursing for a Multi-Ethnic Society*. Buckingham: Open University Press.

Giddens, A. (1993) *Sociology*, 2nd edn. Oxford: Polity Press.

Gill, S.D. (1979) *Songs of Life: An Introduction to Navajo Religious Culture*. Leiden: E.J. Brill.

Glazer, N and Moynihan, D.P. (eds) (1975) *Ethnicity: Theory and Experience*, Cambridge, MA.: Harvard University Press.

Goddard, C. (1996) *Child Abuse and Child Protection: A Guide for Health, Education and Welfare Workers*. Melbourne: Churchill Livingstone.

Goddard, C. and Carew, R. (1993) *Responding to Children, Child Welfare Practice*. Melbourne: Longman Cheshire.

Goffman, E. (1961) *Asylums: Essays on the Social Situations of Mental Patients and Other Inmates*. New York: Anchor Books.

Goldberg, D. (1993) *Racist Culture*. Oxford: Blackwell.

Gramsci, A. (1988) 'Notes for introduction and approach to the study of philosophy and the history of culture.' In D. Forgacs (ed) *A Gramsci Reader*. London: Laurence and Wisharnt.

Gross, R.D. (1987) *Psychology: The Science of Mind and Behaviour.* London, Arnold.

Guéllar, I. and Paniagua, F.A. (2000) *Handbook of Multicultural Mental Health.* Santiago: Academic Press.

Guerin, B. (1998) Religious Behaviours as Strategies for Organising Groups of People: A Social Contingency Analysis. *The Behaviour Analysis 21,* 53-72.

Gurnah, A. (1989) 'After bilingual support?' In M. Cole (ed) *Education for Equality: Some Guidelines for Good Practice.* London: Routledge.

Hall, E.T. (1959) *The Silent Language.* New York, Anchor Press/Doubleday

Hall, E.T. (1966) *The Hidden Dimension,* New York, Anchor Press/Doubleday .

Hall, E.T. (1976a) *How Cultures Collide.* New York, Anchor Press/Doubleday

Hall, E,T, (1976) *Beyond Culture.* New York, Anchor Press/Doubleday.

Hall, M., Dwyer, D. and Lewis, T. (1999) *The GP Training Handbook,* 3rd edn. Oxford: Blackwell.

Hall, S. (1990) 'Cultural identity and diaspora.' In J. Rutherford (ed) *Identity: Community, Culture, Difference.* London: Lawrence & Wishart.

Hall, S. (1992) 'New ethnicities.' In J. Donald and A. Rattani (eds) *Race, Culture and Difference.* London: Sage.

Hall, S. (1996) 'Introduction: Who needs identity?' In S. Hall and P. DuGay (eds) *Questions of Cultural Identity.* London: Sage.

Hall, S. and Du Gay, P. (eds) (1996) *Questions of Cultural Identity.* London: Sage.

Hall, S. and Jefferson, T. (eds) (1996) *Resistance through Rituals: Youth Subculture in Post-war Britain.* London: Hutchinson.

Hansard (Parliament of Victoria, Australia) (1997) *Apology to Aboriginal People.* Melbourne.

Hargrove, B. (1989) *The Sociology of Religion: Classical and Contemporary Approaches,* 2nd edn. Arlington Heights IL: Harlan Davidson.

Hassan, F. (1999) 'Failure of social services and the Muslims.' *The Muslim News 120.*

Haviland, W.A. (1999) *Cultural Anthropology.* New York: Harcourt Brace.

Haynes, J. (1993) *Religion in Third World Politics.* Buckingham: Open University Press.

Healy, J., Hassan, R. and McKenna, R. (1985) 'Aboriginal families.' In D. Storer (ed) *Ethnic Family Values in Australia.* Sydney: Prentice Hall.

Helman, C.G. (1994) *Culture, Health and Illness.* Butterworth-Heinemann: Oxford.

Henley, A. (1982) *Caring for Muslims and their Families: Religious Aspects of Care.* London: DHSS.

Henley, A. and Schott, J. (1999) *Culture, Religion and Patient Care in a Multi-Ethnic Society.* London: Age Concern.

Hemsi, L. (1967) Psychiatric morbidity of West Indian immigrants, *Social Psychiatry 2,* 95-100.

Heraud, B.J. (1970) *Sociology and Social Work: Perspectives and Problems.* Oxford: Pergamon.

Herrera, J.M., Lawson, W.B. and Sramek, J.J. (1999) *Cross Cultural Psychiatry.* Chichester: Wiley.

Hesketh, T., Shu Hong, Z. and Lynch, M. (2000) 'Child abuse in China: the views and experiences of child health professionals.' *Child Abuse and Neglect 24,* 6, 867–872.

Hewison, J. and Wyke, S. (1991) *Introduction.* In S. Wyke and J. Hewison (eds) (1991) *Child Health Matters: Caring for Children in the Community,* Buckingham: Open University Publications.

Hill, M. and Aldgate, J. (1996) *Child Welfare Services: Developments in Law, Policy, Practice and Research.* London: Jessica Kingsley Publications.

Hillier, S. and Rahman, S. (1996) 'Childhood development and behavioural and emotional problems as perceived by Bangladeshi parents in East London.' In D. Kelleher and S. Hillier (eds) *Researching Cultural Differences in Health.* London: Routledge.

Hoksbergen, R.A.C. (1997) *Child Adoption: A Guidebook for Adoptive Parents and their Advisers.* London: Jessica Kingsley Publishers.

Holm, A., Dodd, B., Stow, C. and Pert, S. (1999) 'Identification and differential diagnosis of phonological disorder in bilingual children.' *Language Testing 16,* 3, 271–292.

Hong, G.K. and Hong, L.K. (1991) 'Comparative perspectives on child abuse and neglect: Chinese versus Hispanics and Whites.' *Child Welfare 70,* 4, 463–475.

Hopkins, A. and Bahl, V. (eds) (1993) *Access to Health Care for People from Black and Ethnic Minorities.* London: Royal College of Physicians.

Horowitz, D.L. (1975) 'Ethnic Identity.' In N. Glazer and D.P. Moynihan (eds) *Ethnicity: Theory and Experience.* Cambridge MA: Harvard University Press.

Hudson, J., Morris, A., Maxwell, G. and Galaway, B. (eds) (1996) *Family Group Conferences: Perspectives on Policy and Practice.* Leichhardt: Federation Press.

Humphreys, C., Atkar, S. and Baldwin, N. (1999) 'Discrimination in child protection work: recurring themes with Asian families.' *Child and Family Social Work 4,* 283–291.

Husain, F. and O'Brien, M. (1996) *Muslim Families in Europe: Social Existence and Social Care, Report of Findings for a Project Funded by The European Commission.* London: University of North London.

Irvine, D. and Irvine, S. (1997) *The Practice of Quality.* Oxford: Oxford Radcliffe Medical Press.

John, M. (ed) (1996a) *Children in Charge: The Child's Right to a Fair Hearing.* London: Jessica Kingsley Publishers.

John, M. (ed) (1996b) *Children in Our Charge: The Child's Right To Resources.* London: Jessica Kingsley Publishers.

John, M. (ed) (1997) *Children in Our Charge: The Child's Right To Protection.* London: Jessica Kingsley Publishers.

Johnson, W. B. and Ridley, C. R. (1992) 'Sources of gain in Christian counselling and psychotherapy.' *Counselling Psychologist 20,* 159–175.

Jones, S. (1994) 'Old ghosts and new chains: ethnicity and memory in the Georgian republic.' In R. S. Watson (ed) *Memory, History, and Opposition Under State Socialism.* Sante Fe: School of American Research Press.

Jones, R. and Menzies, S (1999) *General Practice: Essential Facts.* Abington, Radcliffe Medical Press.

Katbamna, S. (2000) *'Race' and Childbirth.* Buckingham: Open University Press.

Kavanagh, K. H. and Kennedy, P. H. (1992) *Promoting Cultural Diversity.* London: Sage.

Kaye, C. (1999) *Race, Culture and Ethnicity in Secure Psychiatric Practice.* London: Jessica Kingsley Publishers.

Keats, D. (1997) *Culture and the Child: A Guide for Professionals in Child Care and Development.* Chichester: Wiley.

Kelleher, D. (1996) 'A defence of the use of the terms "ethnicity" and "culture".' In D. Kelleher and S. Hillier (eds) *Researching Cultural Differences in Health.* London: Routledge.

Kelleher, D. and Hillier, S. (eds) (1996) *Researching Cultural Differences in Health*. London: Routledge.

Kellner, D. (1997) Critical Theory and Cultural Studies: The Missed Articulation. In J. McGuigan (ed) *Cultural Methodologies,* London, Sage.

Kelly, A. (1992) 'The new managerialism in the social services.' In P. Carter, T. Jeffs and M.K. Smith (eds) *Social Work and Social Welfare.* Buckingham: Open University Press.

Kleinman, A. (1980) *Patients and Healers in the Context of Culture.* London: University of California Press.

Korbin, J. E. (1977) 'Anthropological contributions to the study of child abuse.' *Child Abuse and Neglect 1,* 1, 7–14.

Korbin, J. E. (1979) 'A cross-cultural perspective on the role of the community in child abuse and neglect.' *Child Abuse and Neglect 3,* 1, 9–18.

Korbin, J. E. (1980) 'The cultural context of child abuse and neglect' In C.H. Kempe and R.E. Helfer (eds) *The Battered Child.* 3rd ed. Chicago: University of Chicago Press.

Korbin, J.E. (ed) (1981) *Child Abuse and Neglect – Cross Cultural Perspectives.* Berkeley and Los Angeles: University of California Press.

Korbin, J. E. (1987) 'Child abuse and neglect: the cultural context.' In R. Helfer and R.S. Kempe (eds) *The Battered Child,* 4th edn. Chicago: University of Chicago Press.

Korbin, J. E. (1990) 'Han'ino: child maltreatment in a Hawai'ian–American community.' *Pacific Studies 13,* 3, 6–22.

Korbin, J. E. (1994) 'Sociocultural factors in child maltreatment: a neighbourhood approach.' In G. Melton and F. Barry (eds) *Safe Neighbourhoods: Foundations for a New National Strategy for Child Protection.* New York: Guilford Press.

Korbin, J. E. (1997) 'Culture and child maltreatment.' In M.E. Helfer, R.S. Kempe and R.D. Krugman (eds) *The Battered Child,* 5th edn. Chicago: University of Chicago Press.

Kroeber, A. (1925) *Handbook of the Indians of California.* Bureau of American Ethnology Bulletin 78. Washington DC: Smithsonian Institute.

Lagace, R.O. (1999) Society – PAWNEE, (website): http://lucy.ukc.ac.uk/Ethno Atlas/Hmar/Cult_dir/Culture.7864

Lago, C. and Thompson, J. (1996) *Race, Culture and Counselling.* Buckingham: Open University Press.

Lambeth (1987) *Whose Child? The Report of the Public Enquiry into the Death of Tyra Henry.* London: London Borough of Lambeth.

Langan, M. and Day, L. (eds) (1992) *Women, Oppression and Social Work: Issues in Anti-Discriminatory Practice.* London: Routledge.

Leach, E. (1982) *Social Anthropology.* Glasgow: Fontana.

Lee, M. (1997) 'Relocating location: cultural geography, the specificity of place and the city habitus.' In J. McGuigan (ed) *Cultural Methodologies.* London: Sage.

Lees, R. and McGrath, M. (1974) 'Community work with immigrants.' *British Journal of Social Work 4,* 2, 176–186.

Leigh, J. (1998) *Communication for Cultural Competence.* Sydney: Allyn and Bacon.

Leininger, M. (1978) *Transcultural Nursing, Concepts, Theories and Practice.* New York: Wiley.

Lindesmith, A. R. and Strauss, A. L. (1956) *Social Psychology.* New York: Holt Rinehart & Winston.

Lorenz, W. (1999) 'Social work and cultural politics: the paradox of German social pedagogy.' In P. Chamberlayne, A. Cooper, R. Freeman and M. Rustin (eds) *Welfare and Culture in Europe: Towards a New Paradigm in Social Policy.* London: Jessica Kingsley Publishers.

Lyle, D. (1994) *Counselling in the Pastoral and Spiritual Context.* Buckingham: Open University Press.

McClure, E. (1999) 'Elaine McClure.' In M. Hall (ed) *Orangism and the Twelfth: What it means to Me.* Newtownabbey: Island Publications.

Macey, M. and Moxon, E. (1996) 'An examination of anti racist and anti oppressive theory and practice in social work education.' *British Journal of Social Work 26*, 297–314.

McDonald, S. (1991) *All equal under the Act? - A Practical Guide to the Children's Act 1989 for social workers.* London: Race Equality Unit.

McKay, S. (2000) *Northern Protestants: An Unsettled People.* Belfast: Blackstaff.

McKenzie, K. and Crowcroft, N. (1994) 'Race, ethnicity, culture and science.' *British Medical Journal 309*, 286–287.

McLeod, J. (1993) *An Introduction to Counselling.* Buckingham: Open University Press.

McPhatter, A. (1997) 'Cultural competence in child welfare: what is it? How do we achieve it? What happens without it?' *Child Welfare 76*, 1, 255–278.

McRoy, G., Oglesby, Z. and Grape, H. (1997) 'Achieving same race adoptive placements for African American children: culturally sensitive practice approaches.' *Child Welfare 76*, 1, 85–104.

McVeigh, R. (1995) 'Cherishing the children of the nation unequally: sectarianism in Ireland.' In P.Clancy, S. Drudy, K. Lynch and L. O'Dowd (eds) *Irish Society Sociological Perspectives.* Dublin: IPA.

Maguire, G. (1986) 'A study of an urban Gaeltacht community.' Unpublished PhD thesis. Belfast: Queen's University. Ref. T/986 H80.

Maitra, B. and Millar, A. (1996) Children Families and Therapists: Clinical Considerations and Ethnic Minority Cultures. In K.N. Dwivedi and V.P. Varma (eds) Meeting the Needs of Ethnic Minority Children, London: Jessica Kingsley Publications.

Mares, P. (1982) The Vietnamese in Britain: A Handbook for Health Workers, Cambridge, National Extension College.

Mares, P., Henley, A. and Baxter, C. (1985) *Health Care in Multiracial Britain.* Cambridge: Health Care Education Council.

Marsh, P. and Crow, G. (1997) *Family Group Conferences in Child Welfare.* Oxford: Blackwell.

Marshall, K. (1997) *Children's Rights in the Balance: The Participation–Protection Debate.* London: HMSO.

Masson, J. and Oakley, M.W. (1998) *Out of Hearing: Representing Children in Care Proceedings.* Chichester: Wiley.

May, T. (1993) *Social Research: Issues, Methods and Process.* Buckingham: Open University Press.

Millan, R. (1996) Anti-discriminatory Practice: a Guide for Workers in Child Care and Education. London, Cassells.

Milner, P. and Carolin, B. (1998) *Time to Listen to Children: Personal and Professional Communication.* London: Routledge.

Montagu, A. (1974) *Man's Most Dangerous Myth*, 5th edn. London: Oxford University Press.

Moodie, T. D. (1975) *The Rise of Afrikanerdom: Power, Apartheid, and the Afrikaner Civil Religion*. Berkeley: University of California Press.

Moore, B. (1985) *Black Robe*. London: Jonathan Cape.

Moore, J.D. (1997) Visions of Culture. An Introduction to Anthropological Theories and Theorists. California: Alto Mira Press.

Morgan, M.(1996) The meanings of high blood pressures among Afro-Caribbean and white patients. In D. Kelleher and S. Hillier (eds) *Researching Cultural Differences in Health*, London: Routledge.

Mullan, B. (1997) *Reaching Out To Families*. Swansea: International Centre For Childhood Studies: University of Wales.

Nagel, J. (1997) *American Indian Ethnic Renewal: Red Power and the Resurgence of Identity and Culture*. Oxford: Oxford University Press.

Naik, D. (1991) 'Towards an anti racist curriculum in social work training.' In Central Council for the Education and Training of Social Workers *One Small Step Towards Racial Justice: The Teaching of Anti Racism in Diploma in Social Work Programmes*. London: CCETSW.

Noland, L. J. and Gallagher, T. (1989) 'Cross cultural communication for land managers and planners in Alaska.' *Agroborealis 21*, 1, 18–23.

Noonucul, O. (1984) 'Until our culture ...' Quoted in G. Smallwood (1995) 'Child abuse and neglect from an indigenous Australian's perspective.' Henry Kempe Memorial Lecture. Tenth International Congress on Child Abuse and Neglect. *Child Abuse and Neglect 19*, 3, 281–289.

Northern Ireland Government (1995) *The Children (Northern Ireland) Order, 1995*. Belfast: HMSO.

Northern Ireland Government (1998) *The Agreement*. Belfast: HMSO.

O Corráin, D. and Maguire, F. (1990) *Irish Names*. Dublin: Lilliput Press.

Ó Dónaill, É. and Ní Churraighin, D. (1995) *Now You're Talking*. Dublin: Gill & Macmillan.

Odujinrin, O.M.T. (1995) 'Marital disruption – the welfare of the children thereafter in Nigeria.' *Child Abuse and Neglect 19*, 10, 1233–1244.

O'Hagan, K. P. (1993) *Emotional and Psychological Abuse of Children*. Buckingham: Open University Press.

O'Hagan, K.P. (ed) (1996) *Cultural Competence in Social Work Practice*. London: Jessica Kingsley Publishers.

O'Hagan, K.P. (1999) Culture, cultural identity, an cultural sensitivity in child and family social work. Child and Family Social Work, 4: 269-81(see slight addition and change to original text in your editorial enquiry sheet, p13, to include reference to case of Anna Climbie).

O'Hagan, K.P. and Dillenburger, K. (1995) *The Abuse of Women in Childcare Work*. Buckingham: Open University Press.

Ó Riagáin, D. (1998) *A European Overview, with some Examples:* a lecture in the Ulster Tongues series of events. Belfast: Linen Hall Library.

Paniagua, F.A. (1994) *Assessing and Treating Culturally Diverse Clients*. Thousand Oaks CA: Sage.

Papadopoulos, I., Tiki, M. and Taylor, G. (1998) *Transcultural Care: A Guide for Health Care Professionals*. Salisbury: Quay Books.

Park, R. E. (1934) 'Race relations and certain frontiers.' In E.B. Reuter (ed) *Race and Culture Contacts*. New York: McGraw-Hill.

Park, R.E. (1939) 'The nature of race relations.' In E.T. Thompson (ed) *Race Relations and the Race Problem.* Durham NC: Duke University Press.

Parsons, T. (1952) *The Social System.* London: Tavistock.

Parton, N. (1996) 'Child protection, family support and social work, a critical appraisal of the Department of Health research studies in child protection.' *Child and Family Social Work 1,* 3–11.

Patel, N., Naik, D. and Humphries, B. (eds) (1998) *Visions of Reality: Religion and Ethnicity in Social Work.* London: CCETSW.

Payne, M. (1997) *Modern Social Work Theory.* 2nd Edition, Basingstoke: Macmillan.

Phillips, M. (1993) 'Oppressive urge to stop oppression.' *The Observer,* 1 August.

Pierce, M. and Armstrong, D. (1996) Afro-Caribbean lay beliefs about diabetes: an exploratory study. In D. Kelleher and S. Hillier (eds) *Researching Cultural Differences in Health,* London: Routledge.

Pilgrim, D. and Rogers, A. (1993) *A Sociology of Mental Health and Illness.* Buckingham: Open University Press.

Pincus, L. (1974) *Death and the Family: The Importance of Mourning.* London: Faber.

Poole, D. L. (1998) 'Politically correct or culturally competent?' *Health and Social Work 23,* 3, 164–166.

Prentice, Eve-Ann (2000) 'Burning that may mask murder.' *The Times,* 7 August.

Pringle, K. (1998) *Children and Social Welfare in Europe.* Buckingham: Open University Press.

Purves, L. (2000) 'Why can't we learn about sex education?' *The Times,* 27 June.

Quali, N. and Rea, A. (1995) *Insertion, Discrimination and Exclusion.* Point D'Appui Tef, Dossier 11 (septembre), ch.. 2, Université Libre de Bruxelles.

Qasem, F.S., Mustafa, A., Kazem, N.A. and Shah, N.M. (1998) 'Attitudes of Kuwaiti parents towards physical punishment of children.' *Child Abuse and Neglect 22,* 12, 1198–1202.

Qureshi, B. (1989) *Transcultural Medicine: Dealing With Patients From Different Cultures.* Dordrecht: Kulwer Academic Publishers.

Raftery, M. (1999) *States of Fear.* RTE Television.

Raftery, M. and O'Sullivan, E. (1999) *Suffer the Little Children: The Inside Story of Ireland's Industrial Schools.* Dublin: New Ireland Books.

Rangihau, J. (1986) *Puao-te-Ata-tu (daybreak): Report of the Ministerial Advisory Committee on a Maori Perspective for the Department of Social Welfare.* Wellington: Government Printing Office.

Reber, A.S. (1985) *Dictionary of Psychology.* London: Penguin.

Rees, S. (1991) *Achieving Power: Practice and Policy in Social Welfare.* Sydney: Allen and Unwin.

Reschly, J. and Graham-Clay S. (1989) 'Psychological abuse from prejudice and cultural bias.' In M. Brassard, R. Germain and S.N. Hart (eds) *Psychological Maltreatment of Children and Youth.* New York: Pergamon Press.

Robin, R.W., Chester, B., Rasmussen, J.K., Jaranson, J.M. and Goldmand, D. (1997) 'Prevalence, characteristics, and impact of childhood sexual abuse in a south western American Indian tribe.' *Child Abuse and Neglect 21,* 8, 769–787.

Robinson, L. (1999) 'Racial identity attitudes and interracial communication: implications for social work practice in Britain.' *European Journal of Social Work 2,* 3, 315–326.

Robson, A. (1993) 'Torture, not culture.' *Amnesty*, Sept.–Oct., 8–9.

Rogers, A.Y. and Potocky, M. (1996) 'Evaluating culturally sensitive practice through single-system design: methodological issues and strategies.' *Research on Social Work Practice 7*, 3, 391–401.

Rogers, G. (1995) 'Practice teaching guidelines for learning ethically sensitive, anti-discriminatory practice: a Canadian application.' *British Journal of Social Work 25*, 441–457.

Royal College of Speech and Language Therapists (1996) *Communicating Quality, 2: Professional Standards for Speech and Language Therapists.* London, Royal College of Speech and Language Therapists.

Romaine, S. (1994) *Language in Society: An Introduction to Sociolinguistics.* Oxford: Oxford University Press.

Rutherford, J. (1990a) 'A place called home: identity and the cultural politics of difference.' In J. Rutherford (ed) *Identity: Community, Culture, Difference.* London: Lawrence & Wishart.

Rushdie, S. (1988) The Satanic Verses. London, Viking.

Runnymede Trust (1997) *Islamophobia: A challenge to us all.* London: The Runnymede Trust.

Rwgellera, G.G.C. (1977) Psychiatric morbidity among West Africans and West Indians living in London. Psychological Medicine, 7, 317-29.

Sachs, J. (2000) Marriage is a song for two voices in Harmony. *The Times*, 10th August.

Sanzenbach, P. (1989) 'Religion and social work: it's not that simple.' In N. Patel, D. Naik and B. Humphries *Visions of Reality, Religion and Ethnicity in Social Work.* London: CCETSW.

Sapsford, R. and Abbott, P. (1992) *Research Methods for Nurses and the Caring Professionals.* Buckingham: Open University Press.

Sardar, Z. (1985) *Islamic Futures: The Shape of Ideas to Come.* London: Mansell.

Seden, J. (1995) 'Religious persuasion and the Children Act.' *Adoption & Fostering 19*, 2, 7–15.

Segall, M.H., Dasen, P.R., Berry, J.W. and Poortinga, Y.H. (1990) *Human Behaviour in Global Perspective: An Introduction to Cross-Cultural Psychology.* New York: Pergamon Press.

Sewpaul, V. (1999) 'Culture, religion and infertility: a South African perspective.' *British Journal of Social Work 29*, 741–754.

Shaver, L.D. (1998) *Communication and Identity Across Cultures.* London: Sage.

Shurmer-Smith, P. and Hannam, K. (1994) *Worlds of Desire, Realms of Power: A Cultural Geography.* London: Edward Arnold.

Sinha, R. (1998) *The Cultural Adjustment of Asian Lone Mothers Living in London.* Aldershot: Ashgate.

Smallwood, G. (1995) 'Child abuse and neglect from an indigenous Australian's perspective.' Henry Kempe Memorial Lecture. Tenth International Congress on Child Abuse and Neglect. *Child Abuse and Neglect 19*, 3, 281–289.

Smith, S. (1990) 'Towards a global culture?' In M. Featherstone (ed) *Theory, Culture and Society.* Newbury Park CA: Sage.

Smyth, M. and Campbell, J. (1996) Social Work, Sectarianism and Anti-sectarian Practice in Northern Ireland. British Journal of Social Work, 26, 77-92.

South East Thames Regional Health Authority (1993) *Healthquest South-East Regional Report.* SETRHA: Bexhill.

Stanner, W.E.H. (1965) 'Religion, totemism and symbolism.' In R.M. Berndt and C.H. Berndt (eds) *Aboriginal Man in Australia.* Sydney: Angus and Robertson.

Stewart, E.C. and Bennett, M.J. (1991) *American Cultural Patterns: A cross-cultural perspective.* Yarmouth ME: Intercultural Press.

Stewart, T. (1997) Historical Interfaces Between Maori and Psychology. In P. Te Whaiti, M. McCarthy and A Durie (eds) *Mai I Rangiatea: Maori WellBeing and Development.* Auckland: Auckland University Press.

Storkey, E. (1991) 'Race, ethnicity and gender.' *Society and Social Science.* Milton Keynes: Open University, Unit 8 of D103.

Stourton, P.C. (1996) *Songlines and Dreamings: Contemporary Australian Aboriginal Art.* Melbourne: Lund Humphries.

Stow, C. and Pert, S. (1988) *The Rochdale Assessment of Mirpuri Phonology.* Rochdale: Sean Pert.

Sumpton, A. H. (1993) 'A difference of culture.' *Community Care,* 17 June.

Survival International (1999) Canada's Tibet - the killing of the Innu. (Website: www.survival.org.uk

Swinton, J. (2000) *Spirituality in Mental Health Care.* London: Jessica Kingsley Publishers.

Syme, G. (1994) *Counselling in Independent Practice.* Buckingham: Open University Press.

Tamura, T. and Lau, A. (1992) 'Connected versus separations: applicability of family therapy to Japanese families.' *Family Process 31,* 4, 319–340.

Tanno, D.V. and González A. (1998) *Communication and Identity across Cultures, International and InterCultural Communication Annual,* vol. *21.* Thousand Oaks CA: Sage.

Thakur, S. (1998) 'The case for religion in social work: an independent view of social work and ethnicity.' In N. Patel, D. Naik and B. Humphries (eds) *Visions of Reality, Religion and Ethnicity in Social Work.* London: CCETSW.

Thomas, D.R. (1986) 'Culture and identity: maintaining the distinction.' *Australian Journal of Psychology 38,* 371–380.

Thompson, N. (1993) *Anti Discriminatory Practice.* Basingstoke: BASW/Macmillan.

Thompson, N. (1997) 'Children, death and ageism.' *Child and Family Social Work 2,* 1, 59–65.

Thorpe, D. (1994) *Evaluating Child Protection.* Buckingham: Open University Press.

Tickner, J.A. (1997) 'Identity in IR theory: a feminist perspective.' In Y. Lapid and F. Kratochwil (eds) *The Return of Culture and Identity in I.R.* London: Lynne Rienner.

The Times (2000) 'Abduction charges to halt forced marriages.' 30 June.

Timms, N. (1991) 'A new diploma for social work or Dunkirk as total victory.' In P. Carter and T. Jeffs (eds) *Social Work and Social Welfare, Yearbook 3.* Buckingham: Open University Press.

Tronto, J. (1993) *Moral Boundaries: A Political Argument for an Ethic of Care.* New York: Routledge.

Vatin, J. (1982) 'Revival in the Maghreb.' In A. Dessouki (ed) *Islamic Resurgence in the Arab World.* New York: Praeger.

Vatuk, S. (1990) 'To be a burden on others: dependency anxiety among the elderly in India.' In O.M. Lynch (ed) *Divine Passions: The Social Construction of Emotion in India.* Berkeley: University of California Press.

Walker, M. (1992) *Surviving Secrets.* Buckinghamshire: Open University Press.

Waller, B. (1998) 'From the front line: a local authority perspective.' In S. Hayman (ed) *Child Sexual Abuse: Myth and Reality*. London: Institute for the Study and Treatment of Delinquency.

Watson, E. (1991) '"Appropriate" use of child health services in East London: ethnic similarities and differences.' In S. Wyke and J. Hewison (eds) *Child Health Matters: Caring for Children in the Community*. Milton Keynes: Open University Press.

Weeks, J. (1995) 'The value of difference.' In J. Rutherford (ed) *Identity: Community, Culture, Difference*. London: Lawrence & Wishart.

Wells, A. E. (1971) *Men of the Honey Bee*. London: Robert Hale.

Werbner, P. (1996) 'The making of Muslim dissent: hybridized discourses, lay preachers and radical rhetoric among British Pakistanis.' *American Ethnologist 23*, 1, 102–122.

White, L. (1949) *The Science of Culture: A Study of Man and Civilization*. New York: Grove Press.

White, L. (1959) *The Evolution of Culture: The Development of Civilization to the Fall of Rome*. New York: McGraw-Hill.

White, R.H. (1990) *Tribal Assets: The Rebirth of Native America*. New York: Holt.

White, R., Carr, P. and Lowe, N. (1991) *A Guide to the Children Act 1989*. London: Butterworths.

Whitehouse, P. (1983) 'Race, bias, and social enquiry reports.' *Probation Journal*, July, 43–49.

Williams, C. (1997) *Nursing Across Cultures*. (Website: www.ihs.gov/nonmedicalprograms/ nursinged/handouts/culture.doc)

Williams, R. (1963) *Culture and Society, 1780–1950*. Harmondsworth: Penguin.

Willows, D. and Swinton, J. (2000) *Spiritual Dimensions of Pastoral Care*. London: Jessica Kingsley Publishers.

Wolcoff, M. (1989) *Cross Cultural Communication*. Anchorage: Association of Stranded Rural Alaskans.

Wolffe, J. (ed) (1993) *The Growth of Religious Diversity in Britain from 1945*. Sevenoaks: Hodder & Stoughton/Open University Publications.

Wood, J. (1998) 'Jewish issues in social work education.' In N. Patel, D. Naik and B. Humphries *Visions of Reality, Religion and Ethnicity in Social Work*. London: CCETSW.

Websites

There are many websites relevant to the contents of this book. Here is a small selection which the author found useful:

Australia's Aborigines: Oral History Project: National Library
www.nla.gov.au/oh/bth/index/html

Australia's National Sorry Day
www.austlii.edu.au/special/rsproject/sorry/
www.rmit.edu.au/About/hotTYPEv2n3/sdlinks.htm

Challenges in the Care of Muslim Patients – focus on siting stomas
http://home.online.no/~w-b-k/page7.html

The Mabo Judgement: Its Implications
www.caa.org.au/publications/reports/MABO/implications.html

Navajo Indians: The Long Walk
www.navajo,org./lwalk.html

Survival International (1999) Canada's Tibet, The Killing of the Innu
www.survival.org.uk/ir%20february.htm

Irish Language Community
www.pobal.org

Nursing across Cultures (C. Williams 1997)
w.ihs.gov/nonmedicalprograms/nursinged/handouts/culture.doc

Subject Index

Author Index

Qasem, F.S. 112
Quali, N. Rea, A. 48
Qureshi, B. 103, 157, 205, 207, 229

Raftery, M. 102, 141
Rahman, S. 162, 241, 242
Rangihau, J. 148
Reber, A.S. 28, 40, 128
Rees, S. 154
Reschly, J. 239
Ridley, C.R. 147
Roberts, S. 145
Robin, R.W. 115.
Robinson, L. 119, 123
Robson, A. 114
Rogers, A. 108, 109, 114, 239
Rogers, C. 109
Rogers, G. 99
Romaine S. 155
Roth, W.E. 98
Rushdie, S. 143, 230
Russell, B. 142
Rutherford, J. 28, 29–30
Rwgellara, G.G.C. 108
Ryan, P.J. 89

Sachs, J. 135
Sanzenbach, P. 140
Sapsford, R. 173
Sardar, Z. 51
Sarsfield, P. 98
Schlesinger, E.G. 118
Schott, J. 105, 135–36, 136, 145, 155, 156,
    157–58, 159, 207, 229, 239, 244, 245,
    247, 253
Seden, J. 22, 134, 136, 139, 145
Sewpaul, V. 239, 240, 243
Shaver, L.D. 65–66
Shu Hong, Z. 112
Shurmer-Smith, P. 36
Sinha, R. 138, 139, 239
Smith, E.E. 40
Smyth, M. 144
Spurloch, J. 111
Sramek, J.J. 109
Standley, I. 86
Stanner W.E.H. 79
Stewart, E.C. 108, 155
Storkey E. 126
Stourton, P.C. 80
Stow, C. 202
Strauss, A.L. 154

Sumpton, A.H. 147
Swinton, J. 147
Syme, G. 147

Tamura, T. 258
Tanno, D.V. 243
Tecumsah (Indian Chief) 63
Thakur, S. 136
Thomas, D.R. 41
Thompson, J. 110, 147, 157, 239, 243, 245,
    247
Thompson, N. 113, 121, 126, 128, 138, 239
Thorpe, D. 84, 85, 90, 112, 218
Tickner, J.A. 30
Timms, N. 241
Togeby, L. 56
Tronto, J. 30
Tylor, E. 32, 33, 41

Varma, V.P. 138
Vatin, J. 45
Vatuk, S. 259
Vaz, K. 143

Walker, A. 114
Walker, M. 141
Waller, B. 113
Watson, E. 160
Weeks, J. 28, 143
Wells, A.E. 80
Werbner, P. 49
White, L. 34
White, R. 22
White, R.H. 67, 68
Whitehouse, P. 118
Williams, C. 70, 71
Williams, M. 54, 55
Williams, R. 31
Willows, D. 147
Wilson, R. 88
Wolcoff, M. 70
Wolffe, J. 135
Wood, J. 146
Wordsworth, W. 37
Wyke, S. 105, 106

Printed in the United Kingdom
by Lightning Source UK Ltd.
112696UKS00001B/82-105